Restless Spirits

&

Popular Movements

Restless Spirits

&

Popular Movements

A Vermont History

Greg Guma

VERMONT RESEARCH BOOKS
University of Vermont

WHITE RIVER PRESS
Amherst, Massachusetts

Copyright 2021 by Greg Guma
All rights reserved.

Published by White River Press, Amherst, Massachusetts
Whiteriverpress.com

ISBN: 978-1-935052-73-9

Design credits: Abby Kaiser (cover) and Emily Anderson (interior)

Photo or other permissions: Greg Guma

Previous publication history:previously published as an eBook titled *Green Mountain Politics: Restless Spirits, Popular Movements*

Library of Congress Cataloging-in-Publication Data

Names: Guma, Greg, author.
Title: Restless spirits & popular movements: a Vermont history / Greg Guma.
Other titles: Restless spirits and popular movements
Description: Amherst, Massachusetts : White River Press, [2021] | "Vermont research books University of Vermont." | Includes bibliographical references and index.
Identifiers: LCCN 2021025588 | ISBN 9781935052739 (paperback)
Subjects: LCSH: Vermont--History--Anecdotes. | Vermont--Biography--Anecdotes.
Classification: LCC F49 .G86 2021 | DDC 974.3--dc23
LC record available at https://lccn.loc.gov/2021025588

For my mother Olga, who made this book possible, and my granddaughter Margot Grace, who made it worth finishing.

Contents

Preface and Acknowledgements i

Milestones
Image and Reality 1
A Man Called Lyon 11
People of the Land 19
Birth of a Republic 29
From Independence to Statehood 41
Rebellions of the Righteous 47
The First Third Party 57
Growing Pains 65
Slow Progress for Women 75
How Vermont Went Republican 83
Paths to the White House 89
Boom and Bust in Working Class Towns 99
Selling the Beckoning Country 105

Breakthroughs
The Age of Burke 113
From Socialism to the American Plan 133

The Parkway That Never Happened 141
The Aiken-Gibson Wing 147
The Man Who Stopped McCarthy 155
The Hoff Effect 161
The Snelling Style 169

Realignments
Encounters on the Culture Front 177
Capital Consequences 197
The Rise of Bernie Sanders 205
Local Democracy and State Power 221
Howard Dean's Moment 227
Re-imagining Independence 235
Power Struggles 241
Land, Politics and People 253

Epilogue 263
Bibliography 269
Illustrations 273
About the Author 275
Index 277

Restless Spirits

&

Popular Movements

Preface and Acknowledgements

After US Attorney General William Barr dismissed the charges against Pres. Donald Trump's former national security advisor Gen. Michael Flynn, in 2020, for his lies to federal officials, CBS correspondent Catherine Herridge asked him a pointed question: "When history looks back on this decision, how do you think it will be written?"

"Well," Barr replied, "history is written by the winners, so it largely depends on who's writing the history." He was misquoting a well-known phrase. The actual wording is "History is written by the victors," attributed to multiple sources including Josef Stalin and Winston Churchill.

So who actually coined the phrase? It's hard to say. "I believe that the adage evolved over time," Garson O'Toole, webmaster of Quote Investigator, notes. "There are versions of the saying in English, French, Italian, and German." But the more important questions are, is it true? And who are the real victors?

To start, history is sometimes written by so-called losers. Much of the historical profession today focuses on recovering and celebrating the stories of once marginalized groups. For example, the initial victors in the settling of North America were clearly European migrants who used terrorism, even genocide to colonize the continent. For centuries their version of the story— upstanding white men defeating and "civilizing" people they referred to as ignorant savages—went largely unchallenged.

But that false narrative is finally being cast aside, and new ones embodied in *The New York Times* racial exploration, the 1619 Project, and other initiatives are becoming the accepted standard. Similarly, Hollywood writers who lost their jobs during the McCarthy era were not victorious at first. But they eventually rewrote the script and are widely viewed today as heroic martyrs of a fascist movement that demonized any form of dissent.

Sometimes losers become winners over time.

In February 1944, George Orwell used the aforementioned phrase as the title for a newspaper column. During the Spanish Civil War, he said, he often felt that "a true history of this war never would or could be written." Accurate reports of what had happened simply could not break through at the time, or as long as Franco dominated Spain and the Cold War made the tragic complexity of the pre-World War II conflict too inconvenient to be honestly faced.

"In the last analysis our only claim to victory is that if we win the war we shall tell fewer lies about it than our adversaries," Orwell concluded. "The really frightening thing about totalitarianism is not that it commits 'atrocities' but that it attacks the concept of objective truth; it claims to control the past as well as the future."

This book is an attempt to revisit Vermont's past with fresh eyes, to recast the drama, correct the record, and reclaim stories lost, distorted or buried along the way.

Vermont's history in the 20th century has at the least been co-authored by progressive movements that repeatedly transformed its politics. The first was the early 1900s reform era led by Burlington's fiery Irish Catholic mayor James Burke. Uniting the city's growing diversity, Burke ushered in public power, experimented with independent politics, and—in the words of a *Burlington Free Press* eulogy—stirred "the smoldering embers of democracy when they seemed to be dying out."

Despite that breakthrough, the state was a Republican bastion for almost a century. Yet the dominant party had its own rebel factions, and forward-thinking reformers who saw a role for government in improving infrastructure and social well-being. Joining forces with Democrats and Independents, they eventually helped elect Phil Hoff in 1962, the first Democratic governor since 1853. This was sparked by a passion for reform and an influx of immigrants—in this case ex-urbanites looking for a higher quality of life. Before it was over,

Vermont became a two-party state with a reputation for environmental innovation and independent thinking.

After redefining Vermont politics in the 1980s, Sen. Bernie Sanders entered the national stage, leading the Progressive Caucus in Congress and battling to mitigate the impacts of economic inequality, climate change, racial injustice, and corporate abuse. After 16 years as Vermont's sole representative in the U.S. House, he in 2006 replaced retiring Sen. James Jeffords, who had concluded his own political career by leaving the Republican Party and becoming an Independent.

Then Sanders ran for president. Twice.

Vermont's story is filled with such rebellious individuals and collective outbursts, people and moments that forged its path as a small, independent state with a strong sense of how to preserve its traditions while changing with the times. *Restless Spirits & Popular Movements* looks at this unique history through memorable events and people who helped create the delicate balance of sovereignty and solidarity, political independence and mutual aid known as the Vermont Way.

That said, Vermont is not some bucolic refuge, a New England Shangri-La without flaws, blind spots and dark corners.

Along with its virtues and achievements, it has at times practiced the provincial politics of exclusion, delay, and judging books by their covers. Case in point: A century after the women's suffrage movement, Vermont politics remains largely a white men's club. The three-member Congressional delegation is all male—and always has been. No woman has ever represented Vermont in Washington. And only one has been governor. Still, the main thrust of its history reveals enduring values like accountability, autonomy, tolerance, balance, equality, conservation, pragmatism, mutual aid and human scale.

This version of the story will explore such tendencies and values through the exploits of Vermonters like revolutionary leaders Matthew Lyon and the Allen brothers; Anti-Mason trailbrazers William Palmer and Thaddeus Stevens and feminist pioneer Clarina Howard Nichols; railroad and marble tycoons, anti-slavery activists, socialist organizers and labor protesters; Vermont-born Presidents Chester Arthur and Calvin Coolidge; political innovators James Burke and Ernest Gibson; modern political leaders including Phil Hoff, Richard Snelling, Madeleine Kunin, James Jeffords, Howard

Dean, and Bernie Sanders; and even one Vermonter who rescued America from Joseph McCarthy.

****

What follows has been taking shape since my on-the-job training as a reporter and photographer for the *Bennington Banner* from 1968–1970. Thanks must go to Tyler Resch, for being a patient and thoughtful editor, and Elizabeth Dwyer, the paper's inimitable editorial page editor and a postgraduate tutor in political science and Vermont values.

Dwyer had a sense of humor, and often joked about erecting a toll booth at the border with New York. The "flatlanders" were finding it too easy to get in, she would say, and it wouldn't hurt to discourage them. A liberal skeptic and compassionate realist with a sense of irony, she stressed the downside of being attractive to outsiders, the pitfalls of progress and the dangers of undervaluing what the state has going for it.

Working as a journalist in southwestern Vermont, and later in Burlington, I developed an urge to understand the underlying who, how and why of what was happening—the backstory. Even if the news was a "first draft" of history, I thought that reporting should incorporate as much context as possible on a deadline.

In 1976, a new approach to writing history was suggested by Robert Mueller, a friend who had written an essay about colonial and post-Revolutionary War Vermont. His idea was to examine myths and profile popular movements, but he needed help completing the project. My partner Jo Schneiderman and friend Roby Colodny contributed material on the women's movement and labor. I wrote about Vermont's second century, and we called the resulting collaboration *Vermont's Untold History*, a "people's history" in the spirit of Howard Zinn.

It was released during American bicentennial celebrations as an issue of *Public Occurrence*, a magazine produced by a collective and financed by our bookstore in Burlington. Support for a second edition came from the Haymarket People's Fund. Six years later, Schneiderman did further research on Clarina Nichols for *Inroads*, a short-lived magazine I edited for Vanguard Publishing.

Another significant step was taken during my time as editor and writer for the *Vermont Vanguard Press*, particularly after Bernie

Sanders became Burlington mayor in 1981. Thanks to new open leadership at City Hall, records once the exclusive domain of the Democratic establishment became more accessible for review. I pored over old minutes, speeches and legal documents, reconstructing the dramatic story of an earlier progressive era led by James Burke, an Irish blacksmith. The Chittenden Historical Society provided an award in 1984 that encouraged those inquiries. The chapter on James Burke in this book offers selected episodes from a larger saga.

In 1989 New England Press published *The People's Republic: Vermont and the Sanders Revolution,* an attempt to describe what I had seen as a reporter, editor, advocate, and columnist in the 1970s and 80s. The chapter included here on Bernie Sanders is a recap and update, with material from a 1998 interview, press conferences in 2011–12, interviews and online coverage of his presidential campaigns.

Thanks also go to mentors, friends and colleagues like Murray Bookchin, Frank Bryan, Dave Dellinger, Phil Hoff, Nora Jacobson, Marcia Marshall, John McClaughry, Louise Michaels, Shay Totten, and Nat Winthrop. Hoff also co-authored an essay for *Vermont Affairs* on the Snelling-Leahy race in 1986. A decade later, Totten provided the chance to reconnect with the Champlain Valley through Maverick Chronicles, a weekly column for *The Vermont Times.*

Robin Lloyd has been an invaluable collaborator on film and publishing projects since 1977. She and Gerard Colby provided feedback on early drafts of some material in this book. When director Nora Jacobson began recruiting collaborators for *Freedom & Unity: The Vermont Movie,* a six-part documentary, Robin and I decided to focus on the Green Mountain Parkway. My research became the basis for a film segment and a May 2012 presentation at the University of Vermont with Frank Bryan and Bruce Post, sponsored by the Center for Research on Vermont.

In August 2012, the Vermont History Center hosted a multimedia presentation in Barre on Vermont's progressive movements. Jamie Franklin, curator at the Bennington Museum, used my articles and photographs for the *Bennington Banner* as a basis to create the 2019 exhibit, Fields of Change: 1960s Vermont.

News organizations have also helped, by providing work and publishing early versions of some stories presented here. Thanks to VTDigger.com and its editor Anne Galloway, and Rob Williams, editor of *Vermont Commons* and *Green Mountain Noise*. Other outlets that supported the research by offering assignments and publishing articles include the *Vermont Vanguard Press, Burlington Free Press, Rutland Herald, Brattleboro Reformer, Vermont Guardian* and *Seven Days*.

I am also grateful for the support and assistance of Richard Watts, director of the Center for Research on Vermont, and Emily Anderson, program coordinator and research director, who supervised the development of this book, along with copy editor Jessie Forand, designer Abby Kaiser, and Linda Roghaar, publisher of White River Press.

After writing about Vermont for more than 50 years, and interacting with many of the state's politicians, activists and thinkers along the way, this is an effort to define some of the state's basic values and traditions, and how upheavals and individuals have affected its development and self-image. It also recounts memorable moments that exemplify the Vermont Way. Some of the opening chapters rely on archival research and previous books about the state; discussion of recent events draws largely from my direct experiences and interviews with those involved. An earlier draft was released online in 2017.

As Ken Burns put it, history is a table around which we can all sit and have a conversation. By having that talk—embracing the past, re-examining, reliving and most of all remembering it—my hope is that constructive, well-informed decisions can be made going forward. In that spirit, *Restless Spirits & Popular Movements* is a modest contribution to a much longer discussion.

— Greg Guma,
May 2021

Milestones

1

Image and Reality

Evening summer breeze
Warbling of a meadowlark
Moonlight in Vermont

In the midst of World War II the name of a small New England state was featured in the title of a frothy, B-grade Hollywood musical. Released in 1943, *Moonlight in Vermont* told the fanciful story of Gwen Harding, fresh off a Green Mountain farm and yearning for an acting career. Out of her element in the big city Gwen enrolls in a snobby New York drama school and falls in love with another student, Slick Ellis. But some of the kids are mean; that is, until they prove their basic decency by showing up unexpectedly at the family farm in Vermont to help with the harvest. It was a perfect, albeit bland and formulaic set up for some songs.

A popular tune of the era took the same name, although it wasn't featured in the film. Written by John Blackburn and Karl Suessdorf, the song began:

Pennies in a stream
Falling leaves of a sycamore
Moonlight in Vermont

Milestones

> *Icy fingers wave*
> *Ski trails on a mountain side*
> *Snowlight in Vermont*[1]

In reality, Vermont has few sycamores—or meadowlarks for that matter. The substitutions may have occurred because Blackburn, one of the lyricists, hailed from Ohio. In any case, after Margaret Whiting recorded *Moonlight in Vermont* in 1944 it became the unofficial state song, reprised for decades at weddings and special occasions. The film and the song combined to create a picturesque view of the state that dominated for decades—down-to-earth, a country haven, wholesomely romantic, just a few farms, mountains and ski resorts, with plain-spoken, relatively guileless folk.

The TV series *Newhart* used Vermont as a backdrop, its main characters a sophisticated ex-urban couple struggling to run a country hotel. For laughs in the 1980s they turned to Larry, Daryl and Daryl, locals who came across like the Marx Brothers on Quaaludes. In the decades since that sitcom stereotype, Vermont has become better and more favorably known for its weekend getaways, boutique products—luxury items like maple syrup, Ben and Jerry's ice cream and custom-made teddy bears—and frequently, liberal politics.

Gloria Jean and Ray Malone in *Moonlight in Vermont*
Inset: label of the popular record

---

1 John Blackburn and Karl Suessdorf, 1944

Few feature films have actually been set in the state. Jay Craven has translated writer Howard Frank Moser's regional stories for the screen and Nora Jacobson created the homegrown 2013 documentary, *Freedom & Unity: The Vermont Movie*, assembling the work of more than a dozen filmmakers into a six-part series. But most films use it as a convenient backdrop or reference point, portraying Vermont as either a rural sanctuary (*The Stranger, Baby Boom, What Lies Beneath, Sweet Hearts Dance*), romantic getaway (references date from *Three Days of the Condor* to countless romantic comedies), period-piece setting (*Dead Poets Society, The Jacket*) or eccentric enclave (*The Trouble with Harry, Super Troopers*).

On the campaign trail in early 1972 for *Rolling Stone*, Hunter Thompson once mused, "Strange country up here; New Hampshire and Vermont appear to be the East's psychic answer to Colorado and New Mexico—big lonely hills laced with back roads and old houses where people live almost aggressively by themselves."[2]

Decades later, at the end of the 2009 sci-fi blockbuster *I am Legend*, two survivors escape to Bethel, where the post-zombie apocalypse colony looks like a typical Vermont town—with the addition of a fortified gate. In the HBO hit *True Blood*, a series that often suggested allegories with the rights of the LGBTQ community, Vermont was the first place to legalize vampire weddings.

Still, beyond the pop culture references, what most non-residents know about Vermont remains limited to a few basics—small, cold, quirky, and isolated. This is accurate, as far as it goes. Size, climate and location have all had an influence on its development and the evolving nature of its image. After more than 200 years as a state, it remains one of the smallest, 43rd in land area. It consumes less energy than any other except Alaska and Connecticut, and, as of 2019, had less violent crime than all but Maine.

At just over $34 billion, Vermont's gross domestic product was about the same as Libya's in 2020. But the African nation had ten times the people—6.7 million versus less than 630,000 in Vermont, a number that put it above only Wyoming.

There is also no denying that the winters are long and frigid, although the relatively short summers are pleasant enough and, due to

---

2 Hunter S. Thompson, *Fear and Loathing at Rolling Stone*, Simon & Schuster, 2011

deciduous forests, fall produces intensely colorful foliage that attracts countless leaf peepers.

Shoe-horned between upstate New York, New Hampshire to the east, Massachusetts to the south, and the Canadian border above, Vermont is landlocked. Before the advent of modern highways, mass communication and the internet, it felt like a world apart, self-consciously different and relatively unspoiled by progress. Even more recently its location has fed an image of the state as an enduring frontier; as the Vermont Historical Society's 2004 state history, *Freedom and Unity* described it, "continuously creating and recreating itself in relative isolation from other states and the nation as a whole."[3]

Beginning in the early 19th century, Vermonters were forced to deal with periodic population shifts and losses as residents found it harder to survive, or sought opportunities and excitement in cities or new territories. The remote location and severe weather helped to nurture an ethic of "rugged individualism" and hard work, but also fed an underlying tension.

On one hand, most Vermonters wanted to maintain traditions and live in harmony with the natural world. On the other, they were lured by the opportunity, convenience and creature comforts of larger, warmer, less isolated places.

Comparisons have been made with Switzerland, another landlocked place with a history of decentralist politics and reputation as a political renegade. Switzerland also has more than ten times Vermont's population, and more diversity because of its location between France, Germany, Austria, Italy and Liechtenstein. Yet like Vermont its geography required it to deal with issues like regional balance, and it too was frequently a haven for political exiles and intellectuals.

One prominent exile with ties to both places was Nobel Prize for Literature winner Aleksandr Solzhenitsyn, who was deported from the Soviet Union in 1974. For a time he lived in Zurich, then moved to the United States and eventually settled in Cavendish in 1976.[4] Attending a Town Meeting there in 1994, Solzhenitsyn said that in Vermont he had observed "the sensible and sure process of grassroots democracy, in which the local population solves most of its problems on its own,

---

3 Michael Sherman, Gene Sessions and P. Jeffrey Potash, *Freedom and Unity: A History of Vermont*, Vermont Historical Society, 2004
4 David Wallechinsky and Irving Wallace, *The People's Almanac*, Doubleday, 1975

not waiting for the decisions of high authorities. Unfortunately, we do not have this in Russia, and that is still our greatest shortcoming."[5]

Up from Oligarchy

Like a perennial flower that defies climatic change, local control has re-blossomed regularly in Vermont since its birth. The forces nurturing this frequently endangered species have changed—from temperance activists and radical populists in the early days to peace activists and greens in the 1980s, conservative Republicans in the late 1990s and the secession-inspired independence movement of recent times. But it never fails to stimulate a spirited response, and sometimes highlights the distance between image and reality.

The enduring image—some call it a myth—is that Vermont has a unique democratic heritage tied to traditions like Town Meeting Day, a citizen legislature, and resistance to centralized power. This is part of Vermont's sense of difference, that indescribable attitude sometimes called the Vermont Way. The term has been used to describe everything from the traditional way to make maple syrup and smart farming practice to a political campaign agenda and the ability to create something out of almost nothing. Sometimes it is extended into the phrase "Vermont way of life."

When he left the Republican Party in 2001, James Jeffords said, "Independence is the Vermont Way." Consuelo Northrup Bailey, a native Vermonter who was the first female attorney admitted to practice before the U.S. Supreme Court and, in 1955, became the first female lieutenant governor in the nation, remarked in her autobiography that the character of Vermont was defined by "everyday, common, honest people who unknowingly salted down the Vermont way of life with a flavor peculiar only to the Green Mountains."[6]

Authors Frank Bryan and John McClaughry tried to capture the idea in their decentralist manifesto, *The Vermont Papers: Recreating Democracy on a Human Scale*. "God-given liberties, hostility to the central power, whatever it may be, their attachment to their towns and

---

5 *Burlington Free Press*, Feb. 28, 2011
6 Consuelo Northrup Bailey, *Leaves Before the Wind: The Autobiography of Vermont's Own Daughter*, George Little Press, 1976

schools and local communities, their dedication to common enterprise for the common good—all these have been among the most cherished Vermont traits, the subject of countless eulogies of Vermont tradition over the years."[7]

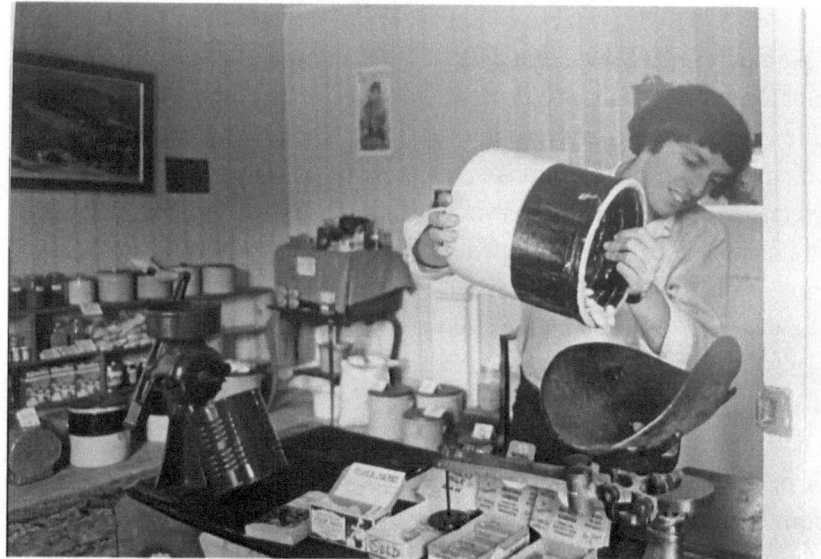

John Jennings weighed peanuts in a Bennington health food store, one of many countercultural enterprises launched as organic farming and natural living made a mark in the 1970s.

Still, these libertarian-leaning thinkers acknowledged that reality is more complex. While the 1777 Vermont Constitution included certain open government provisions, celebrated the consent of the governed—in theory at least, abolished slavery and created a comprehensive education system, it also placed considerable power in the hands of the governor and his council. It has even been argued, notably by historian H. Nicholas Muller III, that "early government in Vermont functioned more like an oligarchy than a democracy."[8] Before the State's senate was created, the council with the governor combined the power of an upper legislative chamber with the executive branch.

---

[7] Frank Bryan and John McClaughry, *The Vermont Papers: Recreating Democracy on a Human Scale*, Chelsea Green, 1990

[8] H. Nicholas Muller III, *Early Vermont State Government: Oligarchy or Democracy? 1778-1815, From Growth and Development of Government in Vermont*, Vermont Academy of Arts and Sciences, Occasional Papers #5, 1970

Today Vermont voters elect statewide officials every two years. Under the original plan, there were annual elections for 16 jobs, including the governor, lieutenant governor, treasurer, and 13-member council. Councilors could simultaneously serve as Supreme Court Justices. The result of this system was closely-held power and few losses for incumbents, leading to longer tenure in office.

After about nine years, but before Vermont joined the United States, the state constitution was amended, creating something closer to what exists today—three separate branches of government with distinct powers. But the Governor's council survived for another half century, and the Council of Censors was also retained. This Federalist-inspired holdover from pre-revolutionary days was supposed to somehow oversee both the governor and legislature, making sure that laws were handled properly and the Constitution was followed. If not, the Censors could call a convention and propose amendments.

Doubts arose early about how Censors were elected, the council's vulnerability to partisan control and proceedings marked by prejudice. Yet Vermont hung onto this unusual institution until 1870. The council also had 13 members, elected at-large every seven years. Some proposed no amendments, but most years they conducted careful investigations and issued informative reports. Some historians argue that, considered in context, the Council of Censors represented advanced political thinking. But their annual conventions rarely sparked change.

In its first 40 years, only one of the censor's proposed amendments was ratified, and that one denied voting rights to foreign-born citizens until they were naturalized. Its most significant recommendation, offered in 1836 after several years with an anti-Masonic governor, led to the creation of the state senate. Another council convention reformed the constitutional amendment process in 1870. In doing so, the censors abolished themselves.

According to Ira Allen, public support for the original Vermont Constitution was limited. Had it been submitted to the people, he wrote in his history of the state, "it is very doubtful whether a majority would have confirmed it." And he would have known. Allen was on the Council of Censors from the beginning, along with his brother Heman, his trusted associate Thomas Chittenden, Thomas Jefferson ally Matthew Lyon, and other business associates. This small group controlled negotiations with the British during the revolution, the composition of the early Supreme Court, and, for several decades, almost everything that made it through the General Assembly.

On the other hand, Vermont had the tradition of Town Meeting. The roots of the idea went back to England and the Massachusetts Bay Colony, eventually spreading through most of New England. In the days of the Bay Colony, the sense that participation was a social obligation was so great that fines were sometimes imposed for non-attendance.[9] But the crucial business conducted by the 19th century was largely appointive. For example, residents would gather to select "tything men" to act as general police, and sometimes pound-keepers or supervisors—known as "reaves"—whose responsibility was to care for hogs and other animals.[10]

The Green Mountains, from Wing Farm, Rochester

That Special Feeling

Vermonters often debate whether the state is somehow exceptional, a sense that has profoundly influenced its self-image. The landscape is certainly extraordinary and, in historical terms, there is a basis for

---

9 Andrew and Edith Nuquist, *Vermont State Government and Administration*, University of Vermont, 1966
10 Ibid.

the idea. After all, it was an independent republic and the first state to ban slavery. Once anti-slavery activism opened the door for the Republican Party, it stayed solidly Republican for a century. At the least this makes it unusual.

The population has remained small and predominantly white, but the political system features the direct democracy of town meeting, short terms for officials, strong environmental laws, and distinction as the first state legislature to legalize gay marriage. On the other hand, the sense of being different has sometimes fed a tendency toward isolationism and even provincial localism.

Dorothy Canfield Fisher once suggested that the whole state could be turned into a new kind of National Park, a place tourists could visit to see how their grandparents once lived. The state history *Freedom and Unity* calls this insight somewhat prescient, since "Vermont represents itself to the rest of the nation as just such a theme park."[11]

When he was getting started politically in Vermont, Bernie Sanders argued that "exceptionalist" thinking was a distraction and a mistake. Like many progressives who came to the state in the 1960s and later, he embraced a political philosophy that defined Vermont as, more or less, a cog in the international capitalist system. But Sanders' perspective shifted once he became Burlington mayor, and in 1990 the state's sole representative in Congress. As the years passed, he often exhorted supporters during his re-election campaigns to "change history," and mused publicly that someday the rest of the country would catch on. In 2016 and 2020, millions of people apparently did, "feeling the Bern" during his extraordinary presidential campaigns.

In their decentralist manifesto Bryan and McClaughry made a case for the proposition that a tiny state like Vermont "can't save the world." But they predicted that it might be able to save itself, and along the way demonstrate by example how to win back democracy.

For political leaders like former Gov. Howard Dean, one of several Vermonters who have run for president, and Bernie Sanders, a socialist convert to exceptionalism who has witnessed both local and national government from the inside, that forecast may prove to be too modest.

---

11 Sherman et al, *Freedom and Unity: A History of Vermont*

The first violent altercation in the U.S. House.

2

A Man Called Lyon

The United States was still a very young nation when French armies marched boldly across Italy and Austria in 1798 under the command of an ambitious young general. Napoleon Bonaparte had already won backing at home to take the fight to Great Britain, although he ultimately opted for Egypt. In Philadelphia debate over the possibility of another armed conflict was underway in Congress Hall.

Until then disputes in the hall had been limited to intense verbal exchanges. But when Roger Griswold, a Connecticut Federalist, viscously attacked the revolutionary war record of Matthew Lyon, a Vermont ally of Thomas Jefferson, the latter statesman strode angrily across the chamber and spat in his critic's face. Griswold replied a few days later with a blow of his cane, which prompted Lyon to defend himself—with a set of fire tongs. They ended up kicking wildly at each other, rolling onto the floor until pulled apart.

It was the first physical fight in the national legislature's history, an early sign of divisive times to come. The Ethics Committee recommended censure, which also made Lyon the first Congressperson charged with such a violation. House members rejected the proposal.

This ornery Vermonter, who became known as "the spitting Lyon," was a printer, farmer and former soldier who had emigrated from Dublin in 1765. Orphaned at 14 years old, he arrived enslaved and was purchased by a Connecticut merchant. He bought his freedom after three years, and moved to Wallingford in 1774, where he organized a militia and joined the Green Mountain Boys. Although court-martialed during the Revolutionary War—a disputed incident of cowardice that Griswold used to attack him—Lyon became a member of the Vermont House of Representatives in 1778. He founded Fair Haven the next year, launching its first mills, a hotel, general store, forges and newspaper.[12]

Rumors of war with France were rampant as the 18th century ended. Some said French troops were moving on Florida and Louisiana. By April 1798 Congress had approved funds to arm merchant ships and fortify harbors. In May it instructed warships to capture any French vessel caught in American waters. Public fears were rising; the pressure for action was intense. According to historian David McCullough's biography of John Adams, even Adams' wife Abigail favored a declaration of war and criticized Congress for acting too slowly.[13]

John and Abigail Adams

Instead, the president and Congress decided to focus on enemies at home. As the summer temperature soared past 90 degrees in Philadelphia, lawmakers went further than Adams hoped, passing the notorious Alien and Sedition Acts. Adams called them war measures. After all, there were more than 25,000 French immigrants in the

---
12 William Doyle, *The Vermont Political Tradition, Northlight Studio Press*, 1984
13 David McCullough, *John Adams*, Simon & Schuster, 2001

country, most survivors of the slave uprising in Haiti on the island of Santo Domingo.

According to McCullough, in Philadelphia there were French newspapers, schools, booksellers, boarding houses and restaurants. "The French, it seemed, were everywhere," he writes, "and who was to measure the threat they posed in the event of war with France?"[14]

The Alien Act increased the period of residency to qualify for citizenship and gave the president the power to deport any foreigner he considered dangerous. But the more consequential law turned out to be the Sedition Act, which made it a crime to stir people up or write anything critical of the government, Congress, or the president.

Editor Noah Webster backed the idea, declaring it time to stop other newspaper editors from libeling public figures. Even George Washington commented privately that some publications deserved punishment for their attacks. War was the pretext, but a little censorship sounded reasonable to many leaders.

Officially, the purpose of the Sedition Act was to crack down on illegal actions that tended to cause the disruption or overthrow of the government. Rather than a foreign spy, however, the first target was Benjamin Franklin's grandson, Benjamin Franklin Bache, an opposition editor in Philadelphia who was arrested for libeling Adams.

In daily attacks he had belittled Adams as "president by three votes," mocking his weight and describing him as a British tool. Bache wasn't convicted, instead he died of yellow fever before he could stand trial.

Matthew Lyon was equally high on Adams' list. After the debate over the Alien and Sedition Acts, the Vermont representative had demanded a roll call vote to see "who are friends and enemies of the Constitution." Jefferson agreed with him, calling the repressive new laws an unconstitutional "reign of terror." But what ultimately triggered Adams into action was a letter to the editor.

Responding to an attack in the Federalist *Vermont Journal*, Lyon said the U.S. should stay out of war with France. The Adams administration, he went on, had forgotten the welfare of the people "in an unbounded thirst for ridiculous pomp, foolish adulation and selfish avarice."

---

14 McCullough, *John Adams*

There was also a comment about Lyon's foot and the seat of the president's pants.

Matthew Lyon

That was enough for Adams and his allies. Lyon was placed on trial in Vermont in front of a judge who had run against him for Congress, convicted of bringing the President and government into contempt. Fined $1,000, sentenced to four months, he was marched to jail in chains through the streets of Vergennes. Rather than being confined at the relatively comfortable state lock up, he was placed in a 12 x 16 foot cell with thieves, murderers and runaway slaves. The sentence was imposed in October 1799, just a month before he was up for re-election.

Adams and the Federalists had made a tactical error, however. They had targeted a hero, an admired figure who had come to the colonies as an indentured servant, fought the British with Ethan Allen, and married one of Allen's cousins. As a result Vermont voters defied the president and re-elected Lyon anyway. Despite his occasionally extreme behavior the arrest had made him even more popular, an early example of the state's outspoken, contrarian—sometimes defiant—independent streak.

Casting the Crucial Vote

The presidential race of 1800 was unique. For the only time in U.S. history, the President ran against the Vice President. Since Matthew Lyon's trial for sedition, eleven more people had been convicted under the law. But that didn't stop the anti-Federalist press from calling Adams a monarchist, an old man too impressed with the British. Some claimed he was insane.

There were equally harsh attacks on Thomas Jefferson, from weakling and French intriguer to libertine and unrepentant atheist who mocked Christian religion. But the attacks on Adams came from both anti-Federalist Republicans, who considered him a warmonger, and Federalists who said he was too cowardly to confront the French.

Lyon was out of jail by then and back in Congress. Vermont voters hadn't held his jail time or anti-war views against him. In fact, he was considered a martyr for free speech, someone who had refused to beg for a pardon and served out his time. But after his release he needed help paying the fine. General Steven Thompson Mason, a senator from Virginia and a friend, took care of that. Collecting contributions from allies like Jefferson, James Madison and James Monroe, Mason rode from his home in the south to Vergennes to deliver the required $1,000 in gold coins.

When Lyons was finally released from jail and departed for Middlebury, legend has it that crowds lined the streets for 12 miles to cheer him on.

The presidential race turned out to be closer than anyone expected. Adams did well enough in New England, but lost in New York, the West and South. The outcome in New York was largely the result of Aaron Burr's influence in New York City. Counting up electoral votes from the nation's 16 states, Jefferson had 73 to 65 for Adams and 63 for Charles Pinckney, a Federalist stalwart from South Carolina. But Burr, who was ostensibly running to be Jefferson's Vice

President, also had 73 votes, which technically created a tie. And meant that the decision went to the House of Representatives.

Burr's refusal to step aside and clear the way for Jefferson soon fueled suspicions that he was privately bargaining with the Federalists. Alexander Hamilton distrusted both men but preferred Jefferson, the current Vice President. "Mr. Burr loves nothing but himself, thinks of nothing but his own aggrandizement," Hamilton charged, "Jefferson is in my view less dangerous than Burr."

In the end, the tie-breaking vote was cast by Lyon, the same person whom Adams had targeted under the Sedition Act. Lyon respected Burr as a New York power broker, but was philosophically allied with Jefferson. Thus, it surprised few people when he picked the Virginian over Boston's first citizen to be the next president. After Burr shot Hamilton about four years later, Lyon suggested that he move to Tennessee and run for Congress. Burr was already thinking about western secession.

Compatriots at first, Hamilton and Burr ended up in a deadly battle for power. The reasons for their July 11, 1804 duel in Weehawken, NJ were complex, in part about honor and unflattering words. But Hamilton also saw Burr as a threat to the nation, a fear justified when Burr launched a scheme to seize part of the Louisiana Purchase and create a separate country.

In 1801, Adams wrote bitterly about Lyon and those like him. "Is there no pride in American bosoms? Can their hearts endure that (James) Callendar, (William) Duane, (Thomas) Cooper and Lyon should be the most influential men in the country, all foreigners and all degraded characters?" All four had been charged with sedition. Adams labeled them "foreign liars," and also suggested, a bit oddly, that there were "no Americans in America."

Lyon's crucial vote meanwhile added to his fame. He had defied a president and helped install what seemed like a more open, Republican administration. Yet he represented Vermont for just one more year before moving to Kentucky in 1801. There he quickly won more terms as a U.S. House Representative, for his new home from 1803–1811.

After building gunboats for the federal government during the War of 1812, however, he went bankrupt when the Department of War declined to honor its contract with him.

By 1818 Mathew Lyon rebuilt his finances and was looking for a new career. In 1820, he found it when President James Monroe, another friend, sent him as a liaison to the Cherokee Nation in the Arkansas Territory. But Lyon really wanted to return to Congress and soon sought a seat as Arkansas territorial delegate to Washington. This time he lost by less than 60 votes, and unsuccessfully contested the results. He died two years later.

Like other illustrious Vermonters who followed him, Matthew Lyon had planted some righteous seeds and played a timely role, but moved on to follow his dreams.

The Oneida Nation's "Allies in War, Partners in Peace" statue greets visitors to the Smithsonian's National Museum of the American Indian.

3

People of the Land

Long before Matthew Lyon, Samuel de Champlain or any other Europeans set foot in the Green Mountains, Indigenous people lived along the waters later named Champlain and the Connecticut River. Early villages were well established near the areas known today as Winooski, Swanton and Newport, while Barton Landing was often used as a stopping point for river travel.

Central Vermont may not have been much inhabited, but it was certainly used by tribes for hunting and fishing. Cossucks came from the upper Connecticut River and Pequots traveled from the lower. Iroquois and Abenaki people, the latter part of the Wabanaki Confederacy, lived near Lake Champlain and traveled widely by canoe, sometimes encountering Algonquins or Mohawk people, who were part of the Iroquois Confederacy and also used the land.

Early French traders in Quebec called any Indigenous person who did business with them Abenaki. Later, the term was extended to tribes from the Penobscot watershed to Lake Champlain, the Richelieu River, and south into Massachusetts and New Hampshire. But the Abenaki people made distinctions and the tribes had different dialects. In the east were the Kenebecs, Amarascogginns and Penobscots; to the west the Missisquoi, Penacooks and Winnipesaukees of the upper Merrimack, and the Cowasucks and Sokokis of Connecticut. Eastern tribes looked to the coast, western ones more to farming.

The Abenaki people called their homeland Ndakinna, for "our land." Eastern members were mostly based in Maine east of the White Mountains; western Abenaki people lived west of the mountains, across New Hampshire and Vermont to the shores of Lake Champlain. The southern boundaries were near the current northern border of Massachusetts. Maritime Abenaki people occupied St. Croix and the St. John's River valleys near the border between Maine and New Brunswick.

Settlements and war forced many Abanaki people to retreat north into Quebec where communities formed at St. Francois and Becancour near Trois-Rivieres survive to the present day. There are reservations in northern Maine (Penobscot, Passamaquoddy, and Maliseet) and reserves in New Brunswick and Quebec. Other communities of Abenaki people are scattered across northern New Hampshire and Vermont.

First European contact with some Abenaki people may have occurred in 1605 during Samuel de Champlain's visit to a village at the mouth of the Saco River. He certainly visited the lake in July 1609, enchanted by its islands, Vermont's woods, open meadows and abundant game.[15] A decade later Ferdinando Gorges spent a winter in the region after King James gifted him most of what became the State of Maine. But the best evidence suggests that direct contact between Europeans and tribe members living in Vermont didn't occur until decades later.

What early explorers and settlers saw was truly exceptional. In the southwest corner at the eventual border with New York stood Mount Anthony, conical and isolated over a pristine valley, site of Bennington, the first chartered town. On the east rose the Green Mountains, to the west the Taconic range. The Walloomsac River wound around a hill at the center of what became Old Bennington, then ran past revolutionary era battlefields into the Hoosac and on to the Hudson.

Moving north, the valley narrowed toward Castleton, Rutland and Mt. Equinox, while the Battenkill River ran south through the mountains at Arlington and entered the Hudson not far from Saratoga. Another stream, the Otter Creek, flowed north into Lake Champlain

---

15 David Hackett Fischer, *Champlain's Dream*, Simon & Schuster, 2008

and then on into the St Lawrence River. Looking west from Mt. Mansfield at the peak of the mountains, the lowlands descended to an island-dotted lake. The Worcester range lay to the east, and beyond that the White Mountains of New Hampshire.

Indigenous villages were usually located on streams adjacent to the Connecticut River on the east and Lake Champlain on the west. Others lived on high bluffs, good lookout spots to protect against raids. In the winter villagers lived on maize, nuts, dried berries and meats, and wild plants. Hunting season could begin in February. The territories used to hunt were defined by a system of water-related trails, each controlled by a family band. No one else was supposed to hunt there without permission, although it was rarely denied to a relative. Moose and deer, which had difficulty moving around in deep snow, were popular prey, but bear, muskrat, otter, and beaver were also fair game.

As spring approached the focus shifted back to the villages, and toward maple tree tapping by women and children. Crops were planted by early May, with women responsible for corn, beans and squash while men sometimes cultivated tobacco in separate gardens. In the summer they took white pine canoes to fish the lakes with hooks of stone, bone and wood. This was also the season to travel and visit other bands.[16]

According to Frederick M. Wiseman, an Abenaki Nation member and college professor, the Winoskik Abenaki people congregated near today's city of Winooski for spring fishing. "Following the fish harvest, the intervale valley was an excellent place to grow corn, beans, squash and tobacco. Yearly flooding of the river, tightly controlled today, gave the crops renewed fertile soil year after year. After the fall harvest the Winooski people dispersed upriver to hunting camps, returning to the main river for the winter. The coming of maple sugaring heralded the spring fish run and the cycle continued."[17]

The French built the earliest European outpost on Isle La Motte in 1666; the Dutch and British followed. By 1724 the first British settlement, Fort Dummer, was guarding settlers near present-day

---

16 William Haviland and Marjory Power, *The Original Vermonters: Native Inhabitants, Past and Present*, University of New England Press, 1981

17 Frederick Wiseman, *The Abenaki and the Winooski*, from *The Mills at Winooski Falls*, Onion River Press, 2000

Brattleboro, just west of the Connecticut River. Other settlements crept north along the river into southern Vermont and New Hampshire. Long before that, however, the impact of European contact was felt in the form of imported diseases.

Indigenous people used high lookouts to keep watch over colonial settlements.

Prior to 1535, the indigenous population of New England was possibly more than 90,000, including about 10,000 Abenaki living in what is today Vermont and New Hampshire. An estimated 4,200 were based in the Champlain Valley, and another 3,800 in the upper Connecticut River Valley, according to Dean Snow, an archaeologist at Penn State University. Using waterways and trails, they stayed in touch with other indigenous people who had encountered Europeans. But that was before germs and viruses made their way into Vermont and brought those numbers down.

After an initial epidemic moved along the St. Lawrence valley in 1535, more followed in 1564 and 1570. New England also suffered an apparent typhus outbreak in 1586. There are no reliable estimates on how many Abenaki people in Vermont became victims. But the series of epidemics that ravaged coastal New England from 1616–1619 provide a sense of the potential impact. Estimates of the mortality rate from those outbreaks run as high as 75 percent. Some researchers point to yellow fever as the source, others suggest smallpox, chickenpox, or trichinosis. But it also may have been rodent-infected water from European ships contaminating local water supplies.

The French mainly used trade and religion to conquer the region. They learned the language and offered some Indigenous people muskets for defense. By 1740 about 1,000 French were living in the Champlain Valley. When not fighting British settlers, Abenaki people traded with them. But that made them more dependent on material goods and weapons. Meanwhile, the British extended outposts and trained rangers to fight tribes in both Massachusetts and Vermont.

From 1723–1727, Grey Lock, who was a Massachusetts Woronoke based near Lake Champlain, raided towns and fought British settlers along the Connecticut River. Fort Dummer near Brattleboro was built in response, and used as a base to attack Indigenous settlements. Grey Lock never made peace with the invaders, but the highest peak in the Berkshires bears his name.[18]

Even after the French and English were well-established Abenaki, people continued to live at the mouth of the Lamoille River. In 1765, however, a tribe leased a five-mile strip of land along the lake, near Swanton, to John Robertson. The agreement said that the land was to be returned after 91 years—in 1856.[19] The Abenakis then left to winter with the St. Francis band on the St. Lawrence River and hunt at Lake Memphremagog. The idea of mutual rights to use the land would soon confront the concept of private ownership.

---

18 Cynthia D. Bittinger, *Vermont Women, Native Americans & African Americans: Out of the Shadows of History*, History Press, 2012
19 At least one Abenaki tribe held onto the lease to Robertson.

Robertson's lease granted timber rights on Abenaki lands in exchange for rent in the form of corn and an annual payment in gold. In the aftermath of the American revolution, however, as New York and New Hampshire pursued conflicting claims, surveyors associated with the Allen family divided the land among prominent pioneers.

Without deeds or titles, the Allen-owned Onion River Land Company later sold property inhabited in the past by Missisquoi Abenaki.

In 1798—33 years after the agreement—a group of Abenaki bands sent a delegation to the Vermont Legislature, by then part of the United States. The representatives carried a petition, signed by 20 chiefs on behalf of the Seven Nations of lower Canada, that claimed their territory. This included all of the land west of the Green Mountains and between Ticonderoga and the provincial line.

Vermont's legislature rejected the petition, arguing that the Abenaki people had forfeited their property by revolting from the English and joining the French. Their title had been lost, said the new Vermonters, when the area was ceded to the English by right of conquest. The French had focused on fur trading and made less effort to colonize.

By 1754, New France had 75,000 European settlers while British America had 1.5 million. At the end of the French and Indian War in 1763, the region that ultimately became Vermont fell under British rule. Since the colonists had defeated the British, the government of Vermont claimed ownership of the land. In fact, Ira Allen and other land traders argued that Indigenous people didn't even live in Vermont. They just passed through to hunt and fish. A myth was born.

The Abenaki community's struggle for land rights and tribal recognition has continued for more than two centuries. To date, they do not have formal U.S. recognition, but did briefly have state recognition in 1976 when Thomas Salmon conferred it near the end of his tenure. The next governor, Richard Snelling, rescinded the decision, dismissing Salmon's executive action as surrender to "romantic notions."

Given the contemporary image of the Green Mountain State as a refuge and laboratory for independent and progressive thinkers it can be jarring to look at the not-so-distant past, a time when Vermont was an isolationist white bastion in which Indigenous people had to call themselves gypsies to avoid sterilization.

Although Cynthia D. Bittinger doesn't stress this dark chapter in her book, *Vermont Women, Native Americans and African Americans: Out of the Shadows of History*, the impact of Vermont's eugenics movement clearly points to the need to revisit and update the state's traditional narrative. In the 1930s and later, both immigrants to Vermont and any other "non-Yankees" were widely considered outsiders, at best. Since about half of all residents today are "transplants," there is good reason to reconsider just who was and is a Vermonter, native, "real" or otherwise, and what has been previously omitted or downplayed in telling the state's story.

Even Calvin Coolidge, one of two Vermonters who became U.S. president, had Indigenous blood in his background. It was not uncommon. Unlike many Abenaki people, however, Coolidge did not feel the need to hide his ancestry. In fact, Vermont was viewed in the 1920s as the "last great white hope" of New England. But immigrants, "nomadic tribes" and others did not fit in with this squeaky-clean image and a related so-called "domestic hygiene" movement.

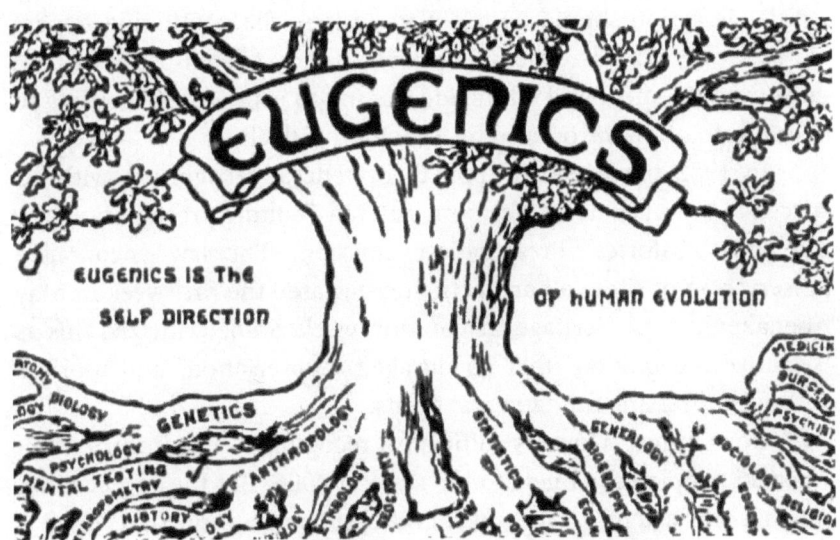

Logo of the International Eugenics Conference in 1921, depicting eugenics as a tree uniting various fields

The state's shameful plunge into control of "human breeding" was apparently driven by a mixture of xenophobia and a confused desire to weed out so-called defects. Harry Perkins, the University of Vermont professor who led the state's Commission on Country Life, publicly justified eugenics as a way to build a healthier society, eliminate poverty and prevent genetic diseases. But he focused specifically on the "hereditary degeneracy" of many Indigenous people and French-Canadians.

"Perkins was judging who was unfit to reproduce," Bittinger writes. "So he drafted a sterilization law that would provide prevention of propagation by consent."[20] Passed in 1931, it promised that the procedure would be "voluntary."

In reality, it wasn't. Although the total number sterilized remains unknown, the impact on the Abenaki community was dramatic. At least 253 cases have been documented, but many records were lost. It took almost half a century for the state to publicly acknowledge this disturbing human rights crime. Vermont's sterilization law remained in place until 1981.

In 2021, state lawmakers discussed issuing an official apology for the program. "The General Assembly recognizes that further legislative action should be taken to address the continuing impact of state-sanctioned eugenics policies and related practices of disenfranchisement and ethnocide leading to genocide," according to a draft resolution introduced by Rep. John Killacky.

In 1982 the Abenaki applied for federal recognition with no success. A decade later Vermont offered "cultural recognition" by the State Historical Preservation Division. The law encouraged preservation of sites and artifacts, and declared the first week in May Abenaki Cultural Heritage Celebration week. Some criticized this as "selective recognition" that encouraged "appreciation" and tourism without addressing fundamental rights.

Gov. James Douglas officially recognized the contribution Abenaki people have made to the state in 2006. But the appreciation still did not extend to legal recognition. The state finally created a commission authorized to recommend tribal recognition in 2010.

---

20 Bittinger, *Vermont Women, Native Americans & African Americans*

This may someday give the Abenaki access to federal funding for education and other benefits.

In 2011, the state officially recognized the Elnu Abenaki, based in Windham County, and the Nulhegan Band of the Coosuk Abenaki Nation in northeastern Vermont. In 2012 the Abenaki Nation at Missisquoi and Koasek Band of the Koas Abenaki Nation were added to that list. Beginning in January, 2021, the Vermont Fish and Wildlife Dept. began issuing free hunting and fishing licenses to certified citizens of Indigneous tribes recognized by the State.

The struggle for full recognition and meaningful reparations continues.

1796 regional map by J. Denison, identifying 11 Vermont counties; today there are 14 counties.

4

Birth of a Republic

In the 18th century, most Europeans who hadn't actually travelled to the "new world" thought Vermont was an untamed wilderness between the colonies of New Hampshire and New York. King George had allowed only small portions of it to be given away. But governors of the bordering colonies knew better, and saw it as a potentially valuable resource.

New Hampshire Gov. Bennington Wentworth took full advantage of this situation. On the instruction of the King, he gave the first of the "New Hampshire Grants" to British veterans, naming the very first—Bennington—after himself. Many of the initial title holders sold their property to land speculators. Wentworth later gave grants for entire towns. In return he took fees and 500 acres of land in every town—in violation of the King's orders. By 1764 he had granted 135 townships in the region that became Vermont.

Catching on to the abuse of Wentworth's authority and concerned about the "independence and unbridled democracy" of Vermont towns, King George instructed the Lt. Gov. of New York, Cadwallader Colden, to take over administration of the territory. This essentially made the future state a colony of New York—and fair game for its speculators. Since New Hampshire speculators weren't willing to stand aside, the stage was set for a battle between the two groups, along with the region's early settlers.

For most New Hampshire grantees, some of whom were defending their homesteads, the rallying cry was property rights. Their natural leaders were the Allens—Ethan, Ira, Heman, Ebenezer and Zimri Allen, along with their cousin Remember Baker—a family that eventually came to control a third of the land between the Green Mountains and Lake Champlain. The standout from the start was Ethan, who arrived around 1764 and established a base in Bennington. An impetuous lover of liberty who sometimes came across as a wild and reckless outlaw, he possessed a robust intellect and considerable persuasive powers. Though a blunt speaker with the potential to become violent, Allen was a natural leader, said to be loved by his followers.

After the King ceded Vermont's towns to New York, a convention of colonists "resolved to support their rights by force" and organized a military force with Ethan Allen in command. According to Edward Swift Isham, who delivered an impassioned address in 1898 defending Allen and colonial resistance, "The practical assertion of independence and the actual autonomy of Vermont date at least from 1764; and it is justly declared to have been the first actual autonomy on either American continent since the wreck of the great Indian monarchies of Mexico and Peru."[21]

Inhabitants of many towns formed committees of defense or safety, usually known as councils of safety, the first semblance of a government. Local groups slowly combined into a general Council of Safety, which began to call conventions. Sometimes a call was confined to a few towns on either the east or west side of the mountains. They were just conferences, but it was generally understood that they might someday lead to a form of civil government. The event that finally brought them together to create the Republic of Vermont was a request from the Continental Congress that the Green Mountain Boys join the army being raised to repel the British.

At first the rebel grantees wrote pamphlets and manifestos protesting a pattern of land seizures by New York. Summing up the basic philosophy, one document explained, "No person or community of persons can be supposed to be under any particular compact or law, except it pre-supposeth, that the law will protect such person or community of persons in his or their properties." But when they were

---

21 Edward Swift Isham, *Ethan Allen: A Study in Civic Authority*

rebuffed by the British and forced to pay additional fees to New York just to keep their land, the colonials soon turned to direct action.

The Catamount Tavern, built in the 1760s, was originally called the Green Mountain Tavern, one of three in Bennington for settlers on their way to frontier homes. When colonial protests began, patrons placed a stuffed catamount on the signpost to taunt Yorkers.

In the eastern section of the territory the first recorded confrontation, in response to a New York plan to replace New England town government with a county administration and courts, became known as the Windsor Riot. Forty residents of the town arrested a

New York Sheriff and his posse in 1770, thus ending the pursuit of four New Hampshire grantees.

Tactics differed in the western section. Here farmers were being evicted for non-payment of rent. But New Hampshire grantees were determined to have the land returned—by force if necessary. Thus, in July 1771 several hundred men blocked an eviction at the Breckenridge House in Bennington. In the inevitable showdown many of the New York Sheriff's deputies refused to advance on the settlers.

In October 1774, the violence that had taken place in Bennington and Windsor was condemned at a county convention in Westminster. Instead, those assembled voted for "manly, steady and determined procedures" to seek justice. But the expression of such principles was not enough to persuade more than a hundred men who stopped 25 New York Sheriff's deputies from establishing a court six months later. On March 13, 1775, deputies seized the courthouse by force and, in what became known as the Westminster Massacre, two New Hampshire grantees were killed. The next morning several hundred residents, led by the Green Mountain Boys, retook the building.

The resistance activities of the Green Mountain Boys were not restricted to sheriffs or their posses. On Jan. 1, 1775, for instance, they arrested a man named Hough. The charge was that he had "dissuaded people from joining the mob" and accepted the office of Justice of the Peace under New York authority. The punishment of an ad hoc court headed by Ethan Allen was 200 lashes on Hough's naked back.

The Green Mountain Boys used many types of force to impose their will, some of which might today be classified as torture or terrorism. Settlers foolish enough to accept land under the New York Grants were compelled to pay the owner of the title under the "officially" void New Hampshire Grants. In such cases the grantee was usually a speculator. If someone refused to pay, Ethan Allen threatened that his "mob would reduce every house to ashes and leave every inhabitant a corpse."

Fundamentally, these early Vermonters were engaged in a struggle for sovereignty and self-government; it was organized citizen resistance to outside authority, a concept that later appeared in the Vermont Constitution. A freeman's oath administered by town governments called on Vermonters "of a quiet and peaceable behavior" to follow their conscience as to "what will conduce to the best good of the (state) . . . without fear or favor of any man."

These revolutionaries understood that when people refuse to cooperate, withhold their help and maintain their position, they deny any opponent the support needed to rule. As Gene Sharp, author of *Social Power and Political Freedom*, has observed, "If they do this in sufficient numbers for long enough, that government or hierarchical system will no longer have power."

The movement toward American independence demonstrated this idea a full decade before the "shot heard round the world" and involved thousands of people. By the time things turned violent, substitute governments and firm alliances were operating in nine colonies.

Early colonial campaigns were often demands, backed by nonviolent actions that forced Britain to change its laws. Through economic boycott and the development of new government structures, John Dickinson wrote in 1767, colonists could pressure parliament by "withholding from Britain all the advantages they get from us." One pamphlet circulating at the time urged colonists to "bid defiance to tyranny by exposing its impotence."

Many colonists were already following this advice, refusing to comply with the new Stamp Act, a direct tax on all sorts of licenses, publications and legal papers, by resisting use of the stamps. According to Britain, the duty would be used to finance British troops "protecting" colonists from Indian "hostility" and French expansionism. Resistance began even before the act was official. This grassroots movement, which essentially nullified the law, involved a massive refusal to import British goods and the beginning of economic self-sufficiency in North America.

The forms of political defiance and direct action included civil disobedience and, in some cases, threats aimed at stamp distributors. No one was killed, but the threats and scattered attacks on property were effective deterrents. By November all the stamp distributors resigned, while ports and newspapers remained open despite the absence of stamps. Debts to British merchants were left unpaid. The Rhode Island Assembly resolved that only colonists could tax colonists. In order to avoid mass prosecution of resistors, however, George Washington advised that colonial courts be closed.

Despite the absence of violence, the threat to British rule was obvious. Power was swiftly being diffused through many substitute governments. Town meetings took to passing laws that were more widely obeyed than British regulations. By early 1768 more than four million pounds was owed to Britain's merchants, who pressured the King and parliament for action. The Stamp Act was repealed, but Britain simultaneously proclaimed that the right to tax the colonies still and would always exist. What couldn't be defended on the ground was brandished on paper.

The Townshend Acts, a 1768 attempt by new British Prime Minister Charles Townshend to impose an external levy, met just as much resistance. The new acts placed a tax on imported goods such as lead, paint, paper, glass, and tea. This time it wasn't merchants who initiated the campaign but mechanics, artisans and workers. The main method was non-consumption, along with development of economic alternatives along self-sufficient lines. When goods weren't bought and those on household shelves weren't used, merchants were forced not to import the boycotted items.

Non-importation put a squeeze on British merchants until the Acts died in 1770. But this time Britain was a bit cleverer: All taxes—except the duty on tea—were repealed. Falling short of total victory, the colonists became divided about the success of their campaign. In the confusion resistance disintegrated as Britain doggedly held onto its right to tax.

Despite the setback, colonial fervor persisted in other resistance efforts. The Committees of Correspondence, established years earlier as underground governments, maintained a network for expressions of solidarity, protests, mutual aid, and new ideas. In 1773, Britain provided the catalyst to test these emerging organs of popular power.

The East India Company, an early international monopoly, was in financial trouble. To help the influential business, Britain's parliament passed an Act controlling prices in order to give East India a colonial monopoly. The law manipulated the market so that even smuggled tea was more expensive. The Boston Tea Party was an early response; Bostonians in Indian garb dumped 342 chests of tea overboard. Britain responded by closing the Port of Boston and increasing repression.

The colonies mobilized, helped by their previous experiences with united action and Paul Revere's rides to "give you all the news." Many communities—New York, Philadelphia, Charlestown, Wilmington and Baltimore among them—pledged moral and economic support. Money, rice and sheep flooded into Massachusetts as Britain tried to undermine self-government.

Defying Britain, a Massachusetts Town Meeting resolved to cut off imports and exports, and called again for economic boycott. Revere rode to New York and Philadelphia with news of the Suffolk Resolves, soon adopted by the Continental Congress. All coercive laws were unconstitutional, the Congress had ruled, and are not to be obeyed. People were urged to form their own governments and deny taxes to the so-called "legal" governments in their regions.

Although the Resolves raised the possibility of war, the thrust remained nonviolent—boycott, tax resistance, non-importation (sometimes including slaves), and development of substitute local governments. The Continental Association, formed at the end of 1774, incorporated these approaches and added legal enforcement of "non-intercourse" along the lines used earlier in Virginia.

Conflicted Loyalties

In the spring of 1776 a revolutionary army ravaged by disease retreated along Lake Champlain to forts at Crown Point and Ticonderoga in New York. It had been a rough year so far. Dysentery and smallpox had undermined an invasion of Canada and spread to civilians. Fearful that it would not be long before British troops and their Indian allies arrived, settlers fled south from the Winooski valley and Lake Champlain. In October, an American fleet was demolished in a battle on the lake.

In the western part of Vermont, people looked to the Allen brothers and the Green Mountain Boys for protection from both the British and New York. But many people in the Connecticut Valley favored association with the Yorkers, while others rejected both them and the Allens. A year earlier a group of western Green Mountain men had gathered in Dorset at Cephas Kent's tavern to talk about terms for independence. They discussed whether New York laws should be recognized and how to deal with "schismatic mobs."

In April, Heman Allen, considered the level-headed brother, presented a petition to the Continental Congress that expressed the view of most western grantees. They wanted to join the fight for freedom, but would have nothing to do with those "monopolizing land traders" in New York. On July 24, a cross-section of colonists gathered in Dorset for their second convention. The stated purpose was to consider the consequences of the Declaration of Independence signed three weeks earlier. It pledged supporters to risk their lives and fortunes to "defend, by arms, the United States." Yet the Vermonters were also confronted with the adoption of a constitution in New York that claimed continued jurisdiction over the region.

Ethan Allen, Remember Baker, Thomas Chittenden and others often met at the Catamount Tavern to plan the activities of the Green Mountain Boys, Council of Safety, and later the Republic of Vermont. It burned down in 1871.

New York's constitution called for administration of the Green Mountain "colony," as well as land granting authority and the power to collect rents. It restricted the right to vote to male property owners and called for lifelong appointment of judges. Such choices in New York effectively ended debate in Vermont over secession from the

Empire State. In a unanimous vote, New Hampshire grantees decided to form a separate district.

The Dorset convention declared basic allegiance to the revolutionary project, and agreed that men from Vermont would join the fight. But support would be withdrawn, the delegates warned, if people were placed under New York command "in such a manner to be detrimental to our private property." The convention had no formal authority, yet it quickly won acceptance as a de facto government, at least for those living in the west, and was inching the region toward being either a state or a revolutionary government.

On Jan. 16, 1777, in a Westminster courthouse, another convention selected the name New Connecticut. This meeting was not as representative, just 26 men from 16 towns. But previous conventions had established the thrust of public opinion. The people were determined to form "a new and separate state." On June 4, 1777, at the suggestion of Dr. Thomas Young, a friend of Ethan Allen's from Pennsylvania, the name was changed to Vermont.[22]

The Council of Safety, which had called for the conventions, also authorized a Declaration of Independence and a Constitutional Convention. By March 1778 the newly independent state had held elections and was calling itself the Republic of Vermont. It promptly began issuing money and raising troops for the war.[23]

Was Vermont's support for revolution a way for land speculators to protect their disputed titles? To some extent, it's true. But similar to the Declaration of Independence, the Declaration of the Rights of Inhabitants that began the state Constitution adopted in July 1877 proclaimed that "all men are born equally free and independent, and have certain natural, inherent and inalienable rights, amongst which are the enjoying and defending of life and liberty; acquiring, possessing and protecting property; and pursuing and obtaining happiness and safety."

The first written constitution for an independent state in North America—also the shortest—Vermont's was the first one to establish

---

22 Lewis H. Meader, *The Council of Censors in Vermont*, address to the Vermont Historical Society, Vermont House Chamber, November 2, 1898
23 Andrew and Edith Nuquist, *Vermont State Government and Administration*

universal male suffrage and abolish slavery.[24] It said that people had the right to establish an independent government for their own protection. It was largely about property and self-determination, ambition and high ideals. The preamble echoed John Locke's assertion that governments should enable people to exercise their natural rights. And if they didn't, "the people have a right, by common consent, to change" them and do whatever "may appear necessary to promote their safety and happiness." The government structure created by the early Vermont Constitution was centralized and incomplete, but the basic philosophical approach was libertarian, flexible and inclusive.

At the same time, the Green Mountain Boys remained eager to please the Continental Congress, a position geared toward winning future statehood. Their plan was to capture Montreal from Gen. Frederick Haldimand, commander of the British army in the colonies. But two invasions failed, and so did negotiations with the new Congress. Large Vermont landowners had joined powerful New York and New Hampshire interests to oppose Vermont's statehood proposal. Action by the Vermont Assembly didn't help much: It accepted the petition of 16 disenfranchised frontier towns in New Hampshire that wanted to be part of Vermont. Heavy pressure from Ethan Allen and threats of attack from the Congress eventually persuaded the Assembly to pull the state's border back.

Ethan Allen and his boys were eager to join the fight for independence. But after a botched attempt to capture St. John in Canada the men reconsidered Allen's leadership and joined the continental army under the command of Seth Warner. Becoming impatient, Allen broke discipline and tried to take Montreal himself with just 100 men. Instead he was captured and spent the next two years as a prisoner of war, in Britain, Ireland and ultimately New York. His tempestuous individualism, invaluable in raising a rebellion, was proving less helpful in winning the war.

George Washington was nevertheless impressed. Observing Allen at Valley Forge he wrote, "There is an original something in him that

---

24 Historians do not agree on whether Ethan Allen had slaves, but his household included at least two Black servants. His brother Levi did practice slavery, and, according to the Ethan Allen Homestead Museum, Ethan's daughter Lucy Caroline Hitchcock illegally kept two slaves brought from an Alabama plantation in her Burlington home.

commands admiration, and his long captivity and sufferings have only served to increase, if possible, his enthusiastic zeal. He appears very desirous of rendering his services to the states and of being employed; and at the same time he does not discover any ambition of high rank."[25]

The Allens are often mentioned as founding fathers. Many people even believe they were among the signers of the Declaration of Independence. On the contrary, Ira Allen repeatedly entertained political overtures from the British. And rather than rejecting them, as a revolutionary patriot might, he opened up the first of the Haldimand negotiations. Allen basically offered the British general the support of Vermont, as long as the British recognized and protected Vermont's independence.

Ira Allen's apparent goal was regional autonomy, the proposal already rejected by the Continental Congress. It may have been a way to push the Congress into accepting Vermont as a state, or perhaps a commercial move to protect future trade with Canada. In any case, the Allen faction felt that their commercial interests would be best served by an independent state under their control. As a result, the radical entrepreneurs formed a strange alliance with British loyalists who remained in the colonies, wooing them to settle in the Allen-controlled Champlain Valley. This put them near British-controlled Quebec and freed them from persecution. Vermont eventually became a safe haven for deserters from both the British and colonial armies.

---

25 Edward Swift Isham, *Ethan Allen: A Study in Civic Authority*

Loyalty to the national government remained in doubt for decades, and many Vermonters opposed the War of 1812. But America's defeat of British forces on Lake Champlain, in only two hours on Sept. 11, 1814, brought the fight home.

5

From Independence to Statehood

Vermont emerged from the American Revolution in the best economic condition of any former colony. It had no state debts, and since the Continental Congress had refused to admit it, no responsibility for the national debt. Its currency was relatively strong and a stream of settlers had begun to arrive. The estimated population jumped from around 20,000 in 1776 to 85,000 when a census was taken 15 years later. In the west, where the Allen family held sway, commercial ties were pursued with Quebec. Timber, potash and meat went through the Richelieu rapids to Canadian markets. On the eastern side people shipped their goods south, down the Connecticut River to the American states.

With land as a foundation the Allen family essentially ran the new republic through their agent Thomas Chittenden, who became Vermont's first governor years before it joined the United States. A farmer and land speculator, possibly the first settler of what became Williston, Chittenden launched the Onion River Company with three Allen brothers. Many people resented their grip on the state. But Chittenden was popular with voters, a practical leader who successfully balanced the factions groping for influence during negotiations with the British and the new Congress.

Despite Chittenden's political gifts, however, repeated attempts to send delegates to the Continental Congress during the revolution were rebuffed. In fact, delegates were treated pretty shabbily, and felt they were being forced to fight both their neighbors and their enemies. Letters from Chittenden to George Washington continued to profess loyalty to the revolution, but also made it clear that Vermont would side with England rather than be swallowed up. Disappointed with treatment by both sides, state government eventually called Vermont's soldiers home and the independent republic adopted a stance of neutrality while leading citizens continued to negotiate for permanent sovereignty.

Bargaining with the British ended with the conclusion of the revolution, at least for the moment. In 1783 American and British representatives signed the Treaty of Paris. The map accompanying the agreement indicated that Vermont was outside the protective boundary of Britain's Canada. However, this didn't obligate Vermonters to join the American fold, and the state's loyalty to the new national government remained somewhat in doubt until the end of the War of 1812.[26]

The Allens wanted to continue building commercial ties with Quebec. But economic interests in the east and southwest had different ideas. This group of speculators, merchants, lawyers, and "Yorkers" began to openly challenge the state's leading family and their governor. Basically, they wanted a greater share of Vermont's land and resources for themselves.

Rebellions and competition wore away at the Allens' influence and holdings for years after independence was won. Farmers and workers meanwhile had their own concerns. They complained, for example, that Vermont had too many merchants, who drained the region's wealth. Many also opposed the harsh tactics used by lawyers and sheriffs to foreclose. Through calculated, expensive legal proceedings encouraged by the state government, poor people were being forced deeper into debt.

Merchants and land speculators were generally doing well, but some were hit hard by a post-revolutionary depression. In response, some inhabitants returned to combat, confronting their new rulers just as they had their previous feudal overseers. A memorable incident was the October 1783 raid on a creditor's house in which a group of Bennington settlers seized notes, obligations and bonds. In November

---

26 Andrew and Edith Nuquist, *Vermont State Government and Administration*

1786 another band tried to close the courts of Windsor and Rutland counties, mainly in order to prevent lawsuits from moving forward.

During the same period the state also experienced its first Watergate-style scandal: Ira Allen was caught with his hand in the till. He had secured ownership of the Town of Woodbridge—now called Highgate—as a favor from Gov. Chittenden. In 1789 the State Assembly investigated. The outcome: Ira lost much of his influence, and Chittenden lost his first election in ten years. But he was back in power just one year later, and remained in office until shortly before his death in 1797.

Ira Allen

The Jeffersonian wing of Vermont's new power structure, originally led by the Allens, was gradually weakened by such controversies. Leaders from other parts of the state meanwhile began to assert more influence. This shift was accompanied by a renewed move toward statehood. New York needed more political allies in Congress, particularly in the Senate, and finally approached the Republic of Vermont. Once former enemies worked out mutually advantageous reasons to drop their disputes and become allies, winning support from the U.S. Congress proved to be little problem.

On Jan. 10, 1791, the state's convention on ratification of the constitution voted yes. Five weeks later, on Feb. 18, the U.S. Congress agreed to admit the region. The independent Republic of Vermont became the 14th state and officially entered the union on March 4, 1791. At this point there were 85,539 people living in 185 towns, according to a general census.

Some leaders promptly tried to stack the electoral deck, pushing unsuccessfully to restrict voting rights to property owners. But as Andrew and Edith Nuquist put it in *Vermont State Government and Administration*, "The inhabitants of Vermont were restless spirits who, having escaped from their former confines, were more than willing to try new ideas and to rebel at restraints normally imposed by society."[27]

Eventually settling in Burlington, Ethan Allen passed away in 1789. His brothers Ira, Levi and Ebenezer, the last of whom resettled in Quebec, continued to look for economic opportunities. But a timber deal with Canada proved disastrous, and Ira's dream of a canal around the Richelieu rapids led to a damaging international incident.

In 1795, Ira went to London to secure support for the canal plan. The point of the project, at this point, was to improve his commercial position and help Britain defend Canada from France. But he was frustrated by the lukewarm response. He also needed money and so moved on to Paris to purchase some guns, ostensibly for the state militia back home. Records suggest Allen actually cut a deal with the French to help bring their recent revolution to Canada.[28]

Caught at sea by the British, he returned to France to obtain official proof of his intentions. But the French doubted his loyalty and threw him in jail for a year. When he finally made it back to Vermont he was a broken man, outcast and in serious debt. Ira deeded his last property to his brother Heman in 1803, then fled the state to avoid imprisonment. In 1814 he died a pauper in Philadelphia.

---

27 Ibid.
28 Sherman et al, *Freedom and Unity: A History of Vermont*

The Ethan Allen Homestead, built a few years before his death, is Allen's only surviving Vermont residence. A modest post-and-beam structure on the floodplain of the Winooski River, it has become a museum.

William Miller spent most of his life along the Vermont-New York border. In his youth, he borrowed books from Matthew Lyon in Fair Haven. After marrying Lucy Smith he moved to Poultney, and was stationed in Burlington during the War of 1812. Then he turned to religion and, through mathematical calculations, predicted the date of Christ's return. His first articles were published in Brandon.

6

Rebellions of the Righteous

The early 19th century was a period of tumultuous change, development and excitement in Vermont, indelibly marked by popular movements against slavery, aristocracy, drunkenness and wage labor that touched most corners of the state. The enthusiasm of these movements was contagious, and almost everyone was affected in some way by the religious revivalism of the post-revolutionary period.

Part of an evangelical surge known as the Second Great Awakening, many revivals centered on Christian prophecies of impending doom. Although the prophecies faded with time, the righteous attitude and enthusiasm promoted by revivals gave energy to diverse popular movements. The basic message was salvation from the many social and personal dilemmas people faced. Revivals offered people a way to stay focused in a confusing time, as well as acceptance by a group of like-minded converts, simple answers to problems, and a sense of purpose in line with a communal form of liberty.

One of the memorable Vermont revivals was led by Rev. Jedediah Burchard, a traveling actor and haberdasher who had been converted in upstate New York. At Burchard's meetings in the 1830s special "anxious seats" were reserved in front for those especially concerned about their souls. Mass prayers were recited for local sinners, often people who didn't care for Burchard. In 1835, one revival in Burlington lasted weeks, with Burchard preaching more than once a day.[29]

Not everyone was a fan. Some people couldn't stand his theatrical approach or the manic excitement he intentionally provoked, according to H. Nicholas Muller and John Duffy in *Jedediah Burchard and Vermont's 'New Measure' Revivals*, a study for *Vermont History*. Occasionally, to get people going, they reported, the former circus performer would do acrobatic stunts, or parade through a crowd on the backs of chairs.

Some disputed his claims to have converted hundreds of people in a single town. And church leaders were concerned that his cathartic approach undermined the essential meaning of religious experience, not to mention church membership. Pastors in Rutland said there was "too little to enlighten the mind" and not enough "sober reflection."

John Humphrey Noyes' boyhood home, known as Locust Grove, in Putney

A more radical religious movement was launched by John Humphrey Noyes, a merchant and Vermont congressman who began an adult bible school in Putney. The school "advanced from a community of faith," he recalled years later, "to a community of property, to a community of households, to a community of affections." Noyes called his faith Perfectionism and compared it to

---

29 H. Nicholas Muller and John Duffy, *Jedidiah Burchard and Vermont's "New Measure" Revivals*, Vermont History, Vol. 46, No. 1, 1978

both the abolitionist and temperance movements. "As the doctrine of temperance is total abstinence from alcoholic drinks, and the doctrine of antislavery is the immediate abolition of human bondage, so the doctrine of Perfectionism is immediate and total cessation from sin," he explained.

The best way to end sin, Noyes concluded, was through communal, communistic living. But in 1847, his neighbors, after investigating the "community of affections" practiced by Noyes and his followers, leveled charges of adultery. The group didn't wait for a verdict, instead jumping bail to resettle across the border in Oneida, N.Y.

John Humphrey Noyes around 1851

What Noyes' persecutors had discovered was an aspect of his "Bible Communism" known as complex marriage. Every male in the community was married to every female, and vice versa. But this wasn't free love or Mormonism. Sexual activity was strictly regulated, largely by Noyes himself, and monogamy was abolished. In Oneida, the community grew into a self-supporting enterprise and conducted the first human eugenics experiments by selecting specific couples for reproduction.[30]

While Noyes was developing the controversial principles of his faith-based movement in Putney, William Miller was preparing his followers for the end of the world. Born in Pittsfield and inspired by revivalism, he believed in the literal fulfillment of biblical prophecy and eventually offered a specific date for the end—1843. He gradually persuaded more and more people, including many Vermonters and a number of ministers, and launched a newspaper, *Sign of the Times,* as his Adventist prediction became a mass movement.[31]

Many of Miller's followers, who eventually narrowed the timing down to the days surrounding March 21, gave away their worldly goods to prepare for Christ's return. When nothing happened Miller explained that he was merely off by a year, due to flawed mathematical calculations. Like many cult movements since then, the failure of the initial prophecy did not deter most believers. In fact, for many the enthusiasm increased. As one of the movement's newspapers, *The Advent Herald,* reported in October, 1844, "Some, on going into their fields to cut their grass, found themselves entirely unable to proceed, and conforming to their sense of duty, left their crops standing in the field . . . This rapidly extended through the north of New England."[32]

Another date—October 22, 1844—passed without incident, then a third was selected. Most of Miller's followers fell away after that deadline also passed, but the movement led within two decades to the birth of the Seventh Day Adventist Church. There was, it turned out, a limit beyond which belief couldn't withstand disconfirmation of the prophecy. But for a long time, there was also cognitive dissonance, as contrary evidence was denied, instead increasing the conviction and enthusiasm of countless true believers.

In contrast, the temperance movement was more "reality based," grounded by and closely connected with traditional Christian churches. Although the Council of Censors began warning about the dangers of liquor as early as 1806, alcohol remained part of most public and private social events, including public debates, sermons and even

---

30 Greg Guma, *Spirits of Desire*, Maverick Books, 2005
31 Leon Festinger, Henry Riecken and Stanley Schachter, *When Prophecy Fails*, Harper Torchbooks, 1956
32 Ibid.

militia training. In response, however, a "General Convention" against alcohol was finally organized in 1827. A year later the Vermont Society for the Promotion of Temperance was formed.

Within 15 years permits to sell liquor became difficult to obtain.

In 1844 William Slade, a former Congressman and anti-slavery activist, proposed a local option for alcohol in his campaign for governor. After his victory a law was passed saying that no liquor licenses would be granted in a town unless it passed a resolution specifically asking the county court for permission. Eight years later prohibition became law after a referendum vote in which western counties said yes, but most eastern counties disapproved.

Despite state action, enforcement remained difficult. So it was not left entirely to the state. The secrecy and discipline of the Sons of Temperance, which grew after the Civil War, made them an independent power that enforced compliance. In 1882 Vermont became the first state to pass a compulsory temperance education law.[33]

Despite a constitutional ban on slavery within Vermont the abolitionist movement had some difficulty getting started. But several factors aided its development. First, Vermont was naturally unsuited for the exploitation of slave labor. Beyond that, it already had a tradition of respecting organized resistance. Thus, petitions were freely circulated and independent newspapers urged agitation.

In 1828 William Lloyd Garrison, perhaps the nation's most famous anti-slavery voice, came to Bennington from Massachusetts to edit the *Journal of the Times*. Within a year he forwarded a petition with more than 2,000 Vermont signatures to Congress calling for abolition in Washington, D.C.

The state's first anti-slavery society, Friends of Equal Rights, was founded in Middlebury in 1834. More soon followed. In its first annual report, Friends of Equal Rights proclaimed itself at war with slavery, adding that "our weapon is truth—our basis, justice—our incentive, humanity—our force, moral power—our watchword, onward—our hope of success, in God."

---

33 Daniel Okrent, *Last Call: The Rise and Fall of Prohibition*, Scribner, 2010

Milestones

More than two million Africans were brought to the Americas by force between 1600-1800, outnumbering Europeans two to one. During the journey they died in staggering numbers. Slavery became a way to save on the cost of labor by turning human beings into machines.

In 1837, a decade before his arrest for adultery and departure for upstate New York, John Humphrey Noyes made a key contribution to the movement. In a letter to Garrison, subsequently published in *The Liberator*, the weekly abolitionist newspaper he published for 35 years—until slavery was abolished—Noyes linked abolition to a much more radical agenda. "I have renounced active cooperation with the oppressor, on whose territories I live," he wrote, "now I would find a way to put an end to his oppression."[34]

---

34 Holly Jackson, *American Radicals: How Nineteenth Century Protest Shaped the Nation*, Crown, 2019

Looking forward to a millennium that would begin "at the overthrow of this nation," Noyes stressed the urgency of starting immediately to live "without being a hypocrite, or a partaker in the sins of the nation." The Bible told believers to "cease to do evil," and even to be "perfect, as your Father in Heaven is perfect." There was no excuse for any form of complicity, Noyes argued forcefully, and anyone who participated as a citizen of the United States—even by voting—was "a subject, and a ruler in a slaveholding government."

Garrison was not a Perfectionist or advocate for "free love." But Noyes' letter confirmed his belief that antislavery activism required public disavowal of the current government.

At first politicians hesitated to press such a controversial issue or even take a position, while the clergy spent much of its time debating whether slavery constituted a "sin" or merely an "evil." But there were exceptions. After receiving petitions, Rep. Slade urged the House of Representatives not to bury the issue. As William Doyle recounts in *The Vermont Political Tradition*, Vermont submitted so many anti-slavery petitions that the Georgia legislature instructed its governor to "transmit the Vermont resolutions to the deep, dank and fetid sink of social and political iniquity from whence they emanated."[35] The Georgia Senate went even further, asking President Franklin Pierce "to employ a sufficient number of able-bodied Irishmen to proceed to the State of Vermont, and to dig a ditch around the limits of the same, and to float 'the thing' into the Atlantic."

Working class churches like the Free Will Baptists openly agitated against slavery. But more conservative churches such as the regular Baptists and Methodists were slower to develop a position, and not all Vermonters opposed it. Still, the Baptists lost so many members during the period of debate that it took 50 years for them to regain the number of members they had in 1843.

Until recently, the impact of African Americans on Vermont's reputation for innovation and independent thinking has been greatly underrated. Among the early Black leaders were Lucy Terry Prince, a former slave who resettled in Guilford and became the first African American poet in the United States; Lemuel Haynes, a minister in Rutland and first African American ordained by a U.S. religious

---

35 Willian Doyle, *The Vermont Political Tradition*

denomination; and Alexander Twilight, the first Black person to serve in any state legislature.

Twilight was a teacher, but also designed Athenian Hall, a school and dormitory that is currently the home of the Orleans Historical Society. In 1836, a crucial transition period in Vermont, Twilight fought to reform education funding in the Legislature. Vermont's record in the struggle to end slavery is certainly laudable, and features a broad range of leaders and strategies. Yet when William John Anderson Jr. became the second black person elected to the state legislature in 1945—more than a century after Twilight's time—he still could not enter the Montpelier Tavern and Pavilion Hotel.[36]

In the 1920s the Ku Klux Klan saw a brief revival in Vermont. There were cross burnings and rallies, but also acts of courageous resistance. In order to go after the KKK's secrecy, Burlington passed an ordinance against wearing masks. Rutland residents responded by staging a boycott of any business owner who dared admit to Klan membership. Frequent condemnation by local newspapers also made a difference.

Founded in 1866, the KKK was an organization of Confederate veterans who dressed in white robes and hoods to look like frightening ghosts of dead soldiers. These armed militias terrorized people with fire, ropes and guns for decades.

---

36 Cynthia Bittinger, *Vermont Women, Native Americans & African Americans*

On the other hand, Kake Walk, a minstrel show performed in blackface, continued at UVM fraternities until 1969. When confronted, UVM President Lyman Rowell was defiant, refusing to "remake the university" for the benefit of Black people. The student senate eventually ended the tradition.

More than a century earlier, deep divisions over slavery already began challenging the traditional political system. In fact, the disenchantment was great enough that a political party could be formed. Called the Liberty Party, it won about 3,000 votes in Vermont as early as 1841. Support jumped to 5,618 by 1844, despite a Whig Party attempt to win over the newer party's voters by adopting a more liberal stand.

Historian John Meyers says "the militant wing of the antislavery movement regarded slaveholding as sinful and saw organization and agitation as necessary to gain adherents and promise hope for destroying the institution." Perhaps the most profound expression of this view was Vermont's Underground Railroad.

Escaping along dark roads, thousands of fugitive slaves hid in secret rooms built within farm homes and barns. In the homes of Vermonters who lived along the Western trunk line, eastern trunk, and cross-state route, fugitives were sheltered from the weather and authorities on their way from southern New York and New Hampshire to Quebec.

During this tumultuous period, some white Vermonters also began to understand and react to their own exploitation. Many were being moved off their farms, forced into dangerous jobs for "slave wages" by mine and factory owners. In the 1830s, Workingmen's Societies started forming in response.

The Working-man's Gazette appeared with the Jeffersonian motto, "All men are treated free and equal." In fact, they were not. But that did not discourage workers from making progressive demands for equal universal education, abolition of imprisonment for debts, elimination of licensed monopolies, revision or abolition of militias— which only drafted working people, a less expensive legal system, and equal taxation of property.

THURSDAY MORNING, June 27.

The Convention met pursuant to adjournment.
Prayer was offered by the Rev. EZRA SPRAGUE, of Montpelier.
The committee appointed to present a nomination for State Officers, submitted the following:

For Governor,
WILLIAM A. PALMER.

For Lieutenant Governor,
LEBBEUS EGERTON.

For Treasurer,
AUGUSTINE CLARKE.

For Councillors,

WILLIAM A. GRISWOLD,	Chittenden County,
HENRY F. JANES,	Washington "
AUSTIN BIRCHARD,	Windham "
ISAAC SHERMAN,	Bennington "
SILAS H. JENNISON,	Addison "
DANIEL COBB,	Orange "
SAMUEL C. LOVELAND,	Windsor "
GEORGE C. CAHOON,	Caledonia "
ZIMRI HOWE,	Rutland "
JOSEPH H. BRAINERD,	Franklin "
JASPER ROBINSON,	Orleans "
RICHARDSON GRAVES,	Essex "

The report was unanimously adopted by the Convention, and the Ticket recommended to the support of the Antimasons of this State at the ensuing election.

On motion of Mr Knapp,
Resolved, That in case of any vacancy in the Ticket for State Officers, which may be occasioned by death or otherwise, the State Committee be empowered to supply such vacancy.

The committee appointed to draft resolutions for the consideration of the Convention, submitted the following

Resolutions.

Resolved, That an institution which veils itself in secrecy and shrinks from the light of truth and public scrutiny—which imposes in its midnight recesses, partial, monopolizing, immoral and illegal oaths, backed by the penalty of death upon its votaries—which confers upon its members aristocratic and kingly titles, directly in the face of the constitution—and which aims in its organization, its obligations, and its whole spirit, at the erection of a privileged order in the land, at the expense of the equal rights of the rest of the community, is anti-republican in all its features and deserving the execration of every friend of his country.

Resolved, That free-masonry is such an institution, and that opposition to it for the purpose of abolishing it, is eminently republican in its character, being in fact a struggle of republican equality against an odious aristocracy.

Resolved, That a coalition between two opposing parties to put down a third at the expense of an abandonment of their distinctive party principles, is a most manifest departure from consistency, integrity and republican independence, and is substituting the blindness of party zeal or the mandates of party leaders, for the honest convictions of truth and a laudable adherence to principle.

Resolved, That such is the character of the coalition now forming between the masonic parties in this state against antimasonry, notwithstanding they shrink from a fair discussion of its principles before the public and dare not meet its advocates in the field of honorable argument,

Resolved, That antimasonry being an opposition to Freemasonry with an intent to abolish it, such a coalition for the sole purpose, as its advocates allege of "putting down antimasonry," is a coalition to save freemasonry from destruction.

Page from the Proceedings of the Anti-Masonic State Convention, June 26-27, 1833, held at the State House in Montpelier

7

The First Third Party

In 1826 William Morgan, a 52-year-old Freemason and printer from Batavia, N.Y., became dissatisfied with his local lodge and announced his intention to publish the details of Masonic rituals. Once his plan became known, however, Morgan was seriously harassed. Things turned darker still in September, when he was seized by unknown parties, taken to Fort Niagara, and never seen again.

Although Morgan's fate remained unknown, it was widely believed at the time that he had been kidnapped and killed by fellow Masons, a suspicion that only increased the existing hostility toward the order and led to the formation of the first national third party in the United States.

Spreading rapidly from upstate New York across New England and west, the Anti-Mason movement introduced innovations like nominating conventions and the adoption of party platforms. By 1831 the new political party was so popular that Vermont elected an Anti-Mason governor, demonstrating both the depth of public opposition to elite power and how far a single-issue movement can go.

There were 20 Masonic lodges in Vermont in 1800, a number that grew to 73 by 1828. Their power rested on tight organization, which included a sworn duty to assist other members. This extended to business and political affairs, an apparent commitment to defend the advantages of a special few. *Liberal Extracts*, a Woodstock newspaper, captured the public mood in July 1829 with this view of the Masons:

> VILLAGE ARISTOCRACY—In almost every village of much importance, there is among certain persons who would be considered, or fancy themselves to be above others, a spirit of pride, or what is called aristocracy, which is one of the greatest evils—we should be pardoned calling it one of the greatest curses that can afflict society . . . For the spirit of aristocracy, could it have its way, would end in nothing short of despotism. There is much of it in our New England villages . . . It is virtually treason against republicanism—against our government; and we should not care if it were made punishable by law.

Morgan's disappearance led more people to conclude that Freemasons were not loyal citizens. And since many were judges, businessmen, bankers and politicians, ordinary folks began to view the group as a powerful, anti-democratic secret society. Others suspected links to the occult and ceremonial magic. One persuasive argument was that the secret oaths administered by lodges could apparently bind members to favor each other over "outsiders." When the trial of the alleged Morgan conspirators was mishandled and Masons successfully blocked further inquiries, even more concluded that they controlled key public offices, abused their power to promote the interests of the fraternity, and violated basic democratic principles

Popular outrage spread as people decided to challenge what they considered a conspiracy. In western New York, citizens attending mass meetings in 1827 resolved not to support any Mason for public office. The National Republicans, heirs of the Jeffersonian faction, were weak in New York at the time, and shrewd political leaders used anti-Mason feelings to create a new party to oppose the rising "Jacksonian Democracy," which favored a more powerful president, expansion of the right to vote, a patronage system, and geographical expansion. The fact that Andrew Jackson was a high-ranking Mason and frequently praised the Order further fueled suspicion.

One of the most prominent Anti-Masons was former President John Quincy Adams, who wrote a series of stern letters condemning the institution after Morgan's disappearance.

Numerous Anti-Masonic papers were published, school readers and almanacs were distributed, and Anti-Mason book stores and taverns opened. In some churches it became a religious crusade. The excitement soon extended as far west as Northeastern Ohio. In some parts of that state, lodge halls were destroyed by mobs; property and records were carried away, Masons were ostracized and their businesses closed.

A national Anti-Mason organization was planned as early as 1827, when New York leaders attempted, unsuccessfully, to persuade Henry Clay, a former Mason, to renounce the Order and head the movement. His slippery reply to an inquiry about his opinion of the group was that he had become a Freemason as a young man, but hadn't given the order any serious attention for a long time. In fact, Clay was a former Grand Master. But the growth of an opposition movement had led him to practically disown it.

In the 1828 elections the new party proved unexpectedly strong, eclipsing the National Republicans in New York State. Within a year it broadened its base, becoming a champion of internal improvements and protective tariffs. In August 1829 Anti-Mason delegates met in Montpelier for what became Vermont's first political convention. When an Anti-Mason convention met in Philadelphia in September 1830 it adopted the following platform:

> "The object of Anti-Masonry, in nominating and electing candidates for the Presidency and Vice Presidency, is to deprive Masonry of the support which it derives from the power and patronage of the executive branch of the U.S. government. To affect this object, will require that candidates besides possessing the talents and virtues requisite for such exalted stations, be known as men decidedly opposed to secret societies."

One of the leading Anti-Masons by then was Thaddeus Stevens, a Vermont native of Danville who made his name in Pennsylvania and later emerged as a leading abolitionist, founder of the Republican Party, and a post-Civil War activist for civil rights and stiff retribution against the south. Attending the Anti-Mason Party's first national convention, he attracted early notice with his strong speeches and oratorical style. In one of them, "On the Masonic Influence Upon The Press," he deplored the lack of publicity given to the convention and attributed that as well to Masonic influence.

Thaddeus Stevens

Stevens' mother Sarah Morill Stevens was a devout Baptist who had "taught the scriptures" to her son. Danville's first Baptist congregation began to meet the year he was born. According to Bruce Levine in *Thaddeus Stevens: Civil War Revolutionary, Fighter for Racial Justice*, Vermont Baptists were strongly egalitarian and democratic, favoring separation of church and state and freedom of religion. "The same concerns led them to demand transparency in government and to oppose fraternal associations, fearing that secrecy could cloak authoritarian and repressive plotting against their rights."

After attending Peacham Academy, Stevens enrolled in Dartmouth College, but spent his junior year at the University of Vermont. His studies exposed him to both Federalist ideas and enlightenment philosophy, as well as strong views about political science, history, and what eventually became known as sociology. At the University of Vermont, he and other students debated slavery and emancipation. Upon graduation in 1814, he moved to Pennsylvania, studied law, and hung his shingle in Gettysburg. That led to investments in real estate and ironworks, and the beginning of his political career.[37]

---

[37] Bruce Levine, *Thaddeus Stevens: Civil War Revolutionary, Fighter for Racial Justice*, Simon and Schuster, 2021

From 1822–1831, Stevens served on the borough council, for a while as its president. In 1833 he was elected to the Pennsylvania legislature on the Anti-Masonic ticket, where his legislative talents quickly revealed themselves. Tall, athletic and intense, he proved to be an excellent debater with a devastating wit that cut his opposition to shreds. He also knew how to maneuver behind the scenes—and bide his time.

In 1830 and 1831, Stevens had attended the Anti-Mason Party's national conventions. He already opposed secrecy in politics, calling it a way to keep people in "total darkness." In 1834, he proposed a Pennsylvania legislative resolution denouncing Masonry because "it secures an undue, because unmerited, advantage to members of the fraternity over the honest and uninitiated farmer, mechanic, and laborer, in all the business transactions of life."

Vermont was already an Anti-Mason stronghold by then, especially Caledonia County, home of Stevens's family. In 1830, when Sarah Stevens learned that her son had joined the movement, she congratulated him for participating in the "good cause," but also warned that the decision might attract dangerous enemies.

Secrets, Oaths and Accountability

William A. Palmer was no newcomer to Vermont politics by 1831. He was a popular Jeffersonian Democrat and a former judge who had represented the state in the U.S. Senate by the time he ran for governor on the Anti-Mason ticket. Vermonters had already elected another Anti-Mason to Congress and chosen more than 30 members of the movement to represent them in the General Assembly. Still, it was a shock to the establishment when Palmer led in the popular vote. It took nine ballots in the state legislature before he won.

The next year, in Baltimore, the national Anti-Mason Party conducted the first presidential nominating convention in U.S. history. Its candidate was William Wirt, a former Mason, who subsequently won 7.78 percent of the national popular vote—and Vermont's seven electoral votes. William Slade, who would later become Vermont governor as a Whig, was sent to Congress as an opponent of Masonry and slavery. Since the state still had one-year terms of office, Palmer also ran and won again, but still couldn't attract a majority of the vote. This time it took 43 legislative ballots before he was re-elected.

William Palmer

In 1834, Palmer won on the first ballot, but only because the other political parties, anticipating the eventual collapse of the Anti-Masons, were competing to win over its constituents. Palmer also led the vote in 1835. But this time he couldn't convince the state legislature. After weeks of wrangling and 63 ballots the lawmakers declared themselves deadlocked and turned to Silas Jenison, a former Anti-Mason official and winner of the lieutenant governor's race. The rest of the Anti-Mason ticket was endorsed by the Whigs. Opposition to Palmer was due primarily to his democratic leanings and a belief that he intended to support Democrat Martin Van Buren for president the next year.

Gridlock in Vermont's General Assembly over Palmer's elections became so disruptive that it led to a Constitutional Convention and the amendment that created the state senate. Criticism of the unicameral legislature wasn't new and proposals for a second chamber dated back to 1793. But in 1836 the idea of reducing the power of the House finally achieved critical mass. The convention stripped it of "supreme legislative power." Crucially, bankers backed the change, mainly with the expectation that two chambers would be easier to handle, circumstantial evidence that in opposing the Masons the movement was also confronting the banks. The general public mainly thought the House had become too arrogant, intransigent and uncooperative.

Gov. Palmer believed that secret societies were "evil." But he didn't take radical stands in public speeches. In his first inaugural address, he declared the intention to appoint only men who were "unshackled by any earthly allegiance except to the constitution and laws," and suggested legislation to prohibit the administration of oaths except "when necessary to secure the faithful discharge of public trusts and to elicit truth in the administration of justice." He wanted to "diminish the frequency" of oaths because of the "influence which they exercise over the human mind."

For Vermont Anti-Masons, the use of secret oaths represented an invasion of the "civil power of a sovereign state" and a violation of liberty. In June 1833, at the height of movement, the Anti-Mason State Convention passed a dozen resolutions defining its position. The first of these, underlining a core commitment to accountability, said "that an institution which veils itself in secrecy and shrinks from the light of truth and public scrutiny—which imposes in its midnight recesses, partial monopolizing, immoral and illegal oaths, backed by the penalty of death upon its votaries—which confers upon its members aristocratic and kingly titles, directly in the face of the constitution— and which aims in its organization, its obligations, and its whole spirit, at the erection of a privileged order in the land, at the expense of the equal rights of the rest of the community, is anti-republican in all its features and deserving the execration of every friend of his country."[38]

In Pennsylvania, the high point of Thaddeus Stevens' Anti-Mason period came on Jan. 18, 1836. Prominent Masons who had previously refused to appear before his committee in the state legislature were finally being compelled to testify. Among them were ex-Gov. George Wolf; George M. Dallas, who was Masonic Grand

---

38 *Proceedings of the Anti-Masonic State Convention*, Montpelier, June 26-27, 1833, Knapp & Jewett Printer

Master of Pennsylvania at the time and ten years later became Vice President under James Polk; and Joseph R. Chandler, editor of the *United States Gazette*, published in Philadelphia. When ordered to answer questions these three powerful men flatly refused. In response they and 23 other witnesses were placed in the custody of the House Sergeant-at-Arms. After several days, however, when some Whigs broke with the Anti-Masons, the prisoners were released and Stevens's campaign for accountability ended.

In 1835, when Pennsylvania's Anti-Masonic Convention endorsed William Henry Harrison for President, Stevens initially refused to accept it because Harrison wouldn't pledge to go after the Masons. By then he already stood almost alone in trying to press the Anti-Masonic agenda on a national basis. Because of his dogged efforts to keep the party alive, he couldn't secure enough support to be elected to Congress again until 1848.

Vermont's Anti-Masons ultimately succeeded in forcing the lodges to close—at least for a while. But that left the state party with less reason to exist. In 1836 Vermont's Anti-Mason leaders, including future Gov. Slade, joined the new, anti-Jacksonian Whig Party.

In Pennsylvania, following the election of an Anti-Mason governor, Joseph Ritner, a state convention was held in Harrisburg to choose Presidential Electors for the 1836 election. The Pennsylvanians picked Harrison for President. Vermont's convention followed suit. But when national Anti-Masonic leaders couldn't get Harrison to say that he definitely wasn't a Mason, they called a separate convention. Held in Philadelphia in May, it was a divisive gathering. A majority of the delegates agreed that the purpose of the party remained anti-masonry but opted not to back a national ticket.

The party's third and final national convention was held in Philadelphia's Temperance Hall in November, 1838. Almost entirely engulfed by the Whigs, the gathering unanimously supported Harrison for president and Daniel Webster for Vice President. When the Whig National Convention chose Harrison and John Tyler, the Anti-Masons did nothing, and soon vanished.

8

Growing Pains

A canal opened at the southern end of Lake Champlain in 1822 and created a new route for trade to the south.[39] To overcome Vermont's rural isolation, entrepreneurs were also forming companies to win monopoly rights of way and establish "toll roads." Burlington entered its first boom period just as most inhabitants of the state were assimilating as "real Americans." The canal was supposed to free Vermont from dependence on Britain's Quebec. And it did open up many new opportunities. But it also made the state more economically dependent on New York.

The forest economy was waning in favor of wool, dairying, mining and small-scale manufacturing. But most people were still able to grow wheat and corn, sugar their own trees, cut timber to build and heat their homes, and sell their sheep and cattle. In short, most of the commodities used by homesteaders were also produced by them. Self-sufficiency reached its pinnacle in the 1830s, a time when production was closely related to use, and not as much about making money.

It was also a time of tremendous agricultural diversity. People worked hard but experienced relative abundance. The soil was productive, especially on the hill farms. The climate was salutary.

---

39 The area was well equipped early, with long wharves, a steamboat shipyard and a drydock in Shelburne. Burlington became the port of entry for the Vermont Customs District in 1822, and a lighthouse was running on Juniper Island by 1826.

Everyone was "useful," from children who helped carry wood to grandmothers knitting sweaters and carding wool.[40]

But the region was heading toward a turning point. In the two decades after statehood the state's population increased from 85,000 to more than 200,000 people, many of them young newcomers. New York City still had less than 100,000 inhabitants at the time. In the next 30 years, however, Vermont's growth slowed dramatically, and at least five counties experienced losses as farm communities emptied out. From 1850-1860, population grew by a tiny 0.3 percent, or just 978 people, while the U.S. as a whole grew by 35.6 percent.[41]

Historian Harold Fisher Wilson described it this way: "In general, no sooner had the towns of northern New England rounded out their growth than they began to find it difficult to maintain their status... the majority of those in the uplands were by the middle of the century entering into a decline from which they were never to emerge."[42]

Life was tough and crops sometimes failed. In 1816 it frosted and snowed every month; at least 1,800 people froze to death that year. And weather wasn't the only challenge. People were continually coping with isolation. To mitigate the effects, farmhouses were sometimes located on the higher plains; that way settlers could at least see neighbors in the distance. But finding someone to talk with could still mean some hard traveling.

Despite the taboos of the time, illegitimate births, sexual promiscuity and alcoholism were common. And, until the vigor of settlement passed and politics became a profession linked to business, participating in local political battles was a popular pastime. But Vermont's post-revolutionary growth period eventually slowed down. As Presidential candidate Stephen Douglas put it, decades after his birth in 1813 and youth in Brandon, "Vermont is a good state to be

---

40 The Vermont Center for Studies in Food Self-Sufficiency, led by James Nolfi and George Burrill, looked at past Vermont agricultural practices as part of research and computer mapping that assessed the potential for self-sufficiency in the 1980s and beyond. In 1975, the Center analyzed energy use in major agricultural sectors and found, for example, that in energy terms maple syrup could be produced efficiently with wood and horses.
41 Andrea Rebek, The Selling of Vermont: From Agriculture to Tourism, 1860-1910, *Vermont History*, Vol. 44, No. 1, 1976
42 Harold Fisher Wilson, *The Hill Country of Northern New England: Its Social and Economic History, 1790-1930*, AMS Press, 1967

born in and a good state to go away from." Douglas left in 1833 at twenty years old.

Many young men went west to farm bigger spreads, search for gold, fight in wars, or just get out of the state. Young women migrated for factory jobs or to sample the excitement and independence of city life in Southern New England. During its first 40 years—from 1790–1830—Vermont's population grew 228 percent. In the next 40, as out-migration escalated, the number of Vermonters rose by only 17 percent. As population growth slowed the few available services deteriorated. And so did public morale.

More Sheep Than People

When French troops under Napoleon invaded Spain in 1808 William Jarvis was representing the U.S. in Lisbon as American Consul. This diplomatic posting allowed him to develop an appreciation of Merino sheep, an ancient breed known for its fine wool. In previous centuries Merinos had helped the Spanish nobility and church maintain a virtual wool monopoly in Europe. Until the 18th century exporting a Merino sheep from Spain was a crime punishable by death.

Famous for their wool, Merino sheep were imported from Spain. By 1840 Vermont had 1.6 million sheep. But competition and better transportation ended "Merino Mania."

Six years earlier Colonel David Humphreys, while U.S. ambassador to Spain, had introduced the strain in Vermont by importing almost 100 rams and ewes. But a British embargo on wool and related clothing in the run up to the War of 1812 created pressure for more local production. In 1808 Humphreys brought over 100 Infantado Merinos. The following year Jarvis began importing the breed in larger numbers. In 1812 about 400 went to a 2,000-acre farm he purchased in Weathersfield, Vt. More than 3,000 sheep imported through Portugal were sold to other farms before war was officially declared.

The Napoleonic wars almost destroyed the Spanish Merino industry. But in Vermont, where farmers turned to sheep grazing to compete in the new world of commercial agriculture, small flocks became huge sheep farms. By 1840 there were an estimated 1,681,000 sheep in the state, outnumbering people almost six to one. Vermonters had found a cash crop that allowed them to buy factory-made commodities.

As the growth of woolen mills in southern New England increased demand, prices rose steadily from the mid-1820s to 1835. The state's first complete woolen factory was built at Winooski Falls, and Vermont became one of the most important sheep raising states.[43] This commercial advance was short-lived, however, and the instability of capitalism soon hit the state. The lowering of protective tariffs, combined with increased use of the Erie Canal and extension of the new railway network, increased competition from the West. As a result, sheep farms began to close, production declined 33 percent by 1850, and large price fluctuations became the norm.

By 1870 Vermont flocks were down to less than 600,000 sheep, a third of the peak number. To adapt, farmers turned to selling and breeding their herds for export to the West. The value of Vermont stock eased the transition out of what had been called "Merino mania," and the best rams were leased for up to $3,000 per season.

Market Forces

Factories like textile mills and small woodworking operations were expanding, often making use of native materials like wool and wood. Many people yearned to escape the "confinement" of rural life and

---

43 Edwin C. Rozwenc, Agriculture and Politics in the Vermont Tradition, *Vermont Quarterly*, Vol. 17, No. 4, 1949

factory production made it possible. Household necessities, once made at home, were now available for a price. But that meant farm production had to generate more cash.

Commercial farming required rationalized production, an agricultural industry that was more scientific, productive, and oriented toward specific markets. The approach was difficult to accept and master at first. The state simply couldn't compete with the great plains of the West. In 1850 a bushel of corn cost between 40–50 cents to produce in Vermont. The same bushel produced out west cost only 12–15 cents. Less than two decades later corn could be bought in New England for 70 cents a bushel, but cost only 10 cents in the West. Staple crops like wheat and corn were being replaced by cows, hay and saleable specialty crops.

Work on the first U.S. railroad began in 1830. In Vermont early construction depended on Irish immigrant labor. By 1848 the Vermont Central was operating from White River Junction to Montpelier as crews finished the northern end to Burlington.

To make things even more complicated, the railroads were coming. They would create a national marketplace in which farmers had to compete directly with the West, even for markets in Eastern cities. The first major integrated industry in the U.S., railroads were the largest enterprise in Vermont until early in the next century. The first line crossed the state from ports on the Atlantic to Canadian and western cities. In 1843 the General Assembly chartered the Champlain,

Central Vermont, Burlington, Rutland and other rail lines. By 1855 more than 500 miles of track crisscrossed the state. But despite an investment of $26 million—a huge number in its day—few dividends were ever paid, although the managers did well.[44]

Most of the routes consisted of segments owned by a half-dozen corporations and covered several jurisdictions. Unfortunately, management was frequently inexperienced or inefficient, the corporate structures were complex, and the financial foundation was weak for such a capital-intensive enterprise. Vermont's railroad industry gradually descended into a labyrinth of bankruptcies, receivership deals, and dreams never realized or dashed by recession.

Wheat production was one of the earliest agricultural casualties of improved transportation. Production dropped 15 percent in the 20 years between 1849 and 1869. In the next three decades it dropped 92 percent—to almost nothing. Portions of improved land in the state also dropped, from 63 percent in 1850 to 45 percent in 1900. Two out of every five Vermonters left the state each decade.

It became common to hear townspeople say, "The only place that's growin's the cemetery!"

Lost Generations

Out-migration began early, from the state and from southern to northern towns. By 1810 the population had peaked in many places. As the soil played out and the west opened up the number of emigrants increased. By mid-century residents were openly expressing fears about the long-term loss of young people.

Some young Vermonters initially resettled in New York and Ohio, but most eventually moved to northern areas of the Midwest, states like Wisconsin and Michigan. After gold was discovered at Sutter's Fort in California in 1848, more than 1,100 Vermonters joined the west coast Gold Rush in the next two years. Some never made it to California. But for those who did complete the journey the west promised independence and the chance of prosperity.

---

44 T. D. Seymour Bassett, 500 Miles of Trouble and Excitement: Vermont Railroads, 1848-1861, *Vermont History*, Vol. 49, No. 3, 1981

Both the state's population and morale were further damaged by the Civil War. Vermont sent more men per capita to fight for the Union than any other state, with the possible exception of New Hampshire. Since most Vermont soldiers were opponents of slavery fighting for a cause, they were often willing to take the lead in difficult situations. As a result, Vermont brigades sustained high casualties. The state that had stayed out of the original Union helped lead the fight to preserve it.

Civil War monuments in Gettysburg honor Col. Francis Randall and Vermont infantry soldiers who fought in the July 1–3, 1863 battle that halted Confederate momentum.

Of the 34,000 who went to war, less than half returned. It took decades for the state to recover from this loss of young manpower. After the war some of them went west, attracted by the promise of cheap and more fertile land. Many of those who did return found rural life tedious and restricting.

Morale took another hit in 1864, when an estimated 23 Confederate soldiers crossed the frontier from Canada to rob more than $200,000 from four St. Albans banks. The mission was to raise money for the war and divert Union troops. The raid itself took less than a half hour, the northernmost land encounter of the Civil War. But in the confusion a telegraph operator sent out a wire erroneously claiming that the town was being burned to the ground as residents were slaughtered in the streets.

It was certainly violent, but actually more of an even fight, as Vermont's First Infantry, on leave, quickly rallied and fought back. Canadian police captured most of the robbers, and their leader, Col. Bennett Young, later surrendered himself. Nevertheless, nearby border towns got nervous, and the state legislature made it a capital crime to take part in such a raid or otherwise make war on Vermont.

Ninety years later the story became a semi-fictional movie, *The Raid,* starring Van Heflin, Anne Bancroft, Richard Boone and Lee Marvin. In the 1954 film, the raid is mainly revenge for Sherman's burning of Atlanta.

Labor and Capital

Residents didn't just move west. They also moved to emerging cities within the state. Rural population declined as urban areas expanded. People were drawn to places with water power for paper, glass, textile and pottery production, metal-working and boat building. Burlington, Winooski, Rutland, Brattleboro, Newbury, Montpelier, and Springfield grew rapidly into large towns and cities.

By 1840 Burlington was the home of all Vermont's boat building, over half its glass production, and a third of its pottery operations. E. L. Farrar, based nearby in Canada, along with Orcutt and Wait of Massachusetts, owned the local potteries; Frederick Smith and William Wilkins ran Champlain Glass Company, the first major manufacturing operation in the area; and Champlain Transportation ran the steamers and sailing vessels. With 4,271 people, the town—not yet incorporated as a city—had three wharfs and three times the population of the average community. About a fifth of the state's banking assets were in two Burlington establishments.

"Nearly all the factory-made small arms, hardware, cutlery, and machinery came from three large towns in the Windsor region and two machine shops in Winooski and Brattleboro," noted T. D. Seymour Bassett in a 1958 article for *Vermont History*, the state's official journal. "Paper mills in Newbury, Bennington, Montpelier, Springfield, Brattleboro and Rutland accounted for over half the product, capital, and labor in that branch." Bennington led in iron furnaces due to the proximity of fuel and ore.

Burlington's waterfront in 1858

Textiles became the most important type of manufacturing at this point, and most of the spindles for weaving cotton were in three towns—Bennington, Middlebury and Springfield. But the most up-to-date machinery was located in Winooski and Northfield.[45]

Vermont's governors were often men like manufacturer Erastus Fairbanks, banker John B. Page, commercial farmer Frederick Holbrook and railroad tycoon John Gregory Smith, one of four railroad builders to manage state government between 1841–1878. The forces of a dynamic but changing market economy had taken root. It didn't do much for working people, but did make some people rich while forcing others to leave their homes.

Smith's life and career exemplifies the influence of leading Vermonters. One of few inhabitants to get a complete education during the period, including Yale, he was practicing law before the age of 25. After his father died in 1858, he moved effortlessly into the family business and almost immediately became a trustee of the Vermont Central and Canada Railroad companies. He later served as president of the Northern Pacific. In 1858 he won his first election, becoming a senator from Franklin County. Two years later he moved to the House of Representatives and was elected speaker within 12 months.

Before the end of 1863, in the midst of the Civil War, he became governor. Bullish on the war, Smith encouraged Vermont's regiments to stand proud. President Lincoln had sent out a call for 300,000 more

---

45 T. D. Bassett, The Leading Villages of Vermont in 1840, *Vermont History*, Vol. 26, No. 3, 1958

men, of which Vermont was expected to supply 3,330. But the state had already sent 20,000 and many residents resented the quota system. Some opposed the draft itself. Smith was unyielding, defending the federal government's right to compel "obedience and respect."

On the other hand, Smith criticized racial discrimination among the Union forces and called unequal pay for Black soldiers a wrong that Congress should address.[46] After the war, he remained a commanding force in state politics for two more decades, chairing the Vermont delegation at three national Republican conventions.

Despite their anti-slavery sentiments, leaders of the Republican Party generally represented businesses, their own and those of large interests building outposts in the Green Mountains. But protests against factory conditions also began. Vermont's first labor newspaper, *The Workingman's Gazette*, was launched in 1830 and agitation followed for collective bargaining.

In 1846, a group of workers, most of them Irish immigrants, launched a strike for two months' back pay. On July 4 the militia was called in to assist management in putting down the rebellion. In 1855, Brattleboro washer women went on strike to raise their rate to 75 cents for a dozen pieces of laundry. A new era of protest and resistance was underway.

A publication called *The New England Farmer* asked as early as 1852, "If it be decided that farming is not profitable, what is to be done? Shall we engage in manufactures…put our labor in equal competition with the pauper labor of Europe…and starve when the wheel of the factory stops?" Men were being freed from the almost total burden of providing shelter, fuel, water and crops for their families and livestock. Women were being liberated from the drudgery of domestic work, production of necessities like meals and clothing. But the price of freedom could be steep.

---

46 Albert R. Dowden, John Gregory Smith, *Vermont History*, Vol. 32, No. 2, 1964

9

Slow Progress for Women

In 1847, a series of articles by Clarina Howard Nichols deploring the lack of property rights for women sparked breakthrough legislation in Vermont that granted married women the right to inherit, own and bequeath property. Two years later her persistence led to even more reforms; specifically, new laws allowing women to insure their husbands' lives, legalizing joint property ownership, and broadening inheritance rights for widows.

Yet Nichols was frustrated. She had already reached the conclusion that until women had the right to vote they would be basically powerless. The laws passed by male legislators concerning women, she wrote in 1849, "show that his intelligence fails to prescribe means and conditions for the discharge of our duties. We are the best judges…and should hold in our own hands, in our own right, means for acquiring the one and comprehending the other…Women must look to the ballot for self-protection."[47]

The Vermont movement for female suffrage had begun in the 1840s with admission of women into the Anti-Slavery Society, but would not gain legislative recognition until 1858. Radicals such as anti-slavery activist Rowland T. Robinson believed that abolition included the slavery of women. When discussing the reasons for admitting women to the Society, he noted that if you substituted the

---

[47] Jo Schneiderman, Clarina Nichols, *Rediscovering Vermont's Common Sense Feminist*, Inroads, 1982

word "woman" for "negro" the description of oppression would be basically the same.

Nichols was born in West Townsend in 1810. Even as a young girl she realized the importance of a "scientific" education for women. For most, if they received any schooling at all, the main lessons focused on home skills like needlepoint, comportment and etiquette. At her graduation in 1829, she delivered a speech titled "Comparative of a Scientific and an Ornamental Education for Women."

Clarina Nichols fought for education and the vote.

After briefly teaching Nichols married Justin Carpenter, a Baptist minister, and the family moved to Herkimer in New York. The next decade was spent raising three children and running a seminary for young women. But in 1840 she returned to Vermont—with the children but not Carpenter—and started writing for the *Windham*

County Democrat.⁴⁸ Three years later she was divorced. Six days after the divorce was final she married George Nichols, the editor and publisher of the *Democrat*.

When her new husband became ill she took over the editing, and under her direction the paper's circulation grew from 100 to 1850. She made it more literary and used its pages to advocate for women's rights and abolition, as well as against the use of alcohol. "It is a fact," she told an 1851 Women's Rights Convention held in Worcester, MA, "that our wearing apparel belongs to our husbands and when they choose to pawn or sell our clothing for drink, they can do so."⁴⁹

Nichols' suffrage work led to a long-standing friendship with Susan B. Anthony but conflict with Vermont's legislative establishment. Her first appearance at the Statehouse—the first ever by a woman—outraged many in the audience. The editor of the *Rutland Herald* threatened to come to the capital with a man's suit and dress her in it.

After Nichols testified in favor of women's right to vote in school district elections, the Education Committee concluded that "women are the proper educators and trainers of the young." But committee members remained "unconvinced that the presence and counsel of women would…contribute to the elevation of the race." Instead of voting on the issue, they recommended that women "entrust advocacy of their views and interests to a male relative or friend."

By this time Nichols had decided that it was time to look for a place where she could be more effective. Another of Vermont's restless spirits was about to move on. She picked Kansas, in part, because a temperate climate might improve her husband's health. But George Nichols died in 1854, only a year after the move. Still, her basic hunch was correct.

In Kansas, she was able to win campaigns to insert many rights for women into the constitution, including voting rights in school elections. Nichols fought relentlessly against alcohol and was instrumental in pushing through a law that gave women custody of their homes and children in cases of chronic drinking. She was also an active abolitionist, and in 1866 moved to Washington, DC with her daughter, where she ran the Home for Colored Orphans.

---

48 Jo Schneiderman, *Beyond Midwifery and Motherhood, Vermont's Untold History, 1976*

49 Ibid., Clarina Nichols

As Cynthia Bittinger notes, while Indigenous women had a "large degree of authority" in their communities in the 18th Century, respected as authorities on sacred matters, tribal history and herbal medicine, early female settlers from Europe "were dominated legally by patriarchy and religious beliefs."[50] They could not own property, sign a contract or keep any wages they earned. Even though Vermont's constitution promised education for all, most women obtained little before becoming parents.

"A woman was only remembered through her connection to her husband," Bittinger wrote.

In fact, the word "relict," meaning a widow but also an inferior person, was carved on tombstones rather than the maiden name of the deceased, a practice demonstrating that women were deprived of identity even in death. Nevertheless, there were pioneers like Mother Ann Lee, a British "shaking Quaker" who resettled near Albany and attracted hundreds of followers during the Second Great Awakening. Among her disciples was Jane Blanchard, who left patriarchy and farm life behind in Norwich after seeing visions and joining the movement.

There was also Emma Hart Willard, who first opened a school for women in her Middlebury home in 1814. Willard may be the first woman to teach other women science and math. However, she found that Vermont wasn't the ideal place to pursue her vision of higher education for women.

At the time, women not only faced discrimination in most areas of employment but were expressly forbidden to hold administrative positions in most institutions. That applied to schools, even though they were permitted to work as teachers. Women physicians couldn't practice in hospitals, and were denied entrance into Vermont's three medical schools until 1920.

Most women who did practice medicine were not actually physicians but rather health practitioners—herbalists, midwives and homeopaths. But several women, educated in New York and other New England states, established outstanding practices. The first woman medical practitioner may have been Elizabeth Whitmore. She and her husband were the second settlers in Marlborough in 1763. She

---

50 Bittinger, *Vermont Women, Native Americans & African Americans*

is estimated to have delivered more than 2,000 babies without losing a mother.[51]

Emily A. Varney-Brownell received her medical degree from the Women's Medical College of Pennsylvania, returning to Vermont to become the State's first woman physician. Already over 30, she practiced medicine for 30 years in Lyndonville, Danville, St. Johnsbury and Concord. Because of the prohibition against practicing in hospitals, Varney-Brownell interned at a health spa in Massachusetts. Like Whitmore, she established an excellent reputation, and maintained a general practice.

In 1854, the same year that Nichols left the state Lucy Stone, a leading voice for abolition and suffrage, gave a fiery speech in Randolph. People should withhold their taxes until women have the right to vote, she urged. But it was her appearance that created the real stir during that visit. Focusing on her attire, Vermont newspapers wondered why attractive young women in the audience were parading around in "unfeminine" bloomers. Stone and other activists had become admirers of Amelia Bloomer's trousered dresses, which permitted women to work more freely, especially when carrying things.[52]

Suffragettes didn't just want the right to vote. They also spoke up for equal employment, equal pay for equal work, property rights, and more access to education. Nevertheless, the first recognition from the Vermont legislature was related to class. In 1858, laws were amended to protect the real estate of divorced or separated women and permit them to use banks. It wasn't an especially progressive step; after all, other states were already considering the vote. But Vermont women continued to struggle for basic rights.

Although the Civil War opened up more jobs, it also suppressed radical activity. Records are spotty for this period, but one recorded strike, in 1866, apparently involved women textile workers in Woodstock. The strikers considered their action an expression of both the feminist and labor movements.

The Vermont Women's Suffrage Association wasn't created until 1869. The bylaws of the group included the assertion that "no distinction or membership or eligibility to office, shall be made on account of sex." This basically meant that men as well as women could

---

51 Schneiderman, *Beyond Midwifery and Motherhood*
52 Ibid.

join and lead. In June 1870, the association brought suffrage to a Council of Censors' convention, where it was defeated 233 to one. The lone dissenter was Harvey Howes of Fair Haven.

Prior to action by the council the issue was reviewed by a committee of legislators; all three members recommended approval. But the suffragettes mounted an active lobbying effort that alienated the press and clergy, making their defeat more overwhelming than it might have been. Afterward Howes found it impossible to obtain a publisher for "A Last Resort," the written defense of his position.

There were some small victories. In 1880, for example, Vermont women won the right to vote in school meetings and hold school office. By 1896 the Suffrage Association had at least 237 active members. Julia Ward Howe, famous as an activist, poet and author of "The Battle Hymn of the Republic," attended the annual meeting that year. The group resolved to petition for municipal suffrage, pushed for election of sympathetic lawmakers, supported Utah's decision to make universal suffrage part of its constitution, and backed similar amendments in California and Idaho.

Vermont's leaders continued to resist giving women the vote. Even when a suffrage bill was finally passed by the state legislature in 1919, Gov. Percival Clement called it unconstitutional and refused to sign. In 1920, when the state was pressured to ratify the 19th amendment, Clement again declined to help, refusing to call a special legislative session. It became the law of the land anyway.

A year later, Edna L. Beard, a former teacher and school superintendent, became the first woman elected to the state legislature. Her first bill aimed to provide funds for women whose husbands were incapacitated. Elected to the Senate in 1923, her first legislation in that body allowed sheriffs to hire female deputies.

Even after the Suffrage Amendment Vermont continued to lag behind on women's rights. Some have argued that the state was just too conservative, and the patriarchy too entrenched. In addition, however, 19th century migration trends too often took the best and brightest out of the state. Even before the Civil War almost 150,000 women left. It took a century until the emergence of women politicians like Consuelo Northrup Bailey and Madeleine Kunin, the state's first two female lieutenant governors.

Madeleine Kunin in 1983

In 2020, attorney Molly Gray became the third, and joined Beth Pearce, who began an extended tenure as state treasurer in 2011. To date, however, Kunin has been the only female governor, and no woman has ever represented Vermont in Congress or the U.S. Senate.

Things have improved considerably in the state legislature. Around 40 percent of the House of Representatives is female, and women do much of the heavy lifting, chairing more than half of the standing committees. In that respect, it is a national leader. But only about a third of the Senate is female, and leadership positions there remain relatively rare. In 2021, Rebecca A. Balint became President pro tempore of the Vermont Senate.

The local level has seen even less progress. As of 2019, only two of the state's larger communities had women mayors. A Sept. 2021, study by the Center for Research on Vermont found that although 79 percent of town clerks were female, they held only a third of selectboard positions and less than a quarter of town manager and administrator jobs. On the other hand, town meeting studies have revealed that 48 percent of local leadership participants are women,[53] so the state may indeed be near a tipping point.

---
53 Bittinger, *Vermont Women, Native Americans & African Americans*

Architect Stanford White considered the Vermont State House the nation's best Greek Revival building. The figure atop its gilded dome is Ceres, goddess of agriculture.

10

How Vermont Went Republican

The convention of Vermont's Whig Party in 1840 was the largest ever staged in New England. Almost 20,000 people came to Burlington and attended an enormous parade in support of William Henry Harrison. During the gathering Vermont Whig leader and U.S. Congressman William Slade encouraged Party members to take a stronger stand on slavery. On Jan. 18, Slade had delivered the first abolitionist address ever made in Congress, calling for the immediate end of human slavery. But he felt that the country wasn't ready yet for an abolitionist president.[54]

Within two years, however, the growth of the anti-slavery Liberty Party convinced Slade to "abolitionize" Vermont's Whigs. In 1842, therefore, the state party's platform called slavery a "moral and political evil" that should be removed.

When Henry Clay emerged as the Whig candidate for president in 1844, Vermonters were rightly suspicious about his position. Clay was equivocating on whether Texas should be annexed since it would eventually become another slave state. To compensate, the Whigs picked Slade to run for governor. Not only did he win, Slade helped Clay carry the state. But Democrat James K. Polk became president.

---

54 This analysis and narrative evolved gradually, beginning with a syndicated newspaper column in April, 1983, Where Do Political Parties Come From?, Public Occurrences, #24, in *Brattleboro Reformer*, etc.

Milestones

As it worked out, annexation of the Lone Star State soon led to a war with Mexico, another decision Vermont Whigs opposed.

William Slade

In 1848, as usual, Green Mountains Whigs were unhappy with their candidate. This time it was Zachery Taylor, a slave owner and hero of the Mexican War. Slade was fed up and decided to move on to the Free Soil Party. An outgrowth of the Liberty Party, it was strongly abolitionist—Free Soil for Free Men, it proclaimed—and drew its leadership from a coalition of Democrats, Whigs and former Liberty Party supporters. Although Carlos Coolidge, a Whig—and distant relative of future president Calvin Coolidge, defeated the new coalition in the governor's race, the opposition of most Vermonters to slavery or its extension into new territories remained undiminished.

Political allegiances were changing fast. From 1849–1853, the state's Democratic Party went into a steep decline. Joining forces with the Free Soilers had undermined its status as a credible alternative to the Whigs. In a desperate move, party leaders chose opposition to temperance as a cause. A temperance referendum had passed, but the vote was close and Democrats felt that it didn't truly reflect public opinion. The real problem, though, was the party's unpopular position on slavery.

The turning point finally came in 1854 after a series of mass meetings was held across the state. The leaders at those spontaneous events weren't the old political players but instead a group of insurgents. The state was at the edge of another political rebellion. That summer the Whigs, split between realists and stalwarts, could only agree on a provisional slate to be headed by Stephen Royce, an abolitionist Supreme Court Judge whose selling point as a gubernatorial candidate was that he had "never mingled in the slightest degree with party politics." The Free Soilers, running this time under the "unionist" banner, looked to an elderly newspaperman, Ezekiel. P. Walton, who announced that he was ready to step aside for someone else.

The Democrats weren't even in the running, further undermined by the nomination of Franklin Pierce for president. Pierce supported the return of runaway slaves under the Fugitive Slave Act, as well as the Nebraska Act, which made slavery a blatant state's right issue. Ironically, the Act had been proposed by former Vermonter Stephen Douglas. Rather than helping Democrats, the Illinois senator's return home for a political appearance in February 1854 accelerated the party's collapse in the state.

The timing was perfect for a new party that could appeal to the many Vermonters disillusioned with the political establishment. In June, Ezekiel Walton called for a mass state convention, and on July 13 around 600 people showed up at the statehouse in Montpelier to form the second state Republican Party in the nation.

"Our rallying cry shall henceforth be the repeal of the Fugitive Slave Law," its platform announced, "the abolition of slavery in the District of Columbia, the prohibition of slavery in all the territories of the United States, and the admission of no more slave states into the Union." Provisional Whig candidate Royce became the new party's gubernatorial nominee and went on to win in November with 62 percent of the vote. By the next year the Republican Party had spread across the northern states and installed one of its own as Speaker of the U.S. House.

Abolitionist meetings were often disrupted with violence, sometimes sanctioned by the police and other state forces. In Boston, William LLoyd Garrison was mobbed, a gallows was built in front of his home, and he was burned in effigy.

There was a brief challenge in Vermont from the American Party, electoral arm of a growing nativist movement known as the Know-Nothings. But the Republicans managed to attract enough nativist support by attacking the Know-Nothing penchant for secrecy while sympathizing with its dislike of Irish immigrants. In a diluted form nativist sentiment was absorbed by the Republican Party, finding expression later in "exceptionalist" rhetoric.

The state's political landscape had been transformed, with confusion replaced by unity. In 1856, John Charles Frémont, the Republican candidate for president, won about 80 percent of Vermont's popular vote. Two years later Pennsylvania reformer Thaddeus Stevens, a native Vermonter, re-entered Congress as a Republican and rapidly assumed leadership of the House, where his strong abolitionist sentiments and legislative skills gave him tremendous power.

Two years after that, in 1860, Vermonters gave Abraham Lincoln the largest margin of victory of any state in the nation. The Green Mountains remained solid Republican territory for the next 100 years.

Elected Vice President in 1880, Chester Arthur became the first President from Vermont the next year—after the assassination of James Garfield.

11

Paths to the White House

Two people born in Vermont have so far become president of the United States—Chester Arthur in 1880, after James Garfield was assassinated, and Calvin Coolidge from 1923–1929. But several others have sought the job.

The earliest Vermont applicant was actually a religious leader, one of those restless spirits who struck out for the west in revival days. Joseph Smith was born in Sharon on Dec. 23, 1805, but moved to New York before he founded the Church of Jesus Christ of Latter-Day Saints in 1831. He said an angel had given him a book of golden plates inscribed with a religious history of ancient peoples. Once "translated" by Smith their contents became the Book of Mormon.

Believers flocked to the new religious movement. But hostile neighbors forced Smith and his followers to keep migrating, first to Ohio, then Missouri and Illinois. In Missouri the tensions broke into outright war. Hostile Missourians thought the Mormons were planning an insurrection and the governor said they should be "exterminated" or at least driven out. Smith led them next to Illinois, where they built a town on some Mississippi River swampland. There Smith became mayor of a Mormon enclave, called Nauvoo, and commanded an impressive militia.

He announced a run for president as candidate of the National Reform Party in early 1844. It was a long shot, since former President Andrew Jackson was engineering the nomination of Tennessee farmer, lawyer and political "dark horse" James Polk. The Whigs were backing Henry Clay, and the big issue was expansion—specifically the takeover of Texas and Oregon.

Smith's new party had emerged from the National Reform Association, a coalition of unionists, locofocos[55] and the Workingman's Party, all of them concerned about depression and "social degradation of the laborer." What most attracted Smith was the Party's main campaign focus—homesteading rights. National Reformers wanted legislation allowing workers and others to acquire public lands free of charge, state laws exempting farm land from seizure to collect debts, and restrictions on ownership of large swathes by the wealthy. Their slogan was "Vote the Land Free."

Joseph Smith was 38 years old when he was arrested during his presidential campaign and 100 angry men invaded the jail where he was held. Once he ran out of bullets, Smith was shot while trying to escape. This image from the Church of Jesus Christ of Latter-Day Saints captures the moment.

But Smith also had some personal baggage; namely, the romantic overtures he had made to the wife of a convert, William Law, a Canadian who had quit the church and publicly attacked the Mormon

---

55 A radical faction of the Democratic Party, the Loco-Focos brought together unionists and libertarians who opposed monopoly and supported free trade.

practice of polygamy in a newsletter. "We are earnestly seeking to explode the vicious principles of Joseph Smith," wrote Law, "and those who practice the same abominations and whoredoms." Accompanied by the Nauvoo city marshal, the prophet responded by destroying his accuser's printing press.[56] The governor charged Smith with inciting a riot and had him jailed.

On June 27, Smith was drinking wine with his brother and friends in a spacious cell in Carthage, Illinois when a mob surrounded the building. He had a gun, a six shot "pepper-box" pistol, but a gang with blackened faces charged into his cell and opened fire, immediately killing his brother and the others. Smith tried to escape out the window. As shots came at him from behind and below he plummeted two stories to the ground.

Afterward, five men were tried for his murder. And all acquitted. But the Mormon movement quickly rebounded when a new prophet emerged—a 43-year-old former house painter and carpenter from Vermont named Brigham Young.

Douglas: Defeated by Slavery

The next Green Mountain native to take a run at the presidency was Stephen Douglas, who at least had better luck resettling in Illinois than his predecessor. Known as the "Little Giant" because of his short stature and "giant" political skills, he became adept at debate and passing laws as a congressman and senator from his adopted home. In 1852, and again four years later, he went after the Democratic Party nomination.

The first time he lost to Franklin Pierce of New Hampshire, a relative unknown chosen over Douglas after 48 ballots. Pierce demolished the Whig candidate in the Electoral College but received only 51 percent of the popular vote. In 1856 Douglas was up against James Buchanan, a former senator, ambassador to Russia and Britain, and secretary of war who had already tried for the nomination three times himself. Douglas lost again.

---

56 David Wallechinsky and Irving Wallace, *The People's Almanac*

Stephen Douglas

The path was finally clear in 1860, but by then the party was hopelessly split. He easily became the Northern Democratic candidate, but the party's southern, pro-slavery wing didn't trust his ambiguous position[57] and separately nominated Vice President John C. Breckinridge. There was also a standard bearer for the Constitution Party, which hoped to avoid civil war through regional compromise. But most of all, there was Abraham Lincoln, who was nominated in Chicago at the Republican Convention. The two men knew each other well, especially from a famous series of debates they had waged when Lincoln challenged Douglas for his senate seat two years before.

Douglas finished second in the popular vote for president with 29 percent but carried only Missouri and half of New Jersey's electors. Breckinridge, the other Democrat, swept the south but won only 18 percent. Lincoln carried 18 northern states, including Vermont and Illinois, and received 39.8 percent, or 1,865,593 of the 4.6 million

---

57 Douglas supported the U.S. Supreme Court's notorious 1857 Dred Scott decision and denied that the South was covertly attempting to introduce slavery in northern states. Yet when President Buchanan and his allies attempted to pass a federal slave code he opposed that move as undemocratic. He didn't condemn slavery in moral terms, but privately deplored it and generally opposed its expansion.

votes cast that year. As soon as he was elected, southern states began to secede. When war came in April 1861 Douglas urged his followers to support the Union. He died a few weeks later. His position on slavery has been disputed ever since.

Arthur: Elevated by Gunfire

Twenty years after Douglas tried and failed, Chester Arthur succeeded without actually running. He was the son of a Baptist minister who had emigrated to North America from Ireland. Arthur's official biography says that he was from Fairfield, a town near the Canadian border, born on Oct. 5, 1830. But there have been persistent rumors that he was actually born nearby in Canada, and that even his birth date may be off by a year. In any case, after college and law school in upstate New York he briefly returned to Vermont in the early 1850s, as principal of an academy in North Pownal, before joining a law firm in New York City.

For a while Arthur was a Whig, but joined the Republicans early and was appointed engineer-in-chief by New York's governor, then acting quartermaster-general for that state during the Civil War. After the war, he rose in the Republican hierarchy, becoming Collector of the Port of New York in 1871 and chair of the Party's state committee in 1879. The following year he backed former President Grant to succeed Rutherford B. Hayes, but the convention delegates in Chicago went with another general, James Garfield.[58] However, Arthur's support for Grant and position in New York politics made him a practical choice to join Garfield on the ticket. The team was elected, and Vice President Arthur began to preside over a U.S. Senate that was so evenly divided that he often had to break ties.

On July 2, 1881, only four months into his term, Garfield was shot at a Washington railway station by Charles Guiteau, an unstable office-seeker. The president lingered on for two months but died from an infection on Sept. 19 after doctors contaminated the bullet wound. The next day Chester Arthur became the first president from Vermont. Guiteau was hanged the following June.

---

58 Messages and Papers of the Presidents, *Bureau of National Literature*, 1911

Milestones

When Garfield and secretary of state James Blaine arrived at the train station Guiteau was waiting for him. He had stalked the president for more than a month. At his trial Guiteau's insanity became apparent. Even after he was sentenced to death he thought he would be set free.

It was a relatively prosperous period for the country. Arthur spent much of his time dealing domestically with building projects, disputes with Indigenous tribes, cowboy violence in the Arizona territory—climaxing with the gunfight at the OK Corral, and hostility to Chinese immigrants. But he frequently took time to address the impact of the Mormon Church, founded and led by fellow Vermonters. In his first Annual Message to Congress on Dec. 6, 1881, he called Mormon polygamy an "odious crime" and a "barbarous system," urging legislation to stop its spread beyond Utah.[59] In reality, Mormons were already established in Idaho, Arizona and other Western Territories. Attacks on polygamy peppered speeches throughout Arthur's presidency.

In 1884, when the Republicans met again in Chicago for their nominating convention, Arthur lost to James C. Blaine, a leading Republican moderate who had briefly been his secretary of state. Chester Arthur died two years later, having served as president for three and half years without winning an election on his own.

Coolidge: Taking Care of Business

The next Vermonter to lead the country also became president due to a death at the top. But there is no dispute about the birthplace of Calvin Coolidge. He was born in Plymouth Notch on July 4, 1872, the only president so far whose birthday is also Independence Day. Like his ambitious predecessors he too left the state to pursue his career. Coolidge moved to Massachusetts and became, first a city official, then mayor, state legislator, lieutenant governor and ultimately governor in 1918. It was a steady and conventional ascent, aside from the decision that brought him to national attention—breaking a police strike in Boston.

"There is no right to strike against the public safety by anybody, anytime, anywhere," Coolidge explained.

When the Republican convention deadlocked two years later, party bosses gathered in what became known as their "smoke-filled room" and selected a little-known Ohio senator, Warren G. Harding. To balance the ticket Coolidge was picked for VP. Disgusted with Woodrow Wilson at the end of World War I, Democrats joined the

---

59 Ibid.

usual Republican base to give Harding the biggest landslide victory in U.S. history—more than 60 percent of the popular vote. Eugene Debs, after serving time in Federal prison during the campaign, won a million votes, his best showing.

The Harding administration soon became infamous for corruption, but Coolidge managed to stay clean. Disillusionment set in and few expected anything to change until the next election. Harding also had a tumultuous private life. Married at 25 to an older woman, Florence DeWolfe, the cold and snobbish daughter of a rich banker known as "The Duchess," he proceeded to have a 15-year affair with the wife of a friend. As Senator and President he was secretly involved with another woman, Nan Britton, who gave birth to a son.

On Aug. 2, 1923, in the middle of a goodwill tour, Harding dropped dead suddenly in San Francisco. Some people suspected that he was poisoned by his wife, perhaps to avoid disgrace or possible impeachment. Her refusal to permit an autopsy reinforced the rumors. But Harding had pronounced his own epitaph in advance: "I am not fit for this office and never should have been here."

In 1924 Coolidge signed the Indian Citizenship Act, which declared that "all non citizen Indians" born in the U.S. were henceforth citizens. In 1927, he was adopted by the Lakota Nation. But his views remained paternalistic, and he argued that "certain divergent people will not mix or blend."

Coolidge was a dramatic change of pace, at least in temperament and style. Harding looked and lived like a Matinee idol. "Silent Cal" was an austere, private family man, legendary for his stinginess and generally incurious nature. But he and his predecessor did have one thing in common—affection for business. Harding called it "the savior of our happiness." Coolidge coined a slogan for the ages: "The business of America is business."

He also endorsed so-called "race science" theories that fueled the eugenics movement. In 1921 he wrote in *Good Housekeeping*, "The Nordics propagate themselves successfully. With other races, the outcome shows deterioration on both sides. Quality of mind and body suggests that observance of ethnic law is as great a necessity to the nation as immigration law." As a result, Coolidge believed that even intermarriage between whites of other "races," not only with nonwhites, degraded the former.[60]

On the surface, he looked like an impressionable handmaiden for outside forces, an accidental president whose taciturn nature was taken for disengagement. But Coolidge was a skilled career politician, clever enough to hold his party together after Harding's Watergate-like scandals and practical enough to stress reducing the national debt. In 1924, he won re-election in a landslide using a slogan that suggested control and awareness of his image, "Keep Cool and Keep Coolidge." Technically, he could have run again. But Coolidge declined with what is likely the shortest political statement ever made by a president: "I do not choose to run for president in 1928."

A year later, Herbert Hoover became president and the nation was about to enter the Great Depression.

---

60 Adam Serwer, *The Cruelty Is the Point: The Past, Present, and Future of Trump's America*, One World, 2021

The early marble business consisted of two main operations: quarrying and sawing marble into slabs. Eventually, workers used block and tackle systems to haul it to the surface, and moved it into mills on sleds. Inside, it was hoisted and sawed with water-powered iron bands. Next came the rubbing beds, covered with sand and water, to remove rough edges, and more rubbing by hand. At this point carvers took over with mallets and chisels. As the need for skilled labor increased, owners turned to Italian immigrants, often hired as soon as they arrived.

12

Boom and Bust in Working Class Towns

As agriculture entered a long, slow decline in the late 19th century, many Vermonters turned to mining and manufacturing. The first marble quarries had been cut in Dorset in 1792 using gunpowder, saws, wagons and sleds. But the industry faltered through various business cycles until 1857, when major business interests raised it from a decade-long standstill.

In 1880, the Sutherland Falls Marble Company merged with the Rutland Marble Company, owned by New York banks and families, to form the Vermont Marble Company, which grew and took over smaller firms under Redfield Proctor. Within a few years it was the state's largest corporation. By 1900 Vermont was producing half the country's marble output.[61]

The benevolent ruler of both the company and a town named after him, Proctor provided workers with access to accident insurance, a company-owned bank and store, and a town library. As "friend and benefactor," he also used his economic power to launch a political career, becoming a state legislator, governor, U.S. secretary of war and senator from 1891–1908. In the Senate, Proctor fanned the flames for

---

61 Robert Gilmore, The Vermont Marble Company: An Entrepreneurial Study, 1869-1939, *New England Social Studies Bulletin*, Vol. 14, No. 2, 1956. Gilmore adds that Vermont marble was later used in Rockefeller Center and on the exterior of the United Nations Secretariat Building.

the Spanish-American War and guided invasions of Chile and Peru. He also chaired the committee that awarded contracts for federal buildings, making certain that their exteriors were built with Vermont marble. The first was Indiana's State Capitol, followed by the U.S. Supreme Court building and Jefferson Memorial.[62]

Redfield Proctor

Following in his father's footsteps, Fletcher Proctor acquired businesses for the Vermont Marble Company in Swanton, Roxbury, Danbury, Brandon, Pittsford and Fletcher. "The ownership of one marble quarry is very precarious," he explained. "The ownership of many marble quarries of diverse kinds and differently located may be fairly stable." Also like his father, Fletcher used business as a springboard to the governor's office.

In 1882, the Proctors invited the first Italian immigrants to Vermont, five sculptors from Carrara. A flow of Italian marble workers and railroad builders into the state was soon underway. But accidents and dust in the quarries claimed lives. Before coming to the U.S. some

---

62 Ibid.

of the newcomers had been members of Italian "mutual aid societies," and many were prepared to defend their rights with radical strategies and ideas. By the early 20th century more than half of Barre's residents were Italian and 90 percent were unionized. There were 15 separate local unions, including laundry workers, musicians and bartenders. A Central Labor Union coordinated the groups, and socialist mayors were elected in 1916 and 1929.[63]

Organizing wasn't restricted to places near the quarries like Barre and Rutland. In June 1883, for example, a confrontation erupted when the Vermont Copper Mining Company's Eli Copper Mine in Vershire tried to bail itself out of financial trouble by laying off some workers. Those still on the job were worried about back pay, which had been held for quite a while. Frustrated, they raided the company store to obtain necessities and, still owed about $25,000, took over the mine boss's mansion. Eventually, they stormed the home of "old man Eli," confronting him with axes, pistols and rocks.

"Gentleman," said the old man, "this mine belongs to the working men. I give this mine to you." And for a while they held onto it, in hopes of recouping what was owed—until uniformed national guardsmen staged a surprise attack and arrested 12 "ring leaders." In the end, no one would testify against the men and they were released. The state attempted to meet the demands of the workers, but only a fraction of the debt was ever paid.

As the state approached its second century labor power was on the rise. In 1866 women at the Woodstock Textile Mill struck for the 10-hour day. Four years later Julia Ward Howe spoke at a women's rights meeting in Burlington. She had just declared the first Mother's Day. Howe returned in 1883, this time speaking to the Vermont Women's Suffrage Association with Lucy Stone and Henry Blackwell. In 1876 the Order of Industrial Reform was founded.

But owners were also active and inventive. Using the cheap labor of prisoners, the National Hydraulic Company (later Jones and Lamson) became the state's first machine shop, producing rifles. That and other shops drew people to the Springfield valley. Jones and Lamson was able to double its capital stock by using a cheap labor pool, working people more than 13 hours a day for six days a week.

---

63 Roby Colodny, *Labor in Barre*, 1900-1941, Vermont's Untold History, Public Occurrence, 1976

Profits improved dramatically when railroad tracks[64] finally reached Springfield in 1897. At this point Jones and Lamson was getting around 10 percent return on invested capital. In the next two years it reached 58 percent, and topped 100 percent by 1900. With such returns, the owners were able to pay their workers relatively well. Business got even better when Fellows Gear began to produce automobiles. In the next ten years these two businesses increased production by 300–900 percent, along the way helping to turn Vermont into a manufacturing state.

When the Great Depression began, many Vermonters still worked in small industries. Employment was divided evenly between mining, quarrying, forestry and machinery production, with somewhat fewer workers in textile mills. New Deal programs tried to prime the pump with public investments, but buying power continued to lag, businesses closed, and unsold goods collected dust.

Some owners used Depression conditions as an excuse for layoffs and pay cuts. When this was attempted in Barre, granite workers launched a bitter two-month strike. Local residents backed the union, tradesmen and farmers distributed free food, and a federal arbitration board looked for a compromise. On April 29, 1933 the Quarry Workers union rejected extension of the old contract for a second time. But the Granite Cutters accepted binding arbitration and the strike was practically settled by May 5.

Two days later the National Guard arrived, creating easier access for strikebreakers. Soon most quarries were back to business as usual. The workers had been demanding union recognition in the open shop quarries. But the presence of the Guard, combined with a sell out by the Granite Cutters union, left many people high and dry. The strike was basically broken during arbitration.

At Vermont Marble the hard times, combined with increased costs, led to reduced services. Management dropped its free medical care and visiting nurses programs. By the mid-1930s the "company town" era had ended in Proctor. Vermont Marble also claimed to be operating at a loss and therefore wouldn't consider any wage increases. The quarrymen didn't believe it, and on Oct. 18, 1935, more than 100 of them decided to strike as a protest of management's decision to stagger

---

[64] The state had more than 1000 miles of railroad track by 1906, plus 122 miles of electric trolley lines.

their hours, which meant work only three weeks out of every four. The workers wanted a 40-hour week, an hourly wage of 50 cents—up from 37, and recognition of their union for collective bargaining.

Within a few days hundreds of other quarry workers were backing their action and demands. But management refused to negotiate. On Nov. 3, at a mass demonstration, 900 workers voted to strike. A week later the *Rutland Herald* declared that "communist influence" might be to blame, its evidence a circular signed by "The Community Party of Rutland County." Four days after that, when a riot broke out, the company responded by bringing in almost 100 sheriff deputies.

That Thanksgiving at least a thousand striking workers and their families marched through Proctor in the rain to draw attention to their cause. This was followed in early December by a clash with the authorities and hired thugs resulting in serious injuries. The strike continued through the winter. But after four months on the picket line about half of the employees returned to work. In the end the workers got a two and a half cent raise and inspired *Vermont Rebels Again*, a play about the campaign that opened in New York City.

By then, however, the Vermont legislature was ready to pick a side, opting to help businesses troubled or threatened by worker militancy. Thus, a bill outlawing sit-down strikes was passed on April 7, 1937, making Vermont the first state to declare it illegal for employees to stop working but remain in their plant until a settlement was reached.

The bill was signed by Gov. George Aiken, who had just been elected on an anti-New Deal platform. But Aiken wasn't happy with the law and subsequently tried to mend fences with organized labor, backing the creation of a state Department of Labor and helping to settle another granite workers strike in 1938.

The dominance of dairy farming was well underway by 1870. Close to 18 million pounds of butter were produced annually, and the St. Albans butter market was nationally recognized. For 75 years cows were the main source of income for Vermont farmers and dairy was the leading industry.

13

Selling the Beckoning Country

The Vermont legislature appointed a commission in 1888 to look into the status of agriculture and manufacturing and offer suggestions for improvement. Regional and national magazines of the time often carried stories about rural problems and abandoned farms in the state. At first the state board of agriculture attempted to repopulate the hillsides by attracting immigrant farmers. But when that strategy fell flat the Board turned to another potential audience—summer visitors.

The Resources and Attractions of Vermont, an 1891 pamphlet developed by the board, suggested looking on the bright side. Instead of thinking about summer fisherman as a nuisance, they pointed at how such visitors "patronize the railroads, and cause better accommodations for everybody. They cause hotels to be built, and bring their families. They hire boats and guides, and patronize country stores...they buy our much abused 'abandoned hillside farms' and make summer homes of them."[65]

This represented a shift in the official line. Two decades earlier, in the *Vermont Historical Gazetteer*, an article had ridiculed city folk who arrived with "long baggage trains" and proceeded to do nothing. Now the state was eager to welcome campers, sportsmen and those wealthy enough to buy or build second homes. The board of agriculture circulated questionnaires to get a sense of what was for sale

---

[65] Andrea Rebek, *The Selling of Vermont: From Agriculture to Tourism: 1860-1910*, Vermont History, Vol. 44, No. 1, 1976

and issued a "list of desirable Vermont farms." The Central Vermont Railroad urged home owners to open their doors to seasonal tourists.

"Vermonters are learning that scenery has economic value," the board claimed. The railroad obviously agreed, connecting the decline of agriculture with the tantalizing prospect that abandoned property could become desirable summer homes. By 1905 summer business was booming. Six years later the legislature funded the Bureau of Publicity, transferring activities until then handled by the agriculture board and railroads to the Department of State.

As a new century began, Vermont was depending less on farming. Wheat production dropped 92 percent from 1869–1899 while corn declined 30 percent. Much of the arable land was being abandoned as relatively unproductive. The value of the remaining farms declined and many people deserted the hillsides. The amount of improved land decreased by 77 percent between 1899–1909.

Between 1840 and 1940 the percentage of Vermont's population classified as rural dropped from 100 to 65 percent, according to the U.S. Census. By then, however, less than half of those residing in rural areas were actually living on farms.

Since the state wasn't able to effectively compete in the market economy with western farms, the remaining farmers tended to concentrate on items that were expensive to ship or perishable if transported from the west. Milk, hay, potatoes, maple products and apples were the favorites; oats, buckwheat and barley passed from the scene. In the 1920s and 1930s some farmers even tried fur farming, with little success. Egg production was also a bit unstable, falling and then rising at the end of the 1920s, and sheep farming dropped to almost zero. Dairy was on the rise.

Maple syrup emerged as a luxury product in competition with sugar syrups. In the first third of the 20th century maple sugar production more than doubled. Yield per bucket, method of sale and product quality all affected the amount a farmer made. An average of at least 450 buckets was the break-even point in those days.

Dairy production became the dominant agricultural sector early in the new century. A railroad shipping station for milk was up and running in Bristol by 1905. Farmers who once depended on butter for dairy income could now send milk longer distances. In 1915, the Boston Chamber of Commerce even launched an advertising campaign encouraging city people to drink it. Within ten years a hundred Boston-owned operations were sending out milk and cream, along with 58 Vermont and 32 cooperative creameries. Three-fifths of Vermont farms focused on dairy production by 1930.

Marketing was a problem at the start, while over-production and frequent price cutting made competition unpredictable. But then farmers organized and launched the Boston Milk War in 1910. The strategy was to hold back 32,000 containers of milk in hopes of spurring higher winter prices throughout the year. After four weeks the dealers agreed to keep the prices constant despite seasonal over-production.

The outcome looked promising until the Sherman Antitrust Act, adopted in 1890, was invoked to tip the scales. The purpose of the Act was progressive enough: to prevent business combination into monopolies and cartels that could harm competition. But it could also be used to target any restraint of competition that tended to restrict production, influence prices, or control a market at the expense of purchasers or consumers. This led the federal government to void the Boston agreement and, as a consequence, uphold the ability of big out-of-state dealers to essentially set milk prices for Vermont farmers.

By the time the "milk war" was declared, farmers in Vermont were no strangers to grassroots action. The Vermont Agricultural Society was incorporated in 1806. But this early attempt to organize was rejected by many rank and file farmers as a "do-nothing" association of rich gentlemen farmers. The Vermont Dairyman's Association, founded in 1868, was more political and educational. By the 1890s it became influential enough to attract the attention of politicians trawling for votes. But its prestige and power declined after World War I as more effective granges, and a more helpful agricultural extension service, attracted the attention and support of small farmers.

Vermont's grange movement started in 1872 and, after slow early growth, surged up to 20,000 members by 1911. Various granges organized co-op buying stores and clubs, sponsored educational activities, and defended the political interests of their members. By the 1890s the movement was prepared to challenge the University of Vermont—over reform of the agricultural college.

Justin Morrill, a progressive merchant who served as a U.S. senator from Vermont for 30 years, was instrumental in creating the land grant system that assisted agricultural colleges. For Morrill, public property was a public trust and, if poor farming practices overtaxed the soil, a scientific approach could protect the fertility that was left. [66] However, Vermont initially made limited use of this opportunity.

Thus, in 1885 a grange resolution stated, "The farmers of Vermont have received no adequate returns or benefits from the government fund for establishment of agricultural colleges." UVM policies had placed children of farm families in a secondary position, it charged; attracting students interested in the humanities and liberal arts was considered a higher priority.

What looked like policies based on class prompted the grange to demand that the agricultural college be separated from UVM. In the end, a compromise was reached. The governor would have the power to select more university trustees, mostly members of agricultural societies, to represent Vermont's farm interests. Having won a short-term demand, the grange continued to watchdog the school, with the Department of Agriculture, and push for rural education reform.

The Vermont Farm Bureau was also a force, particularly in the 1920s when it began to fight for adoption of the income tax "to equalize the tax burden." It passed in 1931. The Bureau also served as guardian angel of the Rural Electrification Program and backed Gov. George

---

66 T.D. Seymour Bassett, *Nature's Nobleman: Justin Morrill, A Victorian Politician*, Vermont History, Vol. 30, No. 1, 1962

Aiken in forming the Public Service Board. One president of the Farm Bureau, a strong advocate of cheap public power, served as chair of the Public Service Board, until he was forced out in a 1941 power play. His departure made room for the first in a long line of chairmen aligned with business. Over time, the board was repopulated by the interests it was originally created to regulate.

Breakthroughs

Wool spinning began in Ludlow shortly after the Civil War. But foreign competition hurt the textile industry. By the 1930s, more than 100 mills still used a "card" system to spin yarn. In 1970, when these photos were taken at Ludlow's Manchester Mills, only a few remained.

14

The Age of Burke

When Theodore Roosevelt visited Burlington in Sept. 1902 he offered some kind words about Vermont. He had been in the Queen City a year before, on the very day he found out that President William McKinley had been shot by what the newspapers were calling a "crazed anarchist." But now the "wild man," that "damned cowboy" hated by Wall Street, vice president under McKinley for less than a year, returned as president.

Burlington Mayor Donley C. Hawley stood with Roosevelt at the train barn near the waterfront, surrounded by flags and bunting. The president told the Vermonters, "You have always kept true to the old American ideals—the ideals of individual initiative, of self-help, of rugged independence, of the desire to work and willingness, if need, to fight." Republicans like Hawley were suspicious of "their" president. His rhetoric about a "square deal" for working people and control of big business sounded radical. But Democrats like James Burke were unabashed admirers.

At the time Burke was just beginning to promote a fusion movement with dissident Republicans. Like Roosevelt, he projected himself as a pragmatic reformer, thriving on idealism, moral outrage and an ability to inspire the masses. Born in Williston on May 4, 1849, he admired the famous Irish-born politician Edmund Burke[67] and took the political plunge in 1893 as an emerging leader of the new Irish, Democratic opposition in the city.

---
67 Interview with Burke's granddaughter, Ruth Cask, 1984

Breakthroughs

His first victory[68] was election to the board of aldermen from Ward 4, then the city's waterfront area. Two years later he was appointed to the Board of Police Examiners. But in 1899 he couldn't recapture his aldermanic seat, and his first two runs for mayor, in 1900 and 1902, also failed.

To many local "puritan" Yankees he was a dangerous "papist," yet Burke found loyal supporters at the foot of University Hill—in low-income neighborhoods, tenements near the railroad tracks and along the waterfront. These were the city's ethnic neighborhoods, populated not only by the Irish but also Germans, Italians, Jews, and French-Canadians.

Six months after Roosevelt's visit, on March 3, 1903, the hotly contested mayoral race between Burke and incumbent Republican Hawley drew an overflow crowd to the city clerk's office. The men—only males could vote at that point—perched on windowsills or stood on the rail that surrounded the aldermanic table. As the results for each ward were announced the winning side cheered. Hawley, a surgeon, came out on top in the affluent areas, but Burke's persistence was paying off in the immigrant wards. And he had two compelling issues: a proposed city-owned light plant and local licensing of saloons.

For James Burke politics meant face-to-face talks and lots of walking—in dozens of campaigns over 40 years.

---

68 *Burlington Free Press and Times*, April 4, 1893

When the final votes were tallied, Hawley had a three-vote margin. But the reason was that City Clerk Charles Allen refused to count ballots that had been marked twice. Burke was livid. "Those who laugh last laugh best," he shouted. "There are many men who voted today for me and whose ballots were thrown out. We propose to have them counted." Good to his word, he took the matter to the Vermont Supreme Court and won, gaining certification of an 11-vote victory by early summer.

In the years that followed Burlington hosted "progressive era" reforms like a public dock and restrooms, an attractive train depot with modern amenities, playgrounds for children, and a public wharf—the latter despite determined opposition from the Central Vermont Railroad. And, in 18 citywide races between 1903 and 1937, Burke lost only twice in Burlington's immigrant wards. They were also the base for his five-year foray into "third party" politics during the depression—the Citizens Party.

He soon brought Burlington a municipally-owned electric plant. Two years after his first mayoral victory, during his third term, Burke's daughter Loretta pressed a button at the bandstand in City Hall Park energizing two circuits of streetlights with power from the newly built facility.

Municipal power had enormous appeal. In December 1902 the Vermont legislature had authorized the city to furnish electricity, purchase needed land—by eminent domain if necessary, and issue bonds for the work. However, it also approved the incorporation of a privately-owned company, Burlington Light and Power, which would subsequently compete with—and sue—the city over the management of energy distribution.[69]

Burlington Light and Power was founded by B.B. Smalley and Urban Woodbury. In 1892, Smalley, a wealthy Democrat, had run for governor. But his main focus was business, as a corporate lawyer, banker, and president of the Burlington Gas Light Company. Woodbury was his closest business associate, president of the Consolidated Electric Company, a founding board member of Smalley's Burlington Gas Light, and a war hero who had been mayor and lieutenant governor.

---

69 Vermont General Assembly, Nov. 15, 1902

In fact, two years after Smalley ran for governor in 1892 and lost Woodbury ran as a Republican and won.

Only a week after Burke was declared mayor by the Supreme Court he asked the alderman to approve bonds for the light plant. Two days later, on June 11, he staged a special city-wide meeting to vote on a proposed $150,000 investment. Woodbury spoke against the plan, along with Elias Lyman, owner of the area's big coal company and Burlington Traction Company, the local mass transit monopoly. Both men were hissed by members of the audience as they talked.

The voters said yes to public power, and within ten years the city was generating over one million kilowatt hours with a turbine generator. Despite widespread support, however, the owners of the private power company didn't cave in. Instead, when the city was on the verge of expanding its department in 1910, Burlington Light and Power made a competing bid to supply energy for street lights, public buildings and parks. Once it was turned down the private utility company filed an injunction to prevent the city from issuing new bonds.

The lawsuit was dropped after two years, since it wasn't possible to prove that commercial lighting supplied by the city would increase public debt.[70] But Burlington Light and Power did eventually win in court, using a 1904 agreement with the city as the basis for its argument. To avoid duplication as demand for electricity increased, the city had made a deal to share utility pole space with the company. Since the city used Light and Power poles, it was supposed to pay a 20-cent per year fee for each wire attached. But the city stopped paying in 1909, claiming that it had a right to use the tops of all poles without charge. Light and Power cried foul, especially since the city was their chief competitor. The court agreed. No matter what the City Charter said, the light department had to pay up.[71]

That defeat didn't change the direction in which the city was moving, however. When Green Mountain Power offered $1 million to lease the department for 20 years the city declined. During those years public power brought Burlington more than $2 million in profit. In 1953, the department became a city monopoly when it bought Green Mountain Power's franchise.

---

70 *Burlington Free Press and Times*, Feb. 22, 1904
71 Vermont Supreme Court opinion, *Burlington Light & Power v. City of Burlington*, Nov. 19, 1918

The Age of Burke

Burke in 1906: He fought for clean government, playgrounds for children and a downtown public restroom. He opposed "big spending," but backed public ownership of basic resources.

Attempted Fusion

Burke's political vision stretched beyond the borders of the city, and by 1906 he was deeply embroiled in an effort to wrest control of the governor's office from the Republicans. To attempt this he forged a delicate personal alliance with Percival Clement, railroad tycoon and owner of the *Rutland Herald*, who was warring with Proctor marble interests. A joint ticket emerged with Democrat and Independent candidates, and Clement at the top.[72]

That summer, as Burke traveled the state attacking Republican graft and rule, he continued to call President Roosevelt "the greatest Republican since Lincoln and the greatest Democrat since Jefferson."

The Burke-Clement alliance was largely rooted in expediency. Both men wanted to be governor and knew that no Democrat could win statewide. Both had also been mayors, Clement in Rutland, although his control of the Rutland Railroad didn't ease negotiations

---

72 Otto T. Johnson, *Nineteen-Six in Vermont*, privately printed, May 1944

with Burlington over the waterfront, which was owned by Clement's line and Central Vermont. But there was an ideological affinity between them that bridged the class divide. Both were ardent supporters of the "local option" to issue saloon licenses and vocal critics of graft by marble and coal interests dominating the GOP.

Percival Clement

The day Roosevelt found out he would be president he was riding with Clement on his railroad. The vice president had been visiting Vermont Lt. Gov. Nelson Fisk at Isle La Motte when word came through that McKinley had been shot. By 1906, Roosevelt was on the attack against the beef, oil and tobacco trusts; in Vermont Clement was warring with marble interests, especially Fletcher Proctor, the Republican candidate for governor.

Burke had won another term as mayor over Walter Bigelow, the 40-year-old chair of the state Republican Party and night editor at the *Burlington Free Press*. He saw a "bright and glorious future" for the city and wanted people to move beyond "a narrow or partisan point of view." But the logic of progressive reform impelled him to influence the movement Clement was building.

At first it was called the "Bennington idea," referring to the town where a petition first circulated for Clement to lead an independent movement that aimed to "save the state" after 50 years of Republican rule. But Clement's supporters decided that a fusion with Democrats was essential, so they tried to induce Burke to join the ticket. He wasn't persuaded. Giving Clement the Democratic nomination for governor would effectively put him in control of the party. If a Democrat won the presidency in 1908, Clement would get to hand out patronage. Thus, Burke remained a potential candidate for governor himself even after a Barre Democrat agreed to join Clement on a fusion slate. The Democrats were still divided on June 28, the day of both the Independent and Democratic state conventions in Burlington.

While the Independents convened in City Hall and the Democrats met at the armory, a joint committee worked out an agreement to divide the state ticket. The Democrats would field candidates for one half, Independents would take the rest. After accepting the Independent nod Clement walked with Burke to the Strong Theater for a joint assembly. Debate on fusion was heated, some people accusing Burke of opposing the idea because he couldn't head the ticket. Speaking for himself, Burke reminded the audience that he had backed fusion under Clement four years earlier. But the "local option" for alcohol[73] was no longer a galvanizing issue and Clement was, after all, still basically a Republican.

The Democrats rejected Burke's advice and approved a joint slate headed by Clement and Democrat C. Herbert Pape. With more than a thousand people packing the theater, Clement took center stage, Burke at his side, and launched into a fiery attack on the Republican machine, the marble companies, and the inefficiency and graft that was robbing the people.

---

73 In 1902 a referendum gave towns the option of granting licenses. Four years later the authority was transferred to the Secretary of State, and in 1917 to the Commissioner of Taxes. In 1921, the old liquor laws were repealed and replaced by a system that conformed to the 18th Amendment to the U.S. Constitution. When prohibition was repealed in 1933, the state re-assumed the power to regulate the sale and use of alcohol.

Burke actively backed Clement's war on the Proctor Republicans, spending much of his time that summer on the campaign trail. As usual, his rhetoric was rich with praise of Roosevelt.

"Reform is in the air," he shouted from the back of the candidate's private train, "and Vermont will share in the benefits that come from the general revolt being made against ring rule and graft." He envisioned a popular coalition of Lincoln Republicans and Jefferson Democrats that would wipe out party lines. It might even combat corporate lobbying on labor issues like the nine-hour day and minimum wage.

But Fusion was defeated by Republicans united behind Proctor in November. And the following March, Burke came up short in his first mayoral race in five years—to Walter Bigelow. The defeat was devastating for political allies who lost their jobs and watched old opponents return to power. Clement eventually became governor in 1918—as a Republican.

Obstacles on the Path

James Burke's allies thought of him as honest and fearless, driven by high ideals of civic pride and duty. His political enemies just as adamantly questioned his motives and called him a demagogue. He sometimes went after them as "corporate interests" or "foreign capitalists." Burke was no friend of Elias Lyman's coal company, for example, or of the Masons and most railroad owners.

In his 1904 race for mayor, he publicly forced the Republican candidate, Rufus Brown, to deny that his campaign was financed by Burlington Gas Light.[74]

One of the most difficult crusades in Burlington's early progressive era put him at odds with both the Central Vermont and Rutland Railroads over public ownership of waterfront land. The railroads had owned and controlled the water's edge since Burlington emerged as a commercial center, and weren't willing to let the city take any part of that land for a "public wharf." This was precisely what Burke proposed to do.

Robert Roberts, the Republican mayor before Burke, later claimed that the idea was really his. This does make some sense, since he was

---

74 *Burlington Free Press and Times*, Feb. 22, 1904

on the executive committee of the Lake Champlain Yacht Club. That and the local trolley company were run by Lyman, who also headed the board of trade. But aside from having the idea Roberts did little to pursue it during his time in office.

The first breakthrough came in 1902. In December, only days after the city won a legislative go-ahead for the light plant, it also received approval to operate a "public wharf…for the landing, loading and unloading of boats and vessels."[75] The city also would be permitted to take land by eminent domain. The idea was immediately popular and embraced by candidates of both political parties.

By 1905 Burke was confident that Burlington would have a wharf within a few months. But months ended up stretching into years.

Once the railroads refused to sell the city any land, Burke hunted down some frontage at the foot of Maple Street that had, as he put it, "escaped the eyes of corporate greed."[76] Most land in that area was owned by the Rutland line. In June 1905, as the city sought construction bids, the railroad won a court order to block construction. Filling in the slip would destroy its "property right," the company argued.

The court battle dragged on into the next mayoral election. *The Burlington Free Press*, whose staff member Walter Bigelow ran against Burke several times, urged the city to negotiate with the other railroad, Central Vermont, for a lease while simultaneously accusing the mayor of trying to "make political capital" out of the issue.[77] Burke won anyway, by 140 votes, mainly based on his popularity in waterfront neighborhoods.

In his fourth annual message, he charged that, "The citizens of Burlington are getting impatient over this question (the wharf)…An outraged people will hold us responsible if we show any inclination to shirk our duty in this great battle now going on with corporate interests which are ever vigilant and successful in watching after their own interests."[78]

Despite public opinion or impassioned speeches, Central Vermont aggressively opposed the city's public wharf plans for three more years. In a variety of legal actions, including a 1909 Vermont Supreme Court case, the railroad put its objection this way: first,

---

75 Vermont General Assembly, Dec. 11, 1902
76 Mayor's Message to the Board of Aldermen, April 3, 1905
77 *Burlington Free Press and Times*, June 7, 1905
78 Mayor's Message to the Board of Aldermen, 1906

the city had no legal right to be a "wharfinger"—slang for running a wharf, and the land was already being used for a public purpose—that is, whatever the railroad chose. Second, they claimed that federal approval was required by law—in this case by the Secretary of War, who hadn't spoken. In any case, the state law authorizing the city to seize land was unconstitutional as it denied the railroad due process. And finally, even if taking land on College Street was legal, it wasn't necessary since the city already claimed to own another wharf site at the foot of Maple Street, not coincidentally land also claimed by Percival Clement's Rutland Railroad.

Like the private utilities, the railroads wanted to establish that Burlington had no legal right to run a public business that would "enter into competition with the world at large." The state's top judges disagreed.

Vermont government could, they ruled, "build or aid others in building, wharves for public use and in aid of trade and commerce; and it is equally clear that whatever the state can do in this behalf, it can delegate to a municipality to do."[79] The project didn't have to be within the narrow purpose of local government, said Vermont's High Court. It could be almost anything of special local benefit, anything considered "proper means for promoting the prosperity of its people."

The decision was handed down on Jan. 16, 1909, less than two months before Burke returned to City Hall after defeats in 1907 and 1908. Even journalists like James Tracy, who thought Burke tactless and possibly a dangerous demagogue, had to concede in a *Vermonter Magazine* profile that his persistence and success on the wharf issue had netted him "prestige among the common people who look upon him as a safe leader and wise counselor."[80]

Nevertheless, the negotiations continued to drag on. Optimism that Central Vermont might let go of its College Street property faded when the railroad, after agreeing to sell for $27,500, demanded to retain the right to run tracks across the property. The land was condemned and the corporation went back to court.

Having lost at the ballot box, the economic establishment hoped to win by wearing down the opposition and exploiting technicalities.

---

79 Vermont Supreme Court opinion, *Burlington v. Central Vermont Railway, Co.*, Jan. 16, 1909
80 James E. Tracy, *The Mayor of Burlington*, Vermonter Magazine, March, 1909

By 1910 Burlington was under legal attack by the railroads, Burlington Light and Power, and the Masons. Before all the disputes could be resolved, the politician at the center of them was out of office again. Burke's old rival Robert Roberts had returned to electoral politics after a 10-year absence to defeat the mayor in five of the city's six recently-redrawn wards.

But comebacks were Burke's forte. In 1913 he made yet another, and immediately picked up his discussions with the railroads. Now he linked the purchase of wharf property with plans for a Union Passenger Station nearby.[81] The Public Service Commission was invited into the debate, and the Supreme Court ironed out the details. Both Central Vermont and the Rutland Railroad eventually accepted the city's proposal. In 1915 the city purchased 160 feet of lakefront property near College Street for $8,000.

Waiting for Emma Goldman

You might think someone like Burke, who benefited from the freedom to reach the public with his ideas, would cherish the right of dissent no matter who was speaking. Yet he sometimes revealed a tendency to drown out his opponents. For example, there was the night when the Masons visited the City Council to request tax exempt status on their Church Street property. Hamilton Peck, a former Republican mayor with whom Burke had battled over control of the Street Commission, represented the Masons. But their most influential ally was Board President Taft, who was no fan of the mayor.

When Peck asked to speak, Burke rapped his gavel angrily and refused. Assuming that he spoke for everyone, the mayor told the lawyer that they'd heard as much of his talk as they wanted. Peck accused Burke of denying his right to speak. A board majority decided to give him five minutes.

"The mayor not being a mason," Peck began. That was too much for Burke. "I resent that," he interrupted, "be a gentlemen."

Peck continued, threatening a lawsuit in the process. Burke was defiant, virtually daring the Masons to file. Members in the audience stormed out in disgust. Taft was enraged and demanded to see the

---

81 Mayor's Message to the Board of Aldermen, 1913

resolution denying tax exemption that the board was about to pass. But Burke found it hard to be magnanimous, instead responding petulantly, "You can at least say please as the children are taught to." Then he handed over the papers.[82]

Given his short fuse, it isn't shocking that Burke often found himself in legal battles. Luckily for Burlington, he was frequently sustained in court. That was the case with the Masons, who refused to pay their taxes until 1910, when the Supreme Court ruled against them.[83] But Burke's most infamous moment of intolerance came on Sept. 3, 1909. In the midst of battles with corporate power, he used police power to deny the freedom to speak to a woman whose philosophy he abhorred.

Emma Goldman was one of the most famous radicals in the country, a forceful speaker who had come to Vermont to discuss "antimilitarism" and the truth about anarchism. In Barre and Montpelier, although some people did object, she found public venues. Her audiences paid 25 cents for admission and were certainly educated and entertained, if not persuaded. The night before her Burlington engagement at City Hall, however, Burke sent a telegram to Montpelier telling her that the auditorium wasn't for rent, even though her manager had put down a deposit. On Sept. 2, the *Free Press* printed the mayor's statement:

> "Announcement having been made that Miss Emma Goldman, apostle of anarchy, would speak at City Hall Friday night, I wish to say that she will not be allowed to preach any of her un-American doctrines in any building owned by the city of Burlington; and I would also request that the proprietors of all other halls refuse to let her have them for the above-named purpose, and I believe it is about time that the American people should insist that Miss Goldman while representing her anarchist teachings, should not be allowed to address public audiences."

Burke's hardline position confused the city's small Jewish community. The mayor was fairly popular among them, and Goldman

---

82 *Burlington Free Press and Times*, June 16, 1905
83 Vermont Supreme Court opinion, *Grand Lodge of Masons v. City of Burlington*, Jan. 16, 1911

was, to be sure, a well-known Jew. Some people wanted to hear her. Reacting quickly, her manager Ben Reitman made emergency arrangements for Goldman to speak at Isaac Perelman's Hall on the corner of Cedar and LeFountain Streets. On the day of the talk he distributed red posters around town.

Emma Goldman was a powerful voice for peace, women's rights, and radical politics. Years before her showdown with Mayor Burke, she visited Vermont in 1899 to meet with quarry workers in Barre. The mayor there blocked some events, but only after two speeches to packed houses. She returned in 1907, addressing 500 people at the Barre Opera House.

Emma's topic for the night was supposed to be "Anarchism and What It Really Stands For." She wanted to respond directly to the mayor's attack. To draw the line more clearly, the following words were emblazoned on the publicity flyers:

IS THERE FREE SPEECH AND FAIR PLAY IN BURLINGTON?

Most storekeepers refused the flyers or tossed them out. But a large billboard with the same message was propped against the fence in front of the Unitarian Church.

At 7 p.m. Goldman and her manager arrived at the hall. A large crowd was already inside. Burke was outside with two policemen.

When Goldman tried to enter, the officers took up positions in front of the door and Burke made a speech. She was forbidden to enter, he announced. Attacking her politics again, he added that citizens were angry and at least one merchant in the neighborhood feared violence.

Reitman and Goldman had seen this kind of hostility and disregard for speech rights in other places. Deciding to withdraw, they simply requested that Reitman be permitted to enter alone and address the audience as a member of the New York Free Speech Committee. Burke refused again, ordering both of them "in the name of peace, of society and of law and order" not to speak anywhere in his city.

The next day the anarchists departed for Massachusetts and the mayor proudly claimed that he had done his duty—protecting Burlington from un-American ideas and "treasonable utterances." In all, it was one of Burlington's less progressive moments.

From Reform to Retrenchment

For most people 60 was an appropriate age to slow down. But Burke was just getting started. In 1908 he made a quixotic gubernatorial run against Newport timber man George Prouty. Only 50 people attended his opening campaign speech, delivered during an August electrical storm. In that campaign he called for revision of the tax system, a license law on liquor, new highways throughout the state and an eight-hour day for workers.

The Republicans ignored him and Prouty suggested that so few differences existed between the two parties that "there is danger of more apathy than should be in a presidential year." But Burke's real problem was that Vermont Democrats had turned away from their party's nominee for president, William Jennings Bryan.[84] As a result William Howard Taft, Roosevelt's chosen successor, breezed into office. And so did Prouty, moving up after a term as lieutenant governor under Fletcher Proctor. Nevertheless, just a few months later

---

84 It was Bryan's third run for president and his opponent William Taft was running on Roosevelt's record. At a time of peace, prosperity and Republican trust-busting Bryan's agrarian radicalism had lost some of its appeal. He didn't carry a single state in the Northeast. Bryan's position on evolution was also becoming known. In a 1905 speech, he said Darwinism represented the "law of hate" and that, if it was true, "we shall turn backward to the beast."

The Age of Burke

Burke was mayor again, defeating Walter Bigelow by 18 votes. It was his first two-year term after the city's charter had been amended.

In spite of his populist activism, Burke's support waned again and he was defeated in 1911. Two years later he was back in power, defeating A.S. Drew and calling for a major revision of the city charter. Now he wanted a "commission system" that would place management under the control of a small number of elected administrators.[85]

When Burke became Burlington postmaster in 1915, instead of entering another mayoral race, it seemed a safe bet that his political career had finally ended. He lobbied for women's suffrage and promoted war bonds during the next years, but local politics proceeded without him. Leadership of the Democratic Party passed to a dentist, J. Holmes Jackson, who served four terms as mayor and ran unsuccessfully for governor in 1924. But Burke's retirement turned out to be temporary.

Elected Burlington's sole representative to the state legislature the same year Jackson ran for governor, he immediately began pushing for state approval of a city retirement fund and a Building Department. Within a few months he was running for mayor again— for the 11th time.

Burke posed with a group of business leaders during the 1930s. When Amelia Earhart flew into Burlington for a visit, he was there to greet her.

As it turned out, Burke's political career still had another 10 years to go. But this last phase was in many ways the most difficult

---
85 Mayor's Message to the Board of Aldermen, 1914

and painful. At first his own party wouldn't support him, forcing him to run as a Citizens Party candidate. He attributed the rejection to the presence of Republicans at Democratic caucuses. When Jackson defeated Burke in the Democratic caucus of 1929, the Irish elder protested after the vote.

"I have played the game square," he said. "I came here tonight resolved to abide by the action of the caucus but when I see the place packed with Republicans, I refuse to accept the decision."

Undeterred, he ran as an Independent; Jackson had both the Democratic and Republican lines. Burke argued in vain that the city was overburdened with loans, overdrafts and excessive bonding, and warned about the consequences of the city's growing debt. He lost. But by the end of the year the stock market crashed and the depression was on the horizon.

Burke was back in the state legislature in 1930 and back on the Burlington scene as a Citizens candidate for mayor the following year. This time, with more than 800 people jamming City Hall for the Democratic caucus, he came out on top. A week later his Democratic opponent, Jackson, was nominated as the Republican candidate, and defeated Burke in the general election.

The partisan power plays were signs of a deeper, more ideological struggle. Burke and his "working class" allies were disturbed by the boom-town atmosphere in Burlington, characterized by slogans such as "bigger, busier, better Burlington." During the late 1920s the city had embarked on a building spree in hopes of becoming a convention center. Burke opposed projects such as Memorial Auditorium on economic grounds, and in his mayoral bids called for a "rigid economy," meaning a lean city budget and a less speculative attitude.

In 1933 his time came—again. The Depression had reached its depth, and his nemesis, Jackson, was too ill to seek another term. About 1,000 people attended both the GOP and Democratic caucuses. At the latter Burke, by this time 83 years old, handily defeated his former protégé Hugh Finnegan, who immediately pledged "absolute" support. The candidate promised a "sound economy and honesty." Victory over the Republican hopeful, William Wilson, came easily. Handling city affairs in a time of economic crisis, on the other hand, required hard decisions. Expenditures had to be cut, including municipal salaries, and local government was forced to accept the sad fact that almost $100,000 in unpaid taxes was "uncollectible."[86]

After his final campaign in 1937, Burke spent his retirement writing letters to the editor, attending meetings, and working in his North Union Street garden.

If there was any doubt that this "progressive era" was over, Burke laid it to rest in June 1934 when 500 workers at the Queen City cotton mill went on strike. Local textile workers were in the vanguard of a national protest. But Burlington's mayor, who had enjoyed the support of the Building Trades Union in his early mayoral campaigns, ordered the strikers back to work, warning that they would receive no relief from the city if they refused. The workers held out until the fall. But once the strike was over the union was left divided by discrimination against ex-strikers, disillusionment and ideological battles.

Combining conservative and liberal tendencies, Burke ran a tight local administration while, in his role as city representative, proposing a cooperative savings and investment plan and encouragement of para-professionalism. Still, the strains of the time led to disaffection. Burke was defeated in his 1935 and 1937 mayoral bids, each time by a larger margin. The latter campaign proved to be his last.

---

86 Mayor's Message to the Board of Alderman, 1933

Breakthroughs

Among his fiercely loyal supporters Burke was known as honest, fearless and filled with high ideals. His enemies meanwhile questioned his motives and considered him dangerous. Describing his speaking style, a *Vermonter Magazine* profile noted, "The ideas were expressed with the intensity of conviction that struck a popular chord in the hearts of the proletariat among whom his strength has been greatest." Speaking for himself, Burke proclaimed, "I believe in a progressive spirit, no going backward."

Upon his death in 1943 the *Burlington Free Press*, a frequent critic, called him "the grand old man of Vermont Democrats, a tireless fighter "stirring the smoldering embers of democracy when they seemed to be dying out."[87]

Nothing lasts forever, however, and the Queen City had drifted back toward conservatism by the 1930s. The Irish led a growing

87 *Burlington Free Press*, April 27, 1943

opposition, but Old Americans—"Yankees" with civic and financial power who still clung to their sense of Anglo-Saxon superiority—continued to dominate local culture. Upper class residents, many of whom literally lived up "on the hill," fought against unions and the minimum wage, and offered little charitable assistance through their churches. People should "help themselves," they advised. And they weren't beyond covering up their own faults.

After a housing survey was completed in the 30s it was quickly buried. Some of Burlington's leading citizens, it turned out, owned several of the shabbiest tenements.

The Politics of Cleavage

Sociologist Elin Anderson provided the most vivid portrait of the Queen City during the depression years in her award-winning study, *We Americans*, published by Harvard Press in 1937. The city was conservative, rural and individualist, she concluded, a far cry from the liberal, urban and socially-engaged place it would become half a century later. In the 1903s it had lost personal neighborliness without gaining impersonal mobility.[88]

The dominant social group was still the Old Americans. Leading the opposition were the Irish, who cast their lot with the "have nots." Their Democratic leanings and Catholic faith sent up red flags among the Yankees, and even some French Canadians viewed their leadership as "officious and irksome."

Anderson studied these three groups, along with smaller Jewish, German and Italian communities, for three years. The WPA paid the salaries of six local women who conducted hundreds of in-depth interviews. One odd finding she noted was that the community believed women, more than men, "preserved prejudicial attitudes."

An unusual aspect of the study was the auspices under which it was conducted: the Vermont Eugenics Survey. The eugenicist, explained Anderson in her introduction, is interested in "ethnic adjustment" through "biological blending—intermarriage—of the most desirable qualities of people."

---

[88] Material for this section was originally presented in *The Way We Were*, a cover story written with Sue Burton for *The Vermont Vanguard Press*, Sept. 24, 1987.

In general, eugenics focused on discouraging propagation by the so-called unfit, reflected in laws allowing sterilization of "mental defectives." At its worst, it gave support to the concept of cultivating a "superior" breed or race, an idea linked to the rising Nazi movement in Germany at the time. Anderson made no such connections; in fact, she scoffed at the notion of a "pure" American and denounced both Hitler and Burlington's anti-Semitic Silver Shirts. She also condemned a local nursery school policy that allowed rejection of a child because of Jewish heritage.

Affiliated with UVM's Zoology Department, the Eugenics Survey began in 1925 with a three-year genealogical study of 62 families with "outstanding defects, deficiencies and other bad traits." Included in this group were hundreds of poor people, illegitimate children, and even some blind and paralyzed people. A few years before Anderson arrived in Burlington, the Survey had lobbied the legislature to allow for sterilization of the "feeble-minded."

More constructively, Anderson's study delineated the prevailing social and ethnic "cleavages" and unmasked the community's WASPs, "stripping away some of the pretense by which the people on top rationalize their position," according to UVM sociology professor Jim Loewen. "She emphasizes that the Old Americans set the status hierarchy and that what they value sets the community values. That's pretty hard-hitting. It's saying the Old Americans are racist, ethnicist, and classist, and get away with it because the lower groups have false consciousness."

The impact of "cleavage" between the Irish and French Canadians was revealed in the response to one of Anderson's questions. Should one vote for the person "who is a member of one's own nationality" when deciding between two qualified candidates? The findings said that French-Canadians tended to vote Republican—with Yankees and, most notably, against Irish Democrats.

The city remained divided along Yankee-foreigner, Protestant-Catholic lines until the late 1950s. Political gerrymandering helped maintain Yankee dominance. By the late 1950s, however, a political alliance had been forged between moderate Republicans and conservative Democrats to control city appointments and services. This open conspiracy, known as the Republicrats, ran the city for the next two decades.

15

From Socialism to the American Plan

The Granai clan was like many Italian immigrant families who settled in Barre at the end of the 19th century. By 1912 Cornelius, one of 18 children, was working as a stone cutter for the Jones Brother Company. His parents were ex-followers of Guiseppe Garibaldi, peasant leader and soldier in the wars of Italian unification.

Decades later, in an interview with oral historian Roby Colodny, Granai recalled hearing stories about more than a dozen members of one Garibaldi expeditionary force that settled in Barre. Other immigrants called themselves Republicani, followers of Mazzini, elder statesman of the Italian Republic.[89] Whatever their previous affiliations, however, most considered themselves socialists, and many joined the two main unions for those who cut stone, the Quarry Workers and the Granite Cutters International Association.

Eugene Debs, three-time Socialist candidate for president, came to Barre, as did his successor Norman Thomas in the early 1930s. Fred Suitor, secretary-treasurer of the Quarry Workers from 1911 to 1933, ran for governor as the Socialist Party candidate in 1912, and was later elected mayor of Barre on the Citizens ticket. According to Granai, everyone knew he was a Socialist.

---

89 Robert Mueller, Greg Guma, Jo Schneiderman and Roby Colodny, *Vermont's Untold History, Public Occurrence*, 1976 Colodny conducted the interviews with both Cornelius Granai and John Lawson.

Cover of 1976 "people's history" of the state

Barre was Vermont's third largest city by 1900, right behind Burlington and Rutland. Although a single industry had fueled its growth, no one family or company dominated the local economy or culture. And its population represented a diverse ethnic mix, from French-Canadians to immigrants from Italy, Spain and Scotland.

During the historic 1912 strike of textile workers in Lawrence, MA, organized by the Industrial Workers of the World, at least 200 children of the strikers were sent to the thriving central Vermont city. On Feb. 17, musical bands from Barre, Bethel and Waterbury greeted the kids as they arrived at the train station. Then they were "divvied out" at a crowded Socialist Hall on Granite Street as people sang "son qui" (here I am), the famous duet from *Tosca*, Puccini's opera about Italy's struggle for independence. Even Yankee farmers from the countryside took children in.

In the 1920s the case of Nicola Sacco and Bartolomeo Vanzetti captured broad local sympathy, especially in immigrant neighborhoods. Two self-professed anarchists had been convicted of murder and armed robbery after a controversial trial in which the judge consistently denied the defense motions. As new evidence emerged, more people decided that it was a frame-up, part of the Red Scare that began during the war. Sacco and Vanzetti became a cause célèbre, and attracted worldwide attention and support.

"Barre was never so stirred up," Granai recalled. "They were seen as victims of their beliefs…victimized by circumstances."

When a play about the two immigrant martyrs was performed at the old Barre Opera House, a thousand tickets were sold for 300 seats. But unlike the Lawrence Strike a decade earlier, there was no victory this time. Sacco and Vanzetti were electrocuted shortly after midnight on Aug. 23, 1927.

The ideas and sympathies of the newcomers sounded "radical" to many of their Yankee neighbors. But their agenda was a campaign for bread and butter, a decent home and education for their children. Like many urban areas in the U.S., Barre witnessed frequent agitation for shorter hours, higher wages and improved working conditions, from "squat sheds" and provocations to lockouts and strikes. Silicosis-producing dust sent many granite workers to the sanitarium on Blakely Hill. Accidents due to drilling and dynamite blasting were common.

Barre granite shed

A 40-hour workweek, with Saturday afternoon off, was instituted in 1914. Two years later Robert Gordon became Barre's first Socialist Mayor, winning by 100 votes over the editor of the *Barre Daily Times*. But the political dynamics were fragile. After war was declared against Germany in 1917 it quickly became a battle against militant labor as well, especially the IWW. Most of its top leadership was rounded up and put on trial. As the Red Scare and deportation of suspected foreign radicals escalated the city's socialist movement faded.

A teenager during the war years, John Lawson attended local socialist meetings with his dad. He and his family had reached Barre from Scotland in 1911, and Lawson took it upon himself to revive the Party after the war. It was a lonely task. Most IWW members—called Wobblies—were either in jail or struggling to hold onto union support. Many businesses were tired of dealing with labor demands. By the early 1920s, although the unions were still strong, the socialist movement was in decline and a new slogan was creeping into use—The American Plan. Cloaked in patriotism, the Plan was a business strategy designed to deny recognition, even to well-established unions, and tar almost any demand for better wages or working conditions as "bolshevism."

"The owners were represented by the Quarry Owners Association and the Barre Granite Association," Lawson recalled. "Both were backed up by a common Board of Control which sat in Boston." Through the intransigence of its President James Boutwell, the board strove to preserve a "united front," especially during a lockout that ran for months in 1922 and 1923.

The Quarry Workers and Granite Cutters held out and some of the smaller companies eventually signed union contracts. But the united front strategy was a partial success. Four months after the strike began scabs were brought in from sheds and quarries in Canada and Massachusetts. Some companies even promised them higher wages than the union was demanding. Once they arrived, however, the wages dropped.

By the time the strike ended, open shop working conditions had taken hold. The Rock of Ages Company was launched soon afterward, a rebranding of the older Boutwell, Milne and Varnum Granite Company, and actively promoted the American Plan. By purchasing other smaller companies—a strategy known as growth-by-acquisition—it became the best-known name in the granite industry. Rock of Ages wasn't unionized until 1941.

Organizing in Hard Times

In the years after World War I migration to larger Vermont communities accelerated, prompting a building boom in regional centers like Burlington. Milk production was on the rise, although the number of farms was dropping rapidly. Fruit production was also high, at least for a few years, but less butter, hay and other grains were being produced. Both manufacturing and agricultural diversity declined as tourism took a firmer hold on the economy.

At its peak, a trolley system carried over 16 million passengers around Southern Vermont—until the flood of November 1927. But the flood, which hurt rail travel and reduced trolley passengers to less than 2 million, ended up helping the summer home and winter sports sectors of the recreation industry by spurring highway spending and the building of airports. In the early 1930s half of the state's $12 million annual budget was devoted annually to highway construction. During the same period only $1 million was spent yearly on education and health.

Increased specialization of labor, along with the growth of services industries and transportation systems, drew Vermont more deeply into the national money and credit network. In 1929 that structure collapsed. Unemployment skyrocketed as the standard of living dropped.

In Barre, a two-month strike by granite workers became a "straight out union fight for survival," recalled Lawson. The strike officially began on April 1, 1933, shutting down six major companies within a week. The only exception was E. L. Smith, which paid above union scale and used workers from Canada. Lawson was president of the Graniteville local, while Granai consulted closely with the strike committee as a lawyer.

The union asked the sheriff and his deputies to let the strikers police themselves. "A police force was established by the wearing of white arm bands," according to Granai. But at that point agent provocateurs rode in and workers fought back. In some cases the latter brandished shotguns for self-defense. Some strikers were jailed by anti-union judges.

The protest was losing ground.

Shortly after the strike began, the sheriff had assisted in the use of 150 strikebreakers. But local residents backed the union, tradesmen and farmers distributed free food, and a federal arbitration board sought a compromise. On April 29, the Quarry Workers union rejected extension of the old contract for a second time. But the Granite Cutters accepted binding arbitration and the strike was almost settled by May 5.

Interpretations of why the National Guard was called in vary. As Granai remembered it, Gov. Stanley C. Wilson didn't issue the order. Rather, people connected with the Granite Cutters made the request "to get rid of agent provocateurs." Lawson and others recall the situation differently. "Protests against the guard were lodged by farmers, churchmen, the ACLU, the Vermont federation of labor, and a committee of Barre businessmen," he insisted.

Whatever the reason, the guard's arrival created easier access for strikebreakers. Soon most quarries were back to business as usual. The workers had been demanding union recognition in the open shop quarries, but the presence of the guard, combined with the action of the Granite Cutters union, left many people high and dry.

Members of both unions returned to work on June 1 and agreed to 1932 wages. But the hearings dragged on until August and many lost their jobs. Two of the three quarries now had open shops. One of the only compensations was that the federal government began to clean up the sheds. Suction machines designed to remove silica dust were in use before the end of the decade.

French-Canadian workers played a role in this and other strikes, often as scab labor. They had been coming to the state for mill jobs since the Canadian rebellion of 1837, when reformers rejected the political repression of Britain's parliament. Vermont also provided better farming prospects, and a chance to work in lumbering or on railroad crews. Often called the "Chinese of the Eastern States," these immigrants worked for cheap and asked few questions. But their exploitation as strikebreakers hurt their relations with the Irish.

When mills began to close in the 1930s, many Canadians turned to farming in Franklin, Orleans and Essex Counties at the state's northern end. Others stayed in the Burlington area but avoided union work. By then the Catholic Church in Quebec had declared unions atheistic.

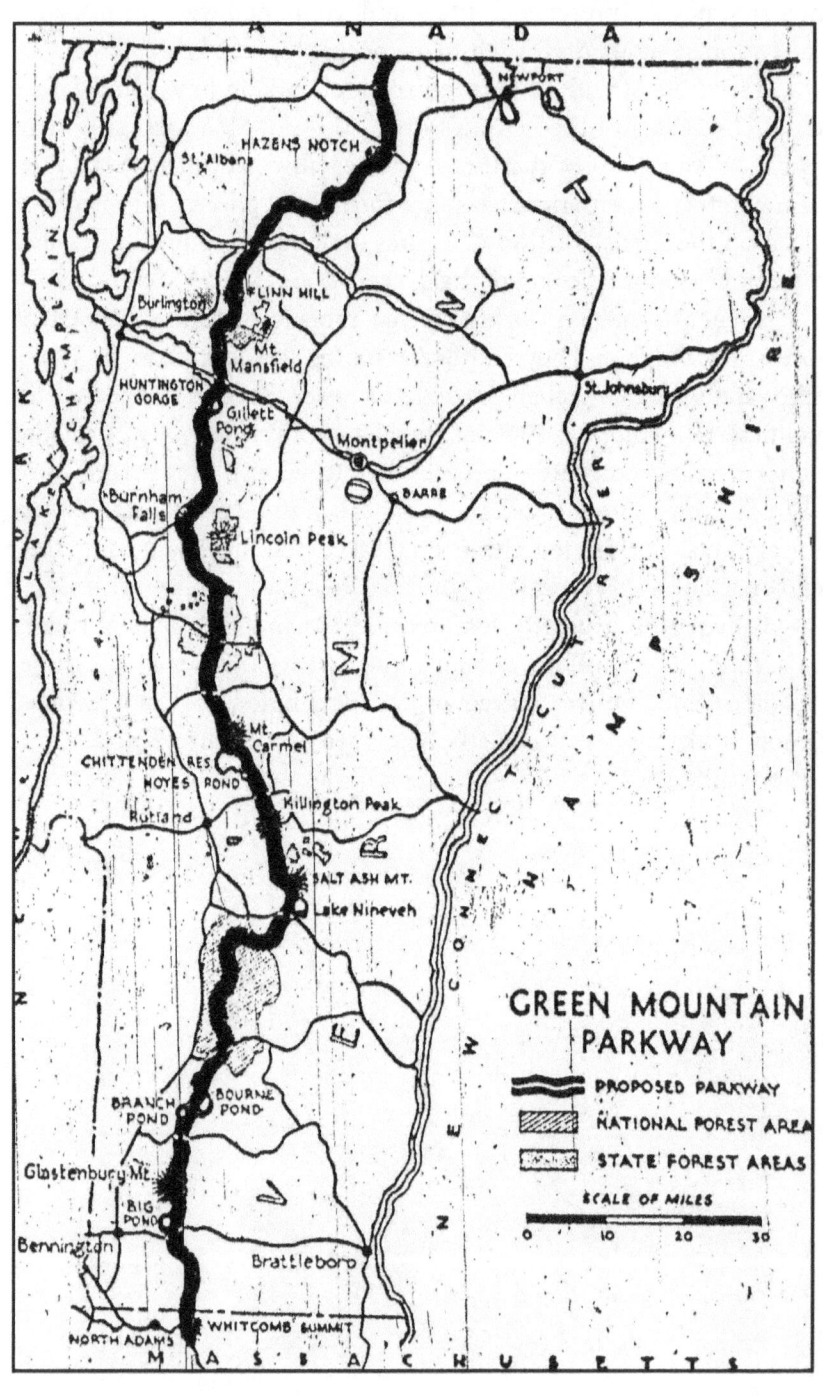

16

The Parkway That Never Happened

Vermont's expanding tourist economy received a sustained push from the Works Progress Administration during the Depression years. That included completion of routes 9 and 7 in southern Vermont, as well as upgrading of state parks and airports.

In 1934, with Vermont House Speaker George Aiken in attendance, the first ski tow rope in the country started operating in Woodstock. All this expanded seasonal employment in the commercial ski industry. Ski trails gradually crisscrossed the state, as wealthy visitors bought farms abandoned by those who could no longer make a living on the land.

One project did hit a snag, however, a proposed Green Mountain Parkway along the ridge of the famous mountain range. Among its main boosters was James Paddock Taylor, Executive Secretary of the Vermont Chamber of Commerce, who envisioned a beautiful, 260-mile ribbon of road extending from Canada to Massachusetts. Washington D.C. wanted it, and, according to Taylor and other supporters, so would most Vermonters once they understood the benefits. A major selling point was that construction would create jobs for some of the 16,000 Vermonters out of work.

All the road's backers needed was legislative approval of half a million dollars to purchase rights of way.[90]

Twenty years earlier, at a talk in Boston, Taylor had described Vermont's mountains as both a blessing and a hindrance. "They have fostered local conservatism and narrowness of interest," he argued, as well as "an excess of individuality."

He saw himself and the project as progressive. Taylor was an optimist who wanted to create a more connected, less insular society and viewed development on the mountains as a way to open minds. He often tooled around the state in a Ford and called it his "chariot of freedom." The Green Mountain Parkway would spur the improvement and beautification of others roads, he believed, and, more profoundly, encourage a "new state of mind," what he called a modern and national outlook.

"The Parkway is a part of that program to get Vermont out of her valley-mindedness into the big view of things which should be expected from a mountain people," he wrote.

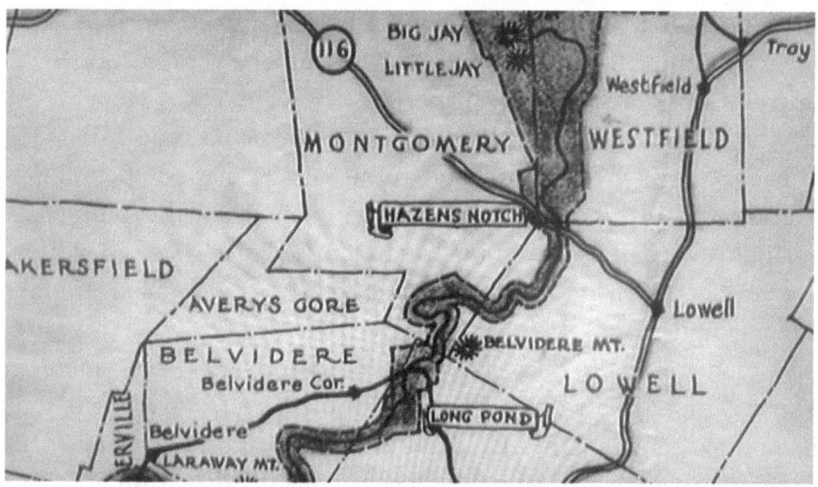

Opponents worried that the parkway would divide the state with a strip of federal territory.

Years after the 1927 flood some roads still weren't repaired. But many Vermonters were suspicious, particularly of President Franklin Roosevelt and the New Deal. They also didn't like the idea that the

---

90 Hal Goldman, *James Taylor's Progressive Vision: The Green Mountain Parkway*, Vermont History, Vol. 63, 1995

federal government would take control of 50,000 acres of land along the ridge of the state's main mountain range, and preferred to see any extra money go toward fixing existing roads and bridges. And some feared that a nationally-controlled parkway would literally cut the state in half.

The Burlington Free Press considered it a fine idea. "If our Washington Santa Claus wants to send us up ten millions to build a road over the side of our old Green Mountains, let's graciously accept it and put the boys to work," the paper chirped in a March 1935 editorial.[91]

Other papers, notably *The Rutland Herald*, weren't so convinced about the benefits. "The parkway would take tourists out of the valleys, where we can sell things to them, into the hills, where we can't," the *Herald's* editors predicted. Half a million dollars was too much to borrow, an editorial added, and "a wilderness area now rich in game will be spoiled for hikes, sportsmen, horseback riders...."[92] The paper also warned that "the state will be split in half, into East Vermont and West Vermont, with a wide strip of U.S. territory in the middle."

Herald headlines of the time often played to public fears:

GASH ON THE MOUNTAINSIDE
ELIMINATION OF THE WOODLANDS
TOLL GATES AT EVERY CROSSROAD

PROCTOR FEARS PARKWAY
WOULD STRANGLE BUSINESS

The last headline introduced a detailed critique by Mortimer Proctor, with an emphasis on the charm of wilderness areas, state sovereignty and the danger of centralized government. Basically, a business-oriented vision of progress was running into what was, in some respects, a conservative, even borderline isolationist backlash.

Beyond those dynamics, there was also the Great Depression, high unemployment and industrial cutbacks. And major strikes—notably by granite workers in 1933 and the Vermont Marble strike in 1935, the same period that the Green Mountain Parkway was being

---

91 *Burlington Free Press*, March 16, 1935
92 *Rutland Herald*, March 2, 1936

Breakthroughs

debated. In November 1935, the *Rutland Herald* added some red-baiting, suggesting that "communist influence" might be to blame for the marble strike. On Thanksgiving a thousand strikers, with their families, marched through downtown Proctor in the rain. By December they were clashing with hired thugs.

The Vermont legislature finally met on Dec. 14, 1935 to consider the Green Mountain Parkway Act, a move designed to give the National Park Service jurisdiction over the necessary land and appropriate matching funds. The debate was spirited. Supporters pointed to 12,000 men on relief, and accused critics of confusing people. One opponent called the promise of jobs propaganda and warned that the bill for construction would be passed on to future generations.

A supporter replied, "Spending $500,000 to get 18 million? I call that a pretty good deal. And as far as the argument that it will become a through way, that's just ridiculous. Mr. Speaker, Franklin County is unanimously in favor, and so is former Gov. Wilson."

One skeptic questioned whether the road would even be completed. "The way it looks now," he predicted, "one of two things will happen—either the whole country will go bankrupt or someone will step in and stop the spending. Either way, we're stuck holding the bag." Another said that people were "sending out an SOS. Heed it, I beg you, and let the people decide."

Pointing to where the parkway would have been, Bruce Post argued in The Vermont Movie that it might have limited the impact of ski resorts.

On March 3, 1936 the final decision was put before voters in a statewide referendum. Actually, the legislature was asking them to choose between two start dates—April 1, 1936, or five years later. But most people understood that it was probably now or never.[93]

In the end, a convincing majority rejected the federal government's $18 million offer. There was strong support for the road in northern counties—Chittenden, Franklin, Grand Isle, Lamoille, and Washington—but it was roundly rejected in the south. As some opponents put it, they simply didn't want the national government to become a large property owner and regulator of land in Vermont. The final count was 31,101 in favor to 43,176 opposed.

"Well, the people have expressed their opinion in no uncertain terms," huffed the *Burlington Free Press.* "So that's that."

Was the decision enlightened or selfish, provincial or progressive, conservative or radical? It is difficult to categorize. Nevertheless, Vermonters had used their unique form of grassroots democracy—Town Meeting. That said, as late as 1960 the National Park Service was still recommending the Green Mountain Parkway as part of an Appalachian Parkway system.

The opposition succeeded in part by appealing to values like independence, resistance to outside control, frugality and distrust. On the other hand, Taylor connected the outcome to a "mysterious psychology" that was limiting the state. In his view, people who opposed the Parkway opposed progress itself. They wanted to remain "different." He saw this as a long-term disadvantage and remained determined to make Vermont more like the rest of the country.

After the release of *Freedom & Unity: The Vermont Movie*, which featured a segment about the Parkway saga, people wondered why such an iconic incident was not more widely known. The simple answer is that it was an embarrassment to the political establishment at the time.

Inspiring to some, it was a defeat for the reigning powers. *The Burlington Free Press,* which had consistently backed the project, certainly had no motivation to spread the word, and as the years passed, Taylor's approach to progressivism gained considerable traction.

In *The Vermont Movie*, former Snelling administration Director of Planning Bruce S. Post speculates that building the Parkway might

---

[93] Hannah Silverman, *No Parking: Vermont Rejects the Green Mountain Parkway,* Vermont History, Vol. 63, 1995

actually have limited the impact of ski resorts on Vermont's mountains, while its absence left a vacuum that was filled by private developers. But UVM political science professor Frank Bryan argues that its defeat in 1936 was "the most democratic expression of environmental consciousness in American history, mythic in its defiance and radical in its implications—a Vermont that is green and rebellious.".

17

The Aiken-Gibson Wing

"America is in peril," warned the Republican Party's 1936 national platform. Unless Franklin Delano Roosevelt and his "socialist" New Deal could be stopped, the country was doomed. Yet when the votes were counted that November, FDR was re-elected with the biggest Electoral College margin in a century and only three states elected Republican governors.

One of those holdouts was Vermont, reliably Republican for more than 70 years. But the new governor represented the Party's progressive wing. By the 1930s George Aiken had built a strong following as an author, horticulturalist, lecturer, and legislator.

After five years in the House, he became lieutenant governor in 1935. But the Democrats were gaining ground and Gov. Charles Smith was a less-than-charismatic 68 year old, so Aiken broke the Republicans' unwritten rotation system and challenged him after just one term, organizing young Republicans, barnstorming the state, and reaching out to Democrats like Burlington's James Burke.[94]

On the other hand, Aiken criticized some aspects of the New Deal, and warned against "the visible and invisible government in Washington, whose thoughts and actions are so alien to the free-

---

94 Samuel B. Hand and D. Gregory Sanford, *Carrying Water on Both Shoulders: George D. Aiken's 1936 Gubernatorial Campaign in Vermont*, Vermont History, Vol. 43, No. 4, 1975

thinking people of Vermont and of the nation; whose policy for the last four years has been one of debt and destruction."

In some respects he sounded like a limited government conservative, arguing that the president was after "more and more control of all of us and our possessions and resources, public and private." On the other hand, he accepted the funds that flowed from New Deal programs, supported Social Security and conservation efforts, and later, as a U.S. senator, was a key author of the Food Stamp program, which benefited both the poor and farmers. As one of few successful GOP governors in the 1930s, Aiken also called for changes in the national party.

George Aiken

By 1937 he was being discussed as a possible candidate for president, a push orchestrated by the publicity director of the National Republican Committee, Vermonter Leo Casey. At a Lincoln's Day dinner organized by the National Republican Club in 1938 Aiken spoke to the nation over the radio and shocked some Republicans with the assertion that Lincoln "would be ashamed of his party's leadership today."

Two years later Wendell Wilkie got the Republican nod and went down to defeat as Roosevelt won a third term.

Ernest W. Gibson, Jr. broke the "Mountain Rule" and served as governor from 1947-1950

Aiken was close to U.S. Sen. Ernest Gibson, Sr., a respected leader of the state's progressive movement, as well as Gibson's son, who became secretary of state soon after finishing law school. When Ernest senior died in office in 1940—he had been representing Vermont in Congress since 1923—Aiken appointed Junior to complete his father's term. It was the beginning of an alliance that became known as the Aiken-Gibson Wing, liberal Republicans united by a moderate philosophy and distaste for the party's Proctor faction.

In Washington, Gibson Junior struck up a friendship with Missouri Sen. Harry Truman and irritated conservatives back home with his support of the New Deal. According to historian Samuel Hand, he was ultimately just keeping "the seat warm until Aiken mounted his own candidacy" for the senate. By the time World War II was declared, Gibson had enlisted in the Army. Aiken meanwhile won the Republican nomination to replace him, beginning an illustrious 36-year run as U.S. senator.

But then, in 1943, Gibson became a war hero in the South Pacific, an achievement magnified by the national publication of a dramatic photo displaying his wounds. By the time he returned home he was a political inevitability.

In 1944, another Proctor, the third since 1878, became governor. Mortimer Proctor's family had been a dominant political force for half a century. Like Republicans before him, he had risen through the legislature and moved from lieutenant governor to the top state job. In following this path he was obeying the unwritten "Mountain Rule," a geographical approach to power sharing in which the office of governor alternated every four years between the east and west sides of the state. Since the winner was always a Republican, it was a way to avoid factionalism and promote "orderly" succession.

Gibson said it was time to end this "rule of succession" and challenged Proctor as leader of a do-nothing "old guard." Once Proctor went down in the primary, effectively ending the family's political dynasty, the general election was a breeze. Gibson not only had the support of most Republicans but also many GIs, populists, some renegade Democrats and the state's poor.

Delivering on his promises was a bit more difficult, since conservatives still controlled the state legislature. He did manage to increase human services, push through a minimum wage and pension plan for teachers, and establish the graduated income tax. He also became "father" of the State police—to the chagrin of county sheriffs. But success was illusive in areas such as public health and welfare. A study commission on occupational diseases appointed by Gibson looked at the health risks of manufacturing and farming—dangerous machinery, dust, asbestos, silicosis, toxic chemicals—but equivocated on improving the state's worker's compensation law. The welfare system was slightly improved, but overseers of the poor, local managers who provided services and ran "poor farms," remained powerful and frightening feudal lords of the impoverished and those with mental health problems.

Before most mainstream politicians, Gibson recognized that public health would inevitably be one of state government's biggest responsibilities. He kept in touch with Aiken, who liked his thinking and brought some of his ideas to Congress. But rank-and-file Republicans never bought into this agenda, and many resented the idea that state government's role should expand to include things like public health and subsidized services for the poor. By 1949 Gibson was fed up and accepted appointment to a federal judgeship by his old friend, and now president, Harry Truman.

Aiken remained in the Senate until 1975, where he won respect as an independent thinker and fought for energy projects that brought affordable hydropower to the state. In the midst of the Vietnam War, a story developed that Aiken had advised that the U.S. should declare victory and bring the troops home. What he actually said was that the nation "could well declare unilaterally that this stage of the Vietnam War is over." The U.S. had "won," he argued—as it turned out, erroneously—because its forces were "in control of most of the field and no potential enemy is in a position to establish its authority over South Vietnam." It was a far-fetched proposal, he admitted, "but nothing else has worked."[95]

The 12-minute speech, delivered during a February 1966 Senate Foreign Relations Committee hearing, generated considerable media heat, and created new tension between Aiken and President Lyndon Johnson, a friend from earlier Senate years. But Mike Mansfield, the Montana Democrat who served as Senate Majority Leader for a

---

95 Richard Ederf, Aiken Suggests U.S. Say It Has Won the War, *New York Times,* Oct. 20, 1966

record-setting 16 years, commented that "the distinguished senior Senator from Vermont has given us a great deal to consider and some additional food for thought."[96]

James Jeffords was another renegade Republicans, an independent thinker in the Aiken-Gibson mold. His career began conventionally, but after a stint as attorney general his path to the top of state government was blocked by Deane Davis, the National Life insurance executive who succeeded Phil Hoff as governor in 1968. Davis preferred Luther Hackett, a fellow insurance man, and Jeffords was defeated in the 1972 Republican primary. He regrouped and replaced Richard Mallory[97] in Congress in 1974.

James Jeffords

---

96 Stephen C. Terry, *Say We Won and Get Out: George D. Aiken and the Vietnam War*, Center for Research on Vermont/ White River Press, 2020

97 Mallory was appointed to fill the state's lone US House seat when Thomas Stafford left for an appointment to the US Senate after the death of Winston Prouty in Sept., 1971. The following January Stafford won a special election to complete Prouty's unexpired term.

From that point onward, Jeffords built his congressional career on defying easy classification and frequently bucked his own party's agenda. In the early 1980s, he opposed Pres. Ronald Reagan's tax cuts, and in 1993 supported the Clinton health care plan. In 1994, despite his defiance of GOP orthodoxy, he succeeded mainline Republican Robert Stafford into the U.S. Senate and continued along a maverick path. One example was his sponsorship of an anti-discrimination bill to prohibit the use of a job applicant's sexual orientation as a basis for hiring, firing, promotion, or compensation. Another was his support of the UN. Neither pleased many of his Republican colleagues.

In October 1997, Jeffords was honored by the UN Association for backing a volunteer system that would give soldiers the "right to choose" UN peacekeeping. A month later he received the Freedom of Choice Award from the Vermont Chapter of the National Abortion Rights Action League (NARAL). Typically the award went to a grassroots activist. But despite his position—senator and lifelong Republican—his name sprang to everyone's lips because of work he had done throughout the late-term abortion ban debate. Standing up for women's right to choose was a risky thing to do, and once again made him unpopular with right wing groups.

But Jeffords was used to being a target, from the left and the right. During a debate on FDA "modernization," for example, he was accused of reducing the labeling requirements for irradiated foods by Food & Water, a Vermont-based environmental group. In offering the legislation, charged the group's director Michael Colby, Jeffords had shown that he was "more concerned with the well-being of big business than with the health and safety of his own constituency."

Nevertheless, he remained one of the state's most popular figures, a liberal maverick who called himself a Lincoln Republican and, near the end of his career, frequently reminded his conservative colleagues that he was the radical right of the Vermont congressional delegation. Confounding ideologues at both ends of the political spectrum, he capped his career with defiance of the Bush administration over tax cuts and his subsequent exit from the Republican Party in 2001. Jeffords ended his career as an Independent.

Although a stalwart Republican, Ralph Flanders helped elect a Democratic Senate majority in 1954 to block the spread of Joe McCarthy's politics.

18

The Man Who Stopped McCarthy

Vermont's habit of questioning authority has rarely been demonstrated more dramatically than at the height of the McCarthy era.

Joseph McCarthy, Wisconsin's ambitious junior senator, had emerged as the country's most powerful anti-communist crusader in 1950 and initiated a modern reign of terror targeting "enemies within," alleged security threats inside the U.S. government, Hollywood and communities across the country. By 1954, having already ruined lives and caused innocent people to be blacklisted and jailed, he was accusing army officers of communist sympathies. Even Pres. Dwight Eisenhower handled him cautiously.

Sen. Ralph Flanders wasn't the most likely candidate to confront McCarthy. A self-educated inventor, businessman and son-in-law of James Hartness, a former governor, Flanders was a pragmatic conservative who enthusiastically defended free enterprise. President of the Boston Federal Reserve Bank before his election to the Senate, he was also a devout Christian who believed "the world seems to be mobilizing for the great battle of Armageddon."[98] But he had heard enough from McCarthy in the Senate to be concerned about the country's direction.

---

98 Sherman et al, *Freedom and Unity*

Flanders was a U.S. Senator from 1947–1959.

In 1948, the dean of Lyndon State College had been forced to resign for supporting Henry Wallace, the Progressive Party candidate for president. Two years later, Rep. Charles Plumley called for the removal of Communists and "sympathizers" from Vermont schools, and Gov. Lee Emerson backed a bill banning "organizations engaged in subversive activities as a political party."[99]

Plumley charged that Vermont had been targeted by the Communists. "Nobody doubts that Vermont was selected and that Vermonters were chosen as a bunch of guinea pigs on which to experiment," he told the *White River Valley Herald.*"[100]

According to *Freedom and Unity*, columnist Westbrook Pegler initially drew McCarthy's eye to the state by writing about a supposed communist cell in the Randolph-Bethel area.[101] Local anti-communist fanatics Lucille and Manuel Miller were accusing public figures, from

---

99 Rick Winston, *A Sinister Poison: The Red Scare Comes to Bethel*, Vermont History, Vol. 40, No. 1, 2012

100 Phil Heller, *Red Scare in the Green Mountains*, Rutland Daily Herald, July 30, 2012

101 Sherman et al, *Freedom and Unity*

Vermont's superintendent of schools to former Gov. Ernest Gibson Jr., by then a federal judge, and even Eisenhower, of communist leanings. Making matters worse, former State Department official Alger Hiss, who was convicted in a notorious espionage case, once owned property in Peacham.

Flanders watched the fear of communism cloud the judgment of state officials, who had attempted to examine textbooks for subversive influences and amend the state's Sabotage Prevention Act, a remnant of World War I. The legislature rejected the proposal to review textbooks, as well as Gov. Emerson's bill to ban "suspect" political parties. But that didn't stop the University of Vermont from dismissing medical school faculty member Alex Novikoff for refusing to discuss his Communist involvement as a student with a Senate subcommittee.

By March 9, 1954 the usually soft-spoken, 66-year-old Flanders had finished watching and started to speak out. Rising on the Senate floor, he mocked McCarthy for spreading confusion and sowing division.

"He dons his warpaint," Flanders said. "He goes into his dance. He emits war whoops. He goes forth to battle and proudly returns with the scalp of a pink dentist." Flanders was referring to an army officer, the only example of a communist sympathizer in the military McCarthy had been able to produce.

Congressional testimony on the alleged threat inside the military began in April. During what became known as the Army-McCarthy hearings the Wisconsin senator accused the Secretary of the Army of interfering with his investigation. The Army countered that McCarthy had sought favors for a military aide. The hearings were broadcast live on television for weeks, the first event of its kind.

Unfortunately, most Vermonters couldn't tune in. The state's first TV transmission tower wouldn't go up until several months later. But Flanders was there, at least in the building, and by June had heard enough.

In another broadside attack, he compared McCarthy to Dennis the Menace and Adolph Hitler. "Were the Junior Senator from Wisconsin in the pay of the Communists he could not have done a better job for them," he charged. On June 11, he further escalated the confrontation, entering McCarthy's hearing room in front of television cameras to hand him a note, an invitation to be present when Flanders spoke in the Senate again.

Flanders confronted Sen. McCarthy and committee counsel Roy Cohn during the Army-McCarthy hearings, hand-delivering his letter about a censure resolution. Flanders' revised motion called for McCarthy to be removed from a committee. This eventually led to his condemnation by the Senate.

Some people considered the Vermonter an oddball, a rural kook who didn't understand the high stakes. As evidence they pointed to his sponsorship of Senate Resolution 87, a proposed constitutional amendment that would effectively bar non-Christians from taking the oath of office. That reflected another aspect of Flanders' world view.

As he explained in his first denunciation of McCarthy, "Now is a crisis in the agelong warfare between God and the Devil for the souls of men." As far as he was concerned, McCarthy was a dangerous distraction from that more important battle. The words harkened back to the revivalism of the early 19th century.

The future of the country was on a knife edge. On one hand, the Supreme Court had ruled unanimously on May 17 that segregation was illegal. In *Brown v. The Board of Education of Topeka*, Chief Justice John Marshall said, "We conclude that in the field of public education the doctrine of 'separate but equal' has no place."

A week later, however, the same court upheld the Internal Security Act, which made Communist Party membership grounds for the deportation of non-citizens. The French garrison at Dien Bien Phu in Vietnam had fallen to insurgent forces led by Ho Chi Minh and Vice President Richard Nixon was urging U.S. intervention. In Guatemala a right-wing coup financed by the CIA overthrew the elected president, Jacobo Arbenz, whose government had nationalized the property of the United Fruit Company.

In this highly charged atmosphere, with public opinion divided—even in Vermont—Flanders went to the Senate floor and introduced a resolution to oust McCarthy from chairmanship of the Senate Oversight Committee. This put the Republican Party in a bind. McCarthy was an embarrassment, but Flanders was going too far, challenging Senate rules regarding committee chairs and seniority. He was at the epicenter of a struggle over the fate of the country. Drawing on his pragmatic side, Flanders consulted with colleagues and took a small but crucial step back. Instead of demanding McCarthy's removal from leadership, he proposed a censure motion.

The struggle continued for months, right into the 1954 mid-term elections. Even though Flanders was a Republican, he worked with the National Committee for an Effective Congress, whose explicit aim was to elect a Democrat majority. The issue was too important to let partisan politics stand in the way. That fall the Republicans lost control of the Senate.

Flanders' resolution initially avoided reference to any specific actions or misdeeds by McCarthy. As he explained, "It was not his breaches of etiquette, or of rules or sometimes even of laws which is so disturbing. It was his overall pattern of behavior."

A special senate committee, chaired by Utah Republican Arthur Watkins, was appointed to evaluate the proposal. It proceeded to weigh 46 complaints itemized by Flanders, other Senate members and witnesses, in the end recommending censure on two counts: that McCarthy had obstructed a Senate Subcommittee attempting to investigate him, and had denounced a fellow senator "without reason or justification" and acted in an "inexcusable" and "reprehensible" manner toward Brigadier General Ralph Zwicker, a witness before his investigating committee.

On Oct. 4, 1954, *Time Magazine* called the outcome "a ringing reassertion of the U.S. Senate's dignity," and a "new landmark in U.S. government."

McCarthy's destructive power had been broken, the beginning of the end of another Red Scare. Within three years "Tail-gunner Joe" died from cirrhosis of the liver, the result of years of alcoholism. Flanders described his contribution afterward with the usual candor and simplicity.

"It became clear that in the outside world McCarthy was the United States and the United States was McCarthy," he recalled. "The conviction grew that something must be done about him, even if I had to do it myself."[102]

Like Matthew Lyon a century and a half earlier, another Vermonter had influenced the nation's course by standing up when others would not. Flanders was no revolutionary and had some unusual ideas. But through bold action at a crucial moment he expressed traditional Vermont attitudes toward authority, dissent and tolerance. Though clearly a New England conservative in many respects he was also part libertarian, part egalitarian, and a persistent advocate for accountability, all in all a prime example of the Vermont Way.

---

102 Neal R. Pierce, *The New England States*, W.W. Norton, 1976

19

The Hoff Effect

For Phil Hoff, one of Vermont's breakthrough governors in the 20th century, the job of an elected leader was to push the envelope of change. "You have to stand up for things," he once said, "and if that results in you being defeated, it's a risk you take."[103]

Hoff was speaking from experience. After three terms as governor in the tumultuous 1960s, he was trounced in a 1970 run for the U.S. Senate by incumbent Republican Winston Prouty. The main reason, as he saw it, was his civil rights activism, particularly sponsorship of the Vermont-New York Youth Project, which brought Black teenagers up from New York to work and play with white Vermonters.

"It was enormously successful for the participants," he said. "But it wasn't well understood, and all the latent racism began to emerge. There's no question it defeated me in the Senate race."

His fight against racism dated to the early 1950s, when he arrived from Massachusetts, just out of Cornell Law School. Hearing that the Black captain of UVM's football team, who had brought his girlfriend up for a weekend visit, was refused a motel room, Hoff joined forces with local clergy and UVM faculty. At the time, such racial discrimination was commonplace. In another case, a Black Air Force officer was refused the right to buy a home when the real estate

---

103 This interview with Hoff, one of several over the years, was conducted in 1998 for an article in *The Vermont Times*. We co-authored a 1986 article on the Leahy-Snelling race for the US Senate.

agent met vociferous local opposition. But the "positive forces" in the community fought back, launching the state's first anti-racist coalition.

"We would go to the neighborhood with a priest, a minister, and a rabbi," Hoff recalled. "And you know, we won every time."

Still, many Vermonters weren't over their prejudice. In the summer of 1968, when someone fired into the home of Reverend David Johnson, a Black minister who had come to the rural town of Irasburg from California, the police focused on the victim and charged him with adultery. Johnson's alleged crime, apparently, was sharing a couch with a white woman. Hoff called for an investigation and discovered that the state police knew the identity of the shooter but didn't go after him. He also discovered that when the public safety commissioner refused to discipline his staff, there was nothing he could do about it.[104]

Years later, Hoff still wasn't pleased about how Vermonters dealt with race. "There's a lot of unrecognized racism, even among people of good will," he said in a 1998 interview. "It's part of the way we were brought up." As a member of the Vermont Advisory Commission on Civil Rights, Hoff attended hearings that year in Burlington and Rutland. "I can't describe how distressing they were," he recalled. "Racial harassment in our public schools is alive, real well, and frightening."

Civil rights activism wasn't the only thing that made Hoff's years as governor special. To start, he was the first Democrat elected in a century—after just one term in the House. It was rough going at first. Facing an overwhelmingly Republican legislature, he thought there was little chance he would be re-elected. "So, why not damn the torpedoes, which I did," he said. "They (voters) wanted us to shake up the establishment."

The Democratic Party had been gaining strength since 1952, when Burlington City Attorney Robert Larrow ran for governor. His 39 percent showing against an incumbent demonstrated the potential to attract Gibson Republicans and win not only in urban areas but statewide. Frank Branon, a Franklin County senator, built on that base in subsequent elections.

---

[104] Joe Sherman, *Fast Track on a Dirt Road: Vermont Transformed 1945-1990*, Countryman Press, 1991

The 1958 race between Bernard Leddy and Republican Robert Stafford was close enough for a recount, while William Meyer, a forester who ran a grassroots campaign, became the first Democratic Congressman in a century. But Meyer was tarred as a "commie lover" for supporting non-intervention in the affairs of China, and defeated after a single term by Stafford, who spent the next two decades in the House and Senate.

Hoff was part of a bipartisan group of legislators known as the "young Turks," an alliance that included Republican Franklin Billings, a Rockefeller-connected lawyer from Woodstock, and Ernest Gibson III, son of the former governor. Hoff claimed that the state had been damaged by a century of one-party rule. The endorsement of Republicans like A. Luke Crispe, a former Gibson law partner from Brattleboro, and T. Garry Buckley helped him to victory. They and other dissident Republicans had joined with Democrats to form the Vermont Independent Party, a strategy for wooing voters away from F. Ray Keyser, the Republican incumbent.

Hoff celebrated in Winooski on election night in 1962.

Larrow, who ran for Attorney General in 1962, was pushing for redistricting of Burlington and, more crucially, reapportionment of the state legislature based on population. Since the founding of Vermont representation in its legislature had been based on the principle of one town-one vote; in other words, a town with only a thousand residents had the same legislative weight as a growing city.

Basing legislative seats in the House of Representatives on population instead would clearly increase representation from urban, Democratic communities like Burlington and Brattleboro. At this point Democrats were winning about 40 percent of the popular vote statewide but had only 20 percent of the legislative seats.

On Jan. 23, 1963, Crispe filed a lawsuit arguing that representation on the basis of towns and counties violated the equal protection clause of the 14th Amendment to the U.S. Constitution. When it reached U.S. District Court the name on the lawsuit was renegade Republican Garry Buckley. One problem the reformers had was the solidly GOP legislature. But they had a friend who was perfect for the job of House Speaker. Just as Crispe filed the reapportionment lawsuit in Brattleboro, Republican Franklin Billings was elected House Speaker with every Democratic vote.[105]

The U.S. Supreme Court eventually agreed with the arguments of Larrow, Crispe and Buckley and ordered the state legislature to make the change. The transition began on May 14, 1965, when the House of Representatives voted to reduce its size from 245 to 150 seats and elect each member based on population rather than geography. Traditionalists warned that small towns would no longer have much influence on the state's direction.

In 1966, Hoff appointed Larrow and Billings to the Superior Court. In the 1970s another Democratic governor, Thomas Salmon, elevated both to the State Supreme Court. Buckley eventually became lieutenant governor.

During Hoff's three terms, the nature and scope of state government dramatically changed. Among other things, those years brought a major expansion of the state college system, the state's

---

[105] Research on the politics of reapportionment was conducted for War in the Courts, a Feb., 1978 investigative cover story for *The Vermont Vanguard Press* that focused mainly on the Vermont Supreme Court and Vermont's Side Judges, a unique aspect of the state's judicial system.

takeover of welfare, urban renewal projects, the first rehabilitation programs at Vermont prisons, and reluctant acceptance that a regional approach to planning was needed. Other initiatives didn't fare as well, but some were just ahead of their time. Regionalized school districts and fair housing legislation, for instance, had to wait.

As Joe Sherman put it in *Fast Lane on a Dirt Road*, "Vermonters seemed willing, at least for a while, to go with the irresistible tug of the American century. They were just climbing on board 60 years late."[106]

Hoff also pushed for a statewide development plan. "It probably wasn't very good," he admitted 30 years later, "but no one had ever done it before." Acknowledging criticism of "uncontrolled" growth, he said that dependence on local tax revenues to support schools was one of the main culprits: "Places like Williston and South Burlington buy into things for the revenues." But he still believed that Vermont needed a statewide development plan. On the other hand, he also concluded that, to keep government closer to people, regional solutions should be considered more seriously.

"In the old days, the parameters of town were about 45 minutes by horse-drawn cart," he mused. "Using that same time frame with the automobile, government can be redrawn in terms of time rather than distance. If you did that, you could divest much of state government to the regions, including health and welfare. And give them as much autonomy as possible. We need a state plan, but one that allows modifications in terms of local circumstances."

What about local control? "Local control is a myth," Hoff said. "Towns are given just enough choice to make people think they're exercising local control. Take education. Do local school districts control educational policy? Like hell. I'd let them do more of it. But if a school district doesn't vote enough money to support its system, the state can take it over. You need some of that."

The cautious, "incremental" approach to governing practiced by Howard Dean during the 1990s didn't appeal to the former governor's "activist" sensibilities. Yet, he had to admit that "Howard is very much in touch with the national mood. He's very careful, especially fiscally, and his agenda stresses children. These are very conservative times."

---

106 Joe Sherman, *Fast Track on a Dirt Road*

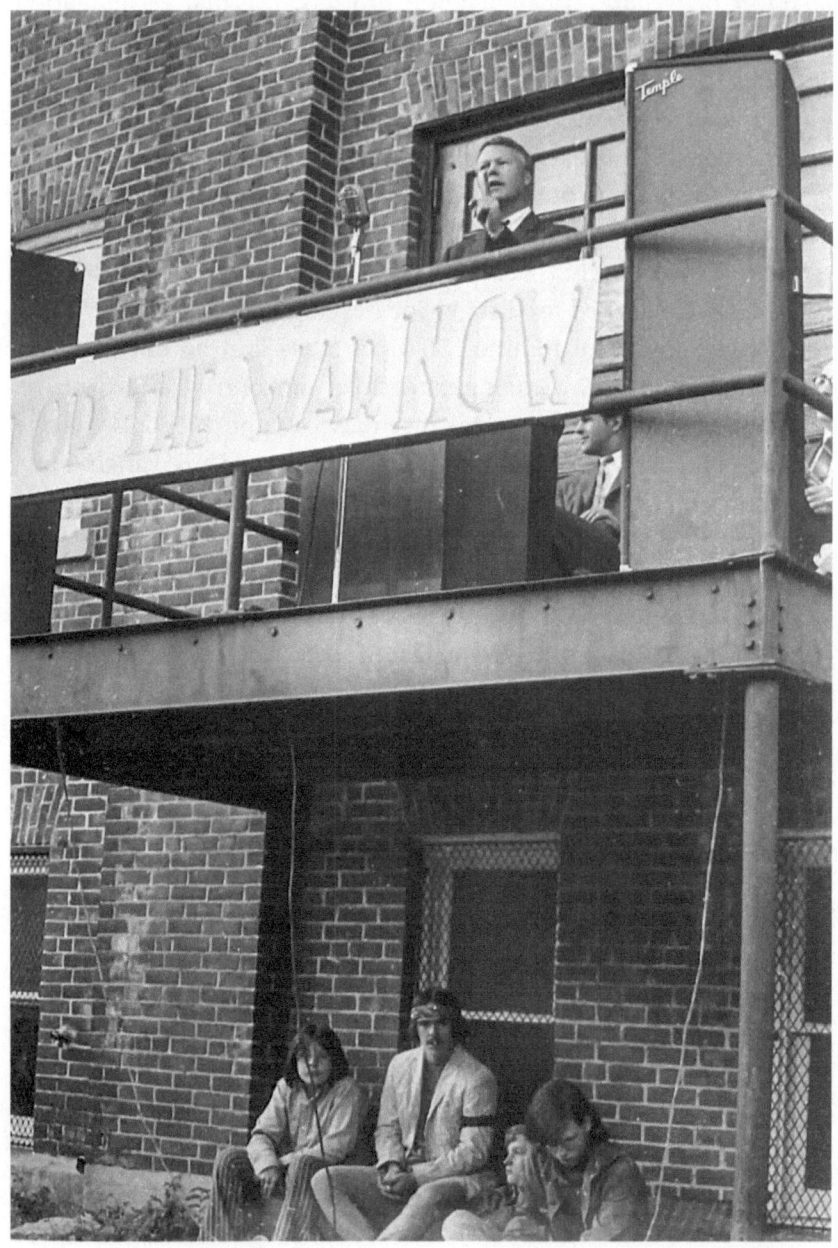

Phil Hoff was the first Democratic governor to break with President Lyndon Johnson over Vietnam. He supported Robert Kennedy's bid for president, and backed Eugene McCarthy after Kennedy was assassinated. Hoff's address at the Bennington Armory on Oct. 15, 1969 was part of the nationwide Moratorium to End the War in Vietnam.

The political landscape changed dramatically after Hoff's glory days. In those heady times, he recalled wistfully, "We were going to revolutionize the country. It fit with the national mood." But in the decades that followed, as "fundamentalists" took the Republican Party to the right, Democrats moved to the middle. What was lost, Hoff felt, was "the left wing of the party, which believes that government is a balancing tool, protector of the ordinary person, and instigator of change."

Political parties weren't as strong as they once were, he said, and most elected politicians were more concerned with looking bipartisan than taking a stand. Meanwhile, the distribution of wealth became worse, while welfare reform moved people into marginal jobs without providing education and training adequate to let them advance.

"We're creating a permanent minority," Hoff predicted. "If you come from a family where the parents barely read and can't finish sentences, you're probably dead before you begin. And that has to do with the distribution of benefits and wealth. It's crazy, and it will do us in."

People don't often embrace change, Hoff argued, and historic moments like the one he seized were few and far between. In Vermont, he suggested, they seemed to come along about every 25 years. "But I like to believe that we're closer to one now than a lot of people think," he added. "What we need is visible leaders who stand for change."

A cover story profiled Richard Snelling during his first term as governor, less than two months after the *Vanguard Press* published its inaugural issue.

20

The Snelling Style

In 1953, a University of Vermont professor and a Burlington lawyer incorporated a TV operation called Green Mountain Television and issued 50,000 shares at one dollar apiece. The company nabbed over 3,000 subscribers for this early "wired" system before WCAX-TV even worked out its licensing problems. One of the early investors in that media startup was Richard Snelling, a Pennsylvania-born Harvard grad who had already run a used car lot in downtown Burlington. Snelling came equipped with a verbal knack, affection for new technology, and the ability to forecast business trends.[107]

The Greater Burlington Industrial Corporation., an association of "concerned businessmen," was also getting started. Over the next decade it would revolutionize countywide employment. Snelling hopped on the bandwagon as a PR man, directed GBIC for seven years, and became its president, then chairman in the early 1960s.

After collecting $250,000 in long term loans, GBIC started building plants on speculation, a godsend when unemployment rose in the 1950s. In short order, 11 towns were kicking in money to support the group's projects.

Snelling was equally adept politically. In 1954 he handled finances for Chittenden County Republicans. The next year, at 28, he was county

---

[107] Much of the material in this chapter was originally developed for The State Business: Snelling's First 500 Days, a cover story for *The Vermont Vanguard Press*, March 7, 1978.

chair. As his political stock rose he cultivated the Horatio Alger image of a self-made man. But his parents were Snelling and Snelling, patent attorneys, and his father, Walter, had invented liquefied petroleum gas. This provided the young man with an inherited interest in invention and financial ties to a Philadelphia bank.

With a winning combination of breeding and a goal-oriented work ethic, Snelling charged into Vermont politics by running for the state's Senate in 1956 and advocating, a decade before its time, a sales tax. He lost, but succeeded in the next cycle with a run for a House seat. Still running GBIC, he also led a new Committee for Economic Progress, a pressure group that wanted to expand the state park, increase UVM's state appropriation, and build up the state's development program. Snelling subsequently pushed through the state park idea, reactivated the Young Republican Club, directed the national Right to Work Committee (to ban "compulsory unionism"), and shifted some of his investments.

Snelling in his factory

As the Eisenhower era ended he made the deal of a lifetime. With the Alling family ready to sell a small tool-making company in

Williston, Snelling sold his GMTV stock and took a gamble on Alling Enterprises. His first move was intensive automation. In 1961, another opportunity opened up when GBIC's real estate arm, Cynosure, built a home in Shelburne for Snelling's Shelburne Industries. He was still running the development group at the time. He dovetailed that move with the purchase of two metal fabricating companies, which he merged and relocated to a new plant. Lining up contracts for assembly work from IBM and GE, he quadrupled sales in four years.

The political track didn't go as smoothly. He had considered a run for lieutenant governor as early as 1960, but waited for four years and lost anyway. In 1966 he made his first run for governor, another uphill battle in the era of Phil Hoff. But there were consolations, especially consistent business gains and the choice that secured his fortune—purchasing Barrecrafter and Barreca Products, which had a line of ski racks, poles and boot-trees. He now had a ripe combination of companies putting out consumer hardware and sporting goods. Sales proceeded to increase by almost 2,000 percent. By the end of the 1960s Snelling was employing about 400 people.

At last he felt ready to move into the political spotlight. Turning over management to a trusted associate, he returned to the legislature and sat on the Shelburne Industries board with his wife Barbara, Vermont's leading commercial developer Antonio Pomerleau, and retired executive C. Herbert Ridgely. As SI stepped up export marketing and bike product sales, its founder set out to lead the state.

One of the first steps was to launch a new group, the Vermont Council for Effective Government, which argued that $10 million could be cut from the state budget. His opponent was the soft-spoken ex-chancellor of the Vermont State Colleges, William Craig. But the real fight came after his primary victory, when he faced Democrat Stella Hackel.

A former state treasurer and commissioner of employment security, Hackel opted to hang her race on a staggering reorganization plan that involved breaking up "super agencies" while strengthening the governor's cabinet and agency of administration. If the legislature wouldn't approve her plans, she threatened to implement them anyway. "One of the first things any governor must realize," Snelling scolded, "is that he or she must be able to work with the legislative branch."

The race was essentially over after that, and by October Snelling was outlining his program.

In office, he was a hard-ball manager, boldly shifting personnel and entire departments. An early attempt to cut welfare was scuttled, but he did succeed in stopping state workers from talking to the press without high-level approval. The opposition called it "muzzling."

When UVM asked for more money, despite his long support for the school he offered only a quarter of the request. When it came to the budget, even his detractors had to admit that he had a magic financial touch. Within two years millions of dollars were saved.

"There are less state employees on the payrolls as well as less authorized positions," he claimed.[108] But House appropriations chair Madeleine Kunin, who challenged his re-election in 1982, saw it as a shell game: authorized positions were merely being replaced, she charged, with "limited service" jobs funded by the feds.

He also kept his promise to attract new industries. The government couldn't create jobs, Snelling explained, but it could create a "reasonable environment" and "direct job growth." Ideally, he believed that job development should be handled locally or regionally. But the rapid growth of Chittenden County had "dislocated some of the most significant attractions to the state." To respond he focused on under-developed regions. Worker morale was another matter, however. When dismissal of state employees rose by 150 percent in Snelling's first year, it produced an atmosphere of caution and gloom in many offices.

After Snelling read his inaugural address, Sen. Russell Niquette said he sounded a lot like a Democrat. In keeping with that description, the governor balanced fiscal caution with flexibility when it came to educational needs and shifting cultural dynamics. In 1982, the *Burlington Free Press* editorial page described him as "a moderate in the best sense of the word. A fiscal conservative, he is more liberal on social issues." Still, his Republican allegiances frequently came through during eight years in office.

Two years after stepping down, Snelling challenged Patrick Leahy in 1986 for his seat in the U.S. Senate. At first Leahy, despite being the incumbent, was considered an underdog facing a four-term

---

108 Snelling Interview, Feb., 1978

governor, a millionaire with savvy and national standing. But as soon as Snelling formally entered the race things changed. Leahy was soon swamping the former governor with a $2 million war chest and an effective campaign plan. Phil Hoff and I assessed the race in an article for *Vermont Affairs*:

"Leahy's forces had been planning for several years and, by the time Snelling announced, had identified over 50,000 strong supporters. Many people were attracted by the senator's activist stance on the arms race. Even more joined after Snelling announced, many of them leftists who supported Leahy as a way to hand Snelling a defeat. Once Snelling started dropping in the polls, his ability to compete financially was also diminished.

"Leahy played the incumbent to the hilt. Ignoring his opponent as often as possible, sending out surrogates to issue his rebuttals, he spoke as senator rather than as candidate, projecting himself via the news in fresh ways. What he did not do, however, was engage in a full-fledged debate or outline his agenda...If Leahy was running against anyone, it was Ronald Reagan."[109]

Snelling's problem was that the political landscape had changed. Vermont was no longer a conservative or Republican stronghold. In defiance of national trends it had moved decidedly left in areas such as the environment, social policy and even foreign affairs. Snelling was in a bind. With an established liberal reputation Leahy sensed the reservations of residents about Reagan policies and seized the Vermont middle.

Although looking like a moderate Snelling decided to move to the right, away from the comfortable center he had occupied in the past. Meanwhile, his decision to focus on deficit reduction drew attention to the $35 million deficit that had accumulated during his own administration. He could explain it, even argue that he had set up the machinery to eliminate it. But the more he talked, the more he was needled—even by conservatives.

By mid-October the race was all but over and the press was issuing post-mortems. Going in, Snelling had seen himself as the savior of his party, returning from a life of ease at the insistence of Republican stalwarts, including Reagan himself. But this had clouded

---

109 Phil Hoff and Greg Guma, *A Clash of Giants*, Vermont Affairs, 1987

his usually keen political vision, while poor advice and deceptive polls kept him from regaining the initiative.

Four years after that defeat, and another attempt at retirement, Snelling returned to the political spotlight for one more close up, winning a fifth term as governor in 1990.

On Aug. 13, 1991, just seven months after the inauguration, he unexpectedly died of heart failure while cleaning his pool one evening. His successor was the lieutenant governor, an ambitious young Democrat named Howard Dean.

Realignments

An Anti-Vietnam War protest was held at the Bennington Monument in October 1969 during a national mobilization. Harvey Carter, then a Republican state legislator, led the pledge of allegiance.

21

Encounters on the Culture Front

Almost two centuries after Bennington's crucial role in the American Revolution it became the site for radical change again, this time in the arts. Beginning in the 1930s Martha Graham and others turned Bennington College into the epicenter of the modern dance world. The Bennington School of Dance, precursor of the American Dance Festival, was an innovative laboratory where pioneers experimented, trained students, and created early works that defined modern dance.

A generation after that, the area became a nexus for modernist art activity. As the story goes, it happened after art critic Clement Greenberg met painter Helen Frankenthaler, then a Bennington College student. Soon joined by painters like Paul Feeley, they were instrumental in connecting the emerging avant-garde movement based at the college with the New York art scene.

By the 1960s, the college community was hosting a veritable artist colony. An article in *Vogue* updated Vermont history by calling painters like Anthony Caro, Kenneth Noland, Vincent Longo and Jules Olitski the new Green Mountain Boys. The school became a small but energetic community of idealists, intellectuals, and artists. Greenberg's idea was that art should be disciplined without sacrificing esthetic vitality, a concept that combined distance with enjoyment and freedom. Not far from urban centers and yet sufficiently removed, Bennington felt like an ideal place to play out this vision.

But the "Golden Age" was winding down by the late 1960s and a conservative political storm was brewing. A few miles from the bucolic college campus, a new public high school had just been built and opened. The year before I began work as a reporter for the local daily in 1968, several school leaders died in a plane crash. The mood, both nationally and in Bennington, was turning dark. Then, just as I was hired, the school superintendent resigned and a dispute emerged, not just over who would replace him but really about where local education was headed.

Covering a Divided Community

The Bennington Banner newsroom was a large, open bullpen filled with manual typewriters and competing conversations. At one end, a picture window loomed over a picaresque main drag. At the other, just this side of the swinging door to production, Bennington Banner Editor-in-Chief Tyler Resch worked over the day's copy. In a corner, the teletype cranked AP reports onto a long roll of yellow paper that spooled onto the floor.

Each weekday morning I would wake up at around 6 a.m. to get downtown, read the Albany papers and develop photos taken the night before by staff. It was my first full-time job in journalism. Since I had commercial photography training, I also ran the darkroom. By 8 a.m. I was checking on the overnight accidents, writing up items for "Over in New York," and printing contact sheets for review. By 9 a.m. I was typing stories on the clanking keyboard of a huge old Remington. The finished newspaper hit the streets shortly after noon.

During my first week on the job, in December 1968, Richard Nixon was back in Washington selecting his cabinet. Vietnam peace talks were stalled in Paris and the Defense Department called up another 33,000 young men to fight the war, bringing the total to half a million troops. My beats in Southern Vermont were far less momentous—district court, local schools, and the Village Trustees.

One night editor Resch accompanied me to a school board meeting, drew a diagram identifying the people around the table, and then left. Now it would be sink or swim. In the grand scheme of things the story mattered little. But for the *Banner*'s readers, it did mean something. Without a local TV station, and long before the internet, my report was their main way to understand what was happening in the school system. If I couldn't explain it I had no business calling myself a reporter.

As luck would have it, a political storm was brewing. Mt. Anthony Union High School, built in the blush of a progressive educational era, was also at the center of Bennington's pain. Its alma mater, "The Impossible Dream," turned out to be prophetic. An idealistic plan for local education was about to be derailed by a cultural backlash.

Pure Lard, a local rock band that performed in the Mt. Anthony Union High School courtyard in 1969, later opened for bands like The Byrds and The Guess Who.

After the school superintendent resigned a dispute had developed over who would replace him as acting chief. The elementary school board wanted Assistant Superintendent George Sleeman. The supervisory union, which combined both the elementary and high school boards, was not so sure. On the surface it looked like a minor bureaucratic fracas, a question of who could sign checks until a permanent chief was selected. But it was actually part of a long-running conflict over the fundamental direction of education and community life.

Lack of experience and limited knowledge made my first stories for the *Banner* less informative than they might have been. But after some tense school board sessions, plus getting the back story from some off-the-record sources, I developed a clearer picture. At the center of it were the Sleemans, the most influential family in the village of Bennington.

Assistant School Superintendent George Sleeman had a brother, Richard, a leading local conservative who chaired the elementary school board, held an administrative job at a nearby college, and supervised local property assessments. The family, which owned more rental property than anyone else in the area, had strong support among the local working class. But the village was literally surrounded by another legal entity, the town of Bennington, a growing suburbia populated by more liberal professionals.

It was a struggle between two factions—working class traditionalists and middle class modernists. Beyond their resentment of Bennington College, the traditionalists disliked the modernists because of the "progressive" agenda they had imposed in the construction and curriculum of the new high school. But their deepest antipathy was reserved for the state's bureaucratic establishment, particularly the commissioner of education, Harvey Scribner.

A no-nonsense teacher from Maine, Scribner came to Vermont after presiding over the integration of Black children into white schools as school superintendent in Teaneck, N.J. In the 1970s, he went on to become chancellor of New York City's school system during its turbulent shift toward local control. But to Vermont conservatives in the late 1960s, Scribner represented the heavy hand of the state. During my second week on the job, he made a fateful decision that turned the traditionalists' simmering discontent into an open feud with long-term local consequences.

To break the stalemate, Scribner—usually a proponent of local control—exercised his authority to merge Bennington's supervisory union with an adjacent board and appoint its superintendent as head of a new "super district." George Sleeman could keep his job, but his promotion was blocked by a state mandate. His allies were stunned and his brother was hopping mad.

Parents and students packed Mt. Anthony Union High School's cafeteria for a heated discussion about the school's curriculum, part of Bennington's ongoing culture war.

For Richard Sleeman, the decision wasn't merely a slap in the face but a sign of things to come. With a superintendent selected by Scribner, the next step would be "open classrooms" and other "dangerous" reforms proposed in the commissioner's Vermont Design for Education. It was, he said:

> An affliction being imposed upon the education system of our fair state. Read it and decide for yourselves. The format could be titled Harvey Scribner meets Matty Mouse. But since use of the Design is voluntary, we can save ourselves and our teachers a lot of spare time by burning the Design for Education on the front lawn of the elementary school. Then we can begin the great work of drawing up our own design forthwith.

Sleeman never got around to a public burning. But his cadre of "concerned citizens" did organize a witch hunt that put progressive education on trial. As the reporter covering schools, it reminded me at times of *Inherit the Wind*, a dramatic film adaptation of the Scopes Monkey Trial.

But Bennington had no Clarence Darrow-type to defend it.

The first flashpoint was a musical production at the high school, an experimental adaptation of *Brecht on Brecht*, George Tabori's sampler of the German artist's plays, essays, poems, aphorisms, and struggles. Students and teachers were attempting to challenge the limits of what high school drama could be, just as Bertolt Brecht had challenged Broadway's theatrical conventions. They were doomed before the curtain went up. On Feb. 1, 1969, I explained in a front-page report:

> A poster advertising Mt. Anthony Union High School's upcoming production of "Brecht on Brecht" has become the center of a controversy involving the U.S. flag, Nazism, advertising and censorship.
>
> That considerable accomplishment was the result of the sign's use of a swastika juxtaposed with sections of Old Glory, symbolizing America's victory over fascism to some—and U.S. police-state inclinations to others.

It was a clever but controversial idea—a swastika over sections of a U.S. flag against a plain black background. At a school board meeting, the Art Department coordinator who had created it, Lon Wasco, explained that the poster's intention was to represent "America's victory over Nazism, with the American flag shining through the swastika." Not everybody saw it that way, however, and the artwork was certainly open to interpretation. To some it suggested police state tactics disguised as patriotism at home. To others it felt insulting and un-American.

Shortly after the show's poster appeared, complaints were lodged with the state police. According to the police, it was illegal under the "uniform flag code" to use the flag or any part of it for advertising. The posters had to come down. Most were never seen again. When the show finally opened, the house was half-full and the audience reaction ranged from nervous laughter to stunned silence. An attempt to dramatize concerns about the state of society instead exposed the gap between the school's avant-garde leanings and the community's growing discomfort.

Unseen for 50 years, the controversial poster for *Brecht on Brecht* was finally exhibited at the Bennington Museum in 2019.

Not long after that, two English teachers made the mistake of teaching a lesson about language with examples that included sexual phrases. The outcry was immediate and overwhelming. This time "concerned citizens" packed the high school cafeteria, heckled the school board and demanded action. At one point, a parent sitting next to Richard Sleeman argued that Broadway plays shouldn't be performed in small towns.

The opening shots of a "moral majority" curriculum war had been fired. What I saw over the next months was instructive. Rather than confront the school's critics, local liberals remained quiet and allowed Richard Sleeman's allies to win control of the high school from the "open education" crowd. After George Sleeman became superintendent, their supporters re-staffed the system. By the early 1970s, the school's football coach was principal. Outside, a fence went up to discourage "loitering;" inside, a crackdown began. It was back to the "basics" and goodbye to "the Bennington College influence."

MS Magazine was banned.

Saving the Butterflies

While reporting and taking photos for the *Banner* I also had the opportunity to cover Vermont's first Earth Day in April 1970.

Locally, the environmental faithful gathered that morning in Barn 1 on the Bennington College campus to help kick off the day's events with a frank discussion on the future of the planet. Inspired by Wisconsin Sen. Gaylord Nelson's call to action, an estimated 20 million Americans nationwide participated in the mobilization the first year.

But three local keynote speakers meant three different viewpoints. Harvey Carter, then a young Republican lawmaker from Pownal, called for community action to influence legislation and elect candidates concerned with the emerging crisis. Local business leader Joseph E. Joseph urged better education and more constructive use of technology. And conservationist John Bischof said the key was each individual's commitment to change society, "even if we have to choose voluntary poverty."

When Bischof explained that he was an organic farmer, the response was a round of applause. "The individual can change society," he said. For me, that related to a "visual pollution" project I had covered for the newspaper. David Wasco, a student at the high school who later became production designer for major Hollywood films, was collecting photos for a display of Bennington's visual deficiencies, things like poorly designed buildings, bad locations, inadequate maintenance, and trash piles. It was original and individual, the kind of thing that often can make a difference.

Several Vermont communities took part in the national "day of concern." At Middlebury College, Gov. Deane Davis, Lt. Gov. Thomas Hayes and Attorney General James Jeffords—all Republicans, at the time—led a discussion of environmental problems with students and teachers.

In Montpelier, Vermont College hosted a two-day observance that began with a speech by Davis on "the aspects of pollution." The second day featured classes, films, and more speakers, culminating in a talk by Reinhold Thieme, the former Vermont commissioner of water resources, who had recently been appointed a deputy assistant in the Interior Department.

Taking the lead from Green-Up Day, a campaign to clear roads of litter, Vermont College students demonstrated the scale of the problem by piling all the garbage normally collected at the school in one week inside a wire mesh enclosure.

Carter was skeptical about Green-Up, claiming it had been "cooked up" by the governor's assistant Al Moulton, and even questioned the effectiveness of pending legislation. Mentioning the Pure Water Act, which gave the water resources board authority to set standards, he noted that it also gave the board the ability to set low standards and permit temporary, or even permanent, pollution of streams.

"I had to have the law amended to protect water near Readsboro," Carter complained.

Vermont had recently adopted what was lauded as the most effective package of environmental controls in the country, a model for other states. It was becoming fashionable to be an environmentalist, especially after mercury was discovered in most of Vermont's waterways. Developers meanwhile pursued quick money by building leisure home tracts, while the attorney general hinted at an organized crime connection.

Politicians, many of whom hadn't heard of ecology a year before, now lined up to pass laws that they claimed would save the state from pollution and threats to the land. The heart of the package was the creation of nine district environmental commissions that would watchdog pollution and control development. Echoing Richard Nixon, Davis called it a chance to "apply our creative localism theory."

Some lawmakers said the new laws weren't strict enough. As David Scribner wrote at the time, "They pointed to certain loopholes, argued that they were drafted without consultation with environmental experts, did not adequately coordinate various state agencies, and particularly, that they excluded a determination of what environmental damage was incurred by government projects."[110]

To many people, the state land use map proposed by the governor looked more like a blueprint for development than a means to define an environmentally sound approach to growth. Beneath the veneer of environmental concern lurked attitudes and assumptions that could open the way toward an ecological crisis down the line.

"The thinking is that we can manage the environment, create problems, and then use technology to solve them," Carter charged. "That is sheer nuttiness."

The Earth Day discussion with Carter, Joseph and Bischof was followed by workshops, with both civil disagreements about whose approach was safest and practical ideas for developing a more self-sufficient community. Despite the prevailing optimism, one participant predicted, "A catastrophe is going to occur."

BE, a new environmental group also based in Bennington, was already working on an ecological survey, with longer-term plans to act as an information center for residents with questions and concerns. Students were meanwhile preparing a personal ecology handbook. Dartmouth College took the opportunity that day to announce a new Environmental Studies Program that would bring students "to grips with the problems of controlling and reversing the damaging encroachments of modern man and technology upon the Earth's ecology." To be co-directed by geology professor Charles Drake and public affairs professor Frank Smallwood, the program was expected

---

110 David Scribner, *From Riverbed to Featherbed*, Quadrille, Vol. 5, No. 1, Fall, 1970

to involve significant research and interdisciplinary undergraduate courses as a supplement in traditional major fields.

During his talk, Carter called Earth Day "a safety value," and hoped to see more political action, specifically support for candidates "concerned with the environment." But Joseph, president of the Bennington Brush Co., remained skeptical, labeling Earth Day "an intellectual approach to the problem. While the community may know what it means, that's as far as it goes."

A campaign to "clean up the world" requires consistent leadership, the businessman advised: "Children in school must be taught not to pollute. All you have to do is drive around the community to see how people live and will continue to live, unless a catastrophe occurs."

It was a surprisingly grim outlook.

About a month after covering Earth Day, I left the *Banner* and went to work for Bennington College as Publications Director. It was the end of a semester marked by environmental engagement and escalating political action. You couldn't visit the campus without hearing phrases like resist the draft, zero population growth, and "man is an endangered species." Best of all, I arrived in time to meet Kurt Vonnegut—and hear him issue this sharp, funny observation in his commencement address:

> The majority of people who rule us, who have our money and power, are lawyers and military men. The lawyers want to talk our problems out of existence. The military men want us to find the bad guys and put bullets through their brains. These are not always the best solutions—particularly in the fields of sewage disposal and birth control.

It certainly captured the mood: serious, ironic, and leaning toward extreme. So did another slogan seen around campus that year:

"The rich and powerful are killing all the butterflies. If your children are to see butterflies you must be a revolutionary and yourself take control of your life and its surroundings."

Two years later, Vermont Yankee, a 540-megawatt nuclear power plant, went online in Vernon. It began malfunctioning within two months. The first incident was a transformer fire, followed by radiation leaks attributed to defective fuel rods, some cooling unit problems, hydrogen explosions, and a shutdown to study vibrations due to cracks in the cooling system.

The plant's performance didn't improve over time: by 1976, there had been more than 100 "abnormal occurrences," as they were called by the industry.

Anti-nuclear activists started protesting almost immediately. But events multiplied, and attracted larger crowds, once connections were made with a related mobilization at the site of the proposed Seabrook nuclear plant in New Hampshire, and especially after the 1979 meltdown at the Three Mile Island nuclear facility in Harrisburg, PA.

Founded by Peter and Elke Schumann, Bread & Puppet Theater moved to Vermont in 1970 and became known for its tree-sized puppets, Domestic Resurrection Circus, and commitment to social change. When protests started at Vermont Yankee, its puppet heads were often on hand.

Nonviolent civil disobedience was part of many protests at Vermont Yankee.

By then a poll conducted by Rep. Jeffords revealed that a majority of Vermonters preferred to develop solar power and other non-nuclear alternatives. Vermont's only congressman concluded that "the people, at least in Vermont, want us to address our energy problems in a decisive, meaningful and well considered manner. There is no cause for political timidity in doing what must be done."

John Froines, one of the "Chicago Seven" defendants in the late 1960s, had moved to Vermont and become state occupational health director. His 1977 reports on the operation and regulation of

Vermont's only nuclear plant became a springboard for a broad and enduring debate over the state government's role in nuclear issues. In a sense, it lasted until the plant closed in 2012.

One of Froine's early reports recommended that Vermont "challenge the federal government's exclusive authority to regulate the construction and operation of nuclear power plants." Another opposed further consideration of the state as a site for nuclear waste storage.[111]

Gov. Richard Snelling responded by appointing a three-person nuclear review committee. All its members had previously worked within the nuclear industry. One had produced a brochure for Yankee, and another was linked with the pro-nuclear U.S. Labor Party led by Lyndon LaRouche.

Pressing Alternatives

Long before the Internet emerged as a tool to distribute independent news and views, many communities had alternative, or sometimes even underground newspapers. Building on a tradition that stretched back to 19th century literary social criticism and early 20th-century investigative journalism ("muckraking," as Theodore Roosevelt called it), utopian community newspapers and radical magazines like *The Masses*, the modern American alternative press officially took off in 1955 with *The Village Voice*. It truly blossomed on the West Coast in the mid-Sixties, and then spread back across the country. Before the 1970s began, most places near a college or a counter-cultural enclave had some voice of "opposition."

Many papers emerged from the anti-war movement (and disappeared once the war wound down), while others focused on the need for local reform, updating the style of early 20th century advocacy journalism.

In Vermont, both trends combined in *Vermont Freeman*, launched in 1969 and based in Starksboro. The format was a tabloid newspaper published twice monthly, circulation around 4,000, sold for 35 cents (as of 1973), and distributed statewide. Thanks to offset printing, a relatively new technology then, copy could be typed in

---

111 Greg Guma, *Public Questioning of Nuclear Power in Vermont*, In These Times & WIN Magazine, Sept., 1977

columns on manual typewriters and pasted onto the layout pages. It gave the publication a hand-made, sometimes ragged look, but also conveyed a relaxed energy and a self-conscious decision to break traditional newspaper rules that computer-generated publications sometimes try to echo.

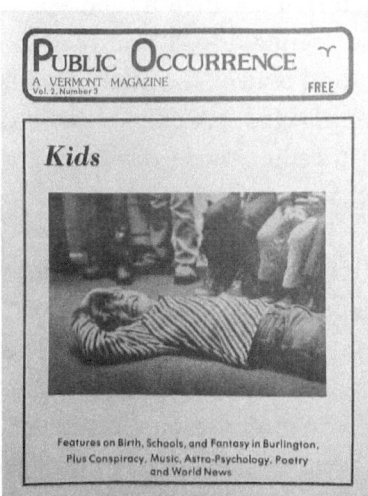

Alternative publications like *Vermont Freeman* and *Public Occurrence* reached thousands but were short-lived. *The Vanguard Press* had a larger impact and lasted from 1978-1990. *Vermont Guardian*, published from 2004-2007, had more than 10,000 print readers and 150,000 online.

Tom Slayton, later the editor of *Vermont Life*, was a *Freeman* associate editor, along with authors such as Lisa Alther and Marty Jezer, media activist Marvin Fishman, and naturalist Beatrice Trum Hunter.

Editor Roger Albright encouraged a wide variety of voices, including Bernie Sanders and myself. *Vermont Freeman* lasted less than a decade, but along the way served as a valuable outlet for against-the-grain thinking, supporting various movements and questioning authority from the height of the Vietnam War to the fall of Richard Nixon.

By the mid-1970s, another wave of alternative publications was underway. Although most weeklies ultimately became part of chains, some guarded their independence, tackled community issues, and helped promote local organizing. Vermont already had a handful of established rural and suburban newspapers, but most of them were politically neutral or conservative.

Not so Burlington's *North Country Star*, which had a circulation of around 6,000 and talked openly about imperialism, sexism and capitalist impacts, everything from medical and housing costs, welfare cutbacks, and local redevelopment to independence for Puerto Rico.

North Country Star was also linked closely with People Acting for Change Together (PACT), a multi-issue organizing group working on behalf of the poor from a small headquarters in Burlington's Old North End. Committed to building a political agenda, PACT and the *Star* focused most of their attention on hot local issues. The interests and impact of the women's movement were reflected in *Commonwoman*, run entirely by women and bringing together those developing a feminist consciousness and working with the local women's center and shelter for women who had experienced domestic violence.

During the same period, The Frayed Page, a Burlington bookstore collective, launched a statewide magazine called *Public Occurrence* (PO), named after the first newspaper in the American colonies. The original was suppressed after just one issue. Like the *Star*, *PO* was a volunteer effort, but its focus differed, combining ecological issues, diverse but mainly radical views and reviews, poetry, and new age ideas. Its most controversial issue was "Women Loving Women," which netted national publicity and cancelation of its typesetting deal with *The Catholic Tribune*. Its most enduring was *Vermont's Untold History*, a bi-centennial response to "official" history.

By the time *PO* folded, bigger plans were in motion. Some ventures, like *The Vermont Journal*, a weekly on statewide issues promoted by John McClaughry, did not materialize. A Republican libertarian, McClaughry envisioned a publication that would be politically independent but have a clear mission: to be "generally critical" of waste of tax money, over-regulation, unresponsiveness in state agencies, and continual centralization of control in Montpelier. Partnering with a liberal Democrat, Sen. Robert O'Brien, he soon after co-founded the short-lived Decentralist League of Vermont.

One newspaper that did briefly get off the ground was *The Eclipse*, launched in mid-1977 by a group of University of Vermont graduates who had worked for the student newspaper, *Vermont Cynic*. The idea was a free weekly for the Champlain Valley that would take on topics like hospital expansion, development plans, and environmental regulation, while also giving voice to the area's youth culture. Predictably, there was no money to pay staff, and no plan for commercial survival.

As *The Eclipse* struggled, another UVM graduate from the same group, Stephen Brown, returned to Burlington from selling ads for *The Boston Phoenix* with enough capital to launch *The Vermont Vanguard Press*.

Brown's plan was a hip and commercial weekly that covered news and the arts, depended on advertising, and paid its writers and staff. Within a few months, he assembled a team that included John Dillon, later to work for syndicated columnist Jack Anderson, United Press International, the *Rutland Herald Times Argus* Sunday paper, and Vermont Public Radio. *The Eclipse* ceased publishing in December 1977; a month later the *Vanguard Press* hit newsstands, lasting more than a decade and influencing the approach of subsequent Vermont weeklies.

By the late 1970s, much of the passion was draining out of weeklies, and a trend toward consolidation and mainstream acceptance was underway. When the owners of two dozen newspapers formed a trade association in 1978, at first they didn't want the word "alternative" in their name.

The Vanguard Press was a bit different—openly alternative, a place where stories, people and ideas not acknowledged by the daily papers were given a platform. By the end of a difficult first year, Nat

Winthrop rescued the publication financially, while Dillon and I became co-editors. Six months later, I went solo, staying several years in various editorial roles, while Dillon worked on investigative pieces.

For a few years, *The Vanguard Press* challenged the political status quo with stories that opened debate on topics like nuclear power plant safety, redevelopment, road building, and local political power. Before the March 1981 mayoral election of Bernie Sanders, it was a leading voice for change. Recognizing the threat, Mayor Gordon Paquette sued the paper for libel after its publication of an investigative feature that examined his banning of rock music. The article suggested that he was intoxicated at the time. Years later, when Paquette was no longer in power, he quietly dropped the lawsuit.

The pay was modest, but the *Vanguard Press*' ability to offer salaries and regularly buy freelance articles allowed it to attract promising writers like Debbie Bookchin, Jeff Good, Alexandra Marks, Barry Snyder, and Peter Freyne, whose long-running column "Inside Track" first appeared in 1982. Weekly editorial meetings were crowded and dynamic. Once Sanders became mayor, the paper's role shifted from opposition voice to skeptical ally of the emerging progressive movement. But it continued to reflect an avant garde sensibility, bringing provocative journalism, social criticism, progressive ideas, and cultural innovations to a growing audience.

The Vanguard Press was published weekly until 1990 with editors like Freyne, Josh Mamis and Pamela Polston. By that time, however, Winthrop was anxious to "stop the bleeding." He wasn't talking about the internal fights, though the publication had its share, but rather cash. Another publisher, Suzanne Gillis, felt much the same. She had been producing the monthly *Vermont Woman* for five years, and was also weary of losing money. A series of private meetings between the two led to a merger that produced *The Vermont Times*.

Their idea was to create a single, stronger publication, a credible news source with "mainstream" appeal. To do that, they avoided the A-word, hired daily newspaper veteran Bill Porter as editor, and geared the tone and coverage to the suburbs. During the next few years, editors changed, new investors took the lead, and the operation was ultimately sold to Denton Publications, an upstate New York printer and publisher.

Polston and Paula Routly launched an expanded arts supplement called *Vox*, and later Shay Totten, a former *Burlington Free Press* reporter, became editor and set out to make the newspaper more hard-hitting.

But Denton wasn't connected to Vermont communities, and more concerned with the immediate bottom line than tapping the emerging culture market or building a strong editorial team. Frustrated, Polston and Routly drew up plans for their own weekly, one that would be commercially viable and focus, at first, on the region's cultural and artistic riches. Their vision, *Seven Days*, was launched in 1995. Within three years, it was the dominant weekly in Northwestern Vermont and the state's first truly sustainable "alternative" publication.

An anti-war protest on Church Street before its transformation into the Burlington Marketplace, led by activists Robin Lloyd and Wendy Coe, founders of the Peace & Justice Center.

22

Capital Consequences

Despite Vermont's recreation and manufacturing boom in the 1960s, workers were underpaid in many industries. The Vermont Marble Company had made substantial profits in World War II, while other employers produced engine parts, boat winches and items for the military. In fact, there was enough spare cash for Vermont Marble to buy more quarries in Tennessee, Colorado, Georgia and Canada. But the highest paid blue collar worker for the company received only $2.21 an hour in 1966, despite rising inflation.

On May Day 1966, members of the United Stone and Allied Products Workers union had enough and voted to strike, demanding a union shop at Vermont Marble and a 15-cent per hour pay increase. The company filed an injunction against the strikers, and Thomas Stafford, brother of U.S. Sen. Robert Stafford, testified on behalf of the company as Vermont Marble director and supervisor of quarries. Former Gov. F. Ray Keyser was the company's lawyer. Some things hadn't changed much in 70 years.

For a short time the workers successfully blocked marble shipments. A Proctor building was burned. After 57 days of confrontation the employees won a 9-cent per hour increase. But Vermont's courts, politicians and local newspapers had lined up against them.

Employees at electronics plants rarely became militant, although workers at Rutland's General Electric plant did agree to a work slowdown in 1972 in reaction to a proposed speed up. Most GE workers agreed to do about 75 percent of their quotas. Construction workers, on the other hand, organized a series of demonstrations that threatened one of the state's largest contractors, Pizzagalli Construction.

When it came to development projects Pizzagalli was the state's undisputed leader, building everything from factories to hotels and hospitals. Beyond the state's borders it constructed sewage treatment facilities in Virginia and Maryland, post offices and parking garages in Maine, and commercial centers from Canada to the Virgin Islands. It also worked with Plaza Realty, a sister corporation that developed package deals involving financing, design, building and leasing. Along the way it sometimes used loopholes in labor law to hire out-of-state, non-union workers at lower wages.

Local 522 of the Building Trades Union began its strike against Pizzagalli and nine other companies on July 7, 1972, receiving strong support from the Laborer's International Union, the Iron Workers, Carpenters and other groups. The issues included wages, hours, overtime, holidays, health insurance and travel pay. Meanwhile, the Associated General Contractors met to find a way back to "open shop" conditions. National and state labor officials petitioned the Democratic Gov. Tom Salmon, who promised to meet with both sides in the conflict.

As workers lost their homes and savings, or faced mace, arrest and harassment by Pizzagalli operatives, Salmon set up a fact-finding committee. But he chose not to veto a $2 million contract with Pizzagalli to build the new Chittenden County Correctional Center— now the Chittenden Regional Correctional Facility. This left the unfortunate impression that the state was taking sides after all. The strike was settled but worker morale suffered.

Salmon had convinced voters that he could preserve the Vermont way of life in 1972. Although Deane Davis was a popular governor and Richard Nixon was soon to be re-elected in a landslide, Salmon's platform of environmental preservation, land use control and tax reform proved irresistible. But the timing turned out to be poor for environmental action or the sales tax increase he proposed.

Soon after Salmon took office both the national and state economy went into a tailspin. Unemployment increased, food and fuel prices spiraled up, retail sales began to slip and a winter of "no gas and no snow" undermined the ski industry. The ensuing recession led to stagnation in just about every economic sector except trades and services. More than 85,000 Vermonters were living below or close to the poverty level, more than a few suffering from untreated medical problems, hunger and malnutrition, substandard housing and inadequate home heating.[112]

Although years of agitation by low-income groups had led to higher welfare payments, Vermont's human services—even after the 1960s expansion—remained limited and financed by a regressive tax structure. The percent of state revenue from business taxes declined as the amount from sales taxes rose. By 1970 the tax breaks for Vermont business properties were already up to $81 million. In the first half of the next decade family income increased by 39 percent, but prices went up by 47 percent. The result was a 5 percent decline in real income. As a consequence of all this, Salmon ended up presiding over an economic bust that made it difficult to deliver on his promises.

Tom Salmon

The reason for Vermont's comparatively low economic standing was no secret. As Michael Parenti, the Liberty Union Party candidate for Congress in 1974, put it, "The poor subsidize the rich

---

112 This was directly observed as a *Bennington Banner* reporter from 1968 to 1970, and subsequently confirmed while working with unemployed teenagers and adults under Department of Labor contracts from 1971 to 1974.

by working for low wages and paying high prices and by carrying a disproportionately greater share of the taxes." Making matters worse, many employees continued to work at great risk to their health and lives. Forty-three workers died in Vermont between 1973 and 1974, crushed, electrocuted and burned. Others reported cancer and other illnesses that were frequently job related.

Liberty Union, the alternative political party founded in Vermont in reaction to the Vietnam War, began running candidates in 1970, taking the fight for social change to the ballot box. Some of its leaders were established figures such as former Democratic Congressman William Meyer and Bernard "Bun" O'Shea, a newspaper publisher from Enosburg Falls who had run a long-shot campaign against Sen. Aiken in 1956. It also attracted young activists, writers, artists and counterculturalists, determined Party organizers like Peter Diamondstone, and effective candidates like Parenti and Bernie Sanders, and took radical positions on utility rates, union fights, human services, and the needs of the poor.

Parenti, one of several UVM faculty members forced out for their political views, talked about community control, worker self-management, and public ownership. When asked if this was socialism he would reply, "We call it democracy." Sanders was an equally dogged campaigner, fighting for equal time, building bridges with unions, and, despite a distinct New York accent, effectively connecting with Vermonters as he challenged the assertions of his major party opponents. After running for the U.S. House and Senate in the early 1970s, his best showing came in his first campaign for governor, more than 11,000 votes, challenging Richard Snelling and Democrat Stella Hackel in 1976. But third party and independent candidates rarely received 10 percent of the statewide vote.

After two terms as Gov. Salmon meanwhile charted a course for Robert Stafford's Senate seat. But with the Democratic Party splitting into factions he was forced into a primary fight with a political newcomer, Scott Skinner, founding director of the Vermont Public Interest Research Group. Skinner had a young, enthusiastic following inspired by a new kind of consumer-oriented environmentalism.

A two-term governor, Salmon was almost defeated in that primary, setting the stage for his Senate loss that November. Low turnout among Burlington Democrats didn't help, leaving him with only 48 percent of the city's vote. It was the start of an extended period of realignment, in which liberals and insurgents challenged the Democratic establishment while conservatives deserted it.

The idea of an "independent Yankee" Vermont had begun to wane in the beginning of the 20th century. Now the State ranked 42nd in per capita income. Out-of-state interests controlled stock in Central Vermont Public Service Corporation and Green Mountain Power. In Montpelier, lobbyists for the utilities, Associated Industries of Vermont, recreation and land development interests, Wholesale Beverage Association, Federated Fish and Game Clubs and Green Mountain Racetrack in Pownal all had a presence. In Burlington, a Canadian development firm named Mondev had demolished a neighborhood to make way for a hotel, office building and underground shopping mall geared to the new tourist economy.

Corporations like GE, IBM, Textron, Litton Industries, Goodyear, Gulf and Western, Johnson and Johnson, Minnesota Mining and Manufacturing, Standard Register and Simmons Precision dominated industrial employment and development.

Vermont's banks and investors focused on the tertiary sector—tourism, retail trade and real estate—or on low-risk stocks and bonds with big corporations. These ingredients were making Vermont a net exporter of capital, a situation common in underdeveloped countries. Businessmen claimed that the "climate" for investment was good, due largely to laws restricting strikes, picketing and boycotts, a low unemployment compensation rate and meager worker's compensation benefits. But for many people the outlook looked as severe as a Vermont winter.

Struggling with Sprawl

In 1969, Vermont took a vanguard role in the emerging environmental movement. Act 250 was a landmark attempt to preserve the state's most valuable asset—its extraordinary physical environment—while promoting "orderly growth and development." But the law's limitations were obvious within seven years, when the plan surfaced to build a large shopping mall in Williston.

Both bustling South Burlington, which had led the suburban wave, and tranquil Richmond, which remained a rural oasis, anticipated major traffic congestion. Winooski was worried about the potential impacts on water quality, transportation, and its own urban renewal dreams. Despite plans for a marketplace district, Burlington warned that the project could "devastate" downtown business. And the newly-formed Citizens for Responsible Growth argued that the project—then known as Pyramid Mall—wouldn't only affect soil, air, and water quality, but also prove to be energy inefficient and aesthetically unpalatable.

While threatening such potential impacts, the mall plan helped crystallize a fundamental debate over large-scale development, and whether the region's rural character could be preserved in the long run. The problem had been identified in a 1968 report by the Vermont Planning Council, chaired by Phil Hoff.

"The traditional rural scene in Vermont, characterized by concentrated settlement in villages and open countryside dotted with farms, is disappearing," concluded the report, called *Vision and Choice: Vermont's Future*. "The sharp distinction between village and countryside is blurring throughout the state. Highways between towns are becoming ribbons of residential and commercial development. Where strip development has become intense, particularly on the outskirts of the larger towns and in the most popular ski and recreation areas, the effects have been highly detrimental."

Thirty years later, the land-use permit for a 550,000-square-foot shopping center near Tafts Corner in Williston was approved. Combined with Wal-Mart, Home Depot, Circuit City, PetSmart, Toys 'R' Us, and a Hannaford superstore already there, Maple Tree Place sealed Chittenden County's suburban fate. It was a cumulative phenomenon, beginning at the edge of traditional centers and then moving out into previous rural areas. Sprawl was land-consuming, auto dependent, and energy and resource intensive.

By the 1960s, Burlington had already become so concerned about fringe commercial development that it decided to "revitalize its city center" by clearing 27 acres of land at the heart of the city. An ethnic neighborhood with more than 100 buildings, once home base for Progressive Mayor James Burke, was torn down as urban renewal began. But commercial development continued to spread along Routes 2 and 7, and residential development filled in nearby, along with strip commercial centers, auto dealers, discount stores and banks. From there growth spread to Williston, Jericho, Shelburne and Milton. Industrial parks also appeared.[113]

Suburban development created a dilemma for many leaders. Progressives agreed with Republicans and Democrats on the need for growth. But they parted company on where it should happen and exactly how to manage it.

Peripheral development began to threaten Burlington's position as the region's commercial center. In response, more than $96 million in public funds was spent between 1972 and 1982 to develop the Church Street Marketplace, renovate historic buildings, rehabilitate others, continue urban renewal and improve the transit system. But sprawl expanded through large lot residential subdivisions, "big box" retail stores, and office parks. Land use controls failed to redirect the pattern of development.

By 1997 there were three major retail centers in the county, plus significant smaller ones. Burlington lost over 237,000 square feet of department store space, as employment in general merchandising

---

113 Sustainability and Growth Center Team, *The History of Sprawl in Chittenden County*, Champlain Initiative, 1999.

dropped steeply. It had happened despite the investment of almost $100 million more in public and private investment.

And Chittenden County was no longer primarily agricultural. By 1992 it had lost 70 percent of its farms, much of its prime farmland, and related wetlands. The trends were positive news for national retailers, property owners ready to sell, lenders who financed the developments, communities that saw increased property tax revenues, and families that wanted a quiet home in the new suburbs. But retail business owners in older shopping centers lost sales, some towns lost part of their tax base, water quality dropped due to runoff, air pollution increased from auto use, and traffic congestion intensified for almost everyone.

Sprawl critic James Howard Kunstler predicted that, having failed to acknowledge the difference between city and country, nature and culture, scenery and civic life, Chittenden County seemed almost resigned to a "cartoon" future in which it looked a lot like Los Angeles.

"Sometimes I think that the mentality in Vermont is that a good traditional Vermont town is a strip mall with a candle shop in it," he joked.

In reality, Williston was slated for suburbanization long before a large mall appeared on the horizon. In the same year Act 250 became law, a report on public investment designated Tafts Corner as a prime commercial site due to interstate access. The only thing lacking, said the experts, was adequate sewage, a problem that could be solved by public funding. The effects of Williston's commercial expansion spun out for miles beyond the town lines. While no one community felt the entire brunt, many were affected. But trying to use the state's land-use law as a regulatory mechanism proved to be difficult, especially since crucial public investments had promoted precisely such an outcome.

A report commissioned by Burlington, *Creating a Sustainable City*, stated the case against suburbanization. Beyond the environmental impacts, it argued, places like Tafts Corner tended to "homogenize the market experience, erasing local customs, traditions, and products." Yet, even in this progressive city, sprawl was still defined primarily as a threat to downtown retail sales, prompting increased pressure to keep up. Thus, the answer to Maple Tree Place and the big boxes remained "saving" downtown by adding another parking garage and attracting a big box of its own.

23

The Rise of Bernie Sanders

Gordon Paquette was a working-class guy from the "inner city" who grew up working on a bread delivery truck and started his political career as a Democratic alderman in 1958. By managing a patronage-based coalition known as the Republicrats he reached what turned out to be the pinnacle of his power as Burlington mayor from 1971–1981.

People knew him around town as Gordie, a street-smart operator who figured out how to satisfy the Irish and French-Canadians while cutting deals with the business class. Comparisons with Chicago's Mayor Richard Daley were not uncommon. But his willingness to demolish an ethnic neighborhood near the Waterfront and a "master plan" to replace it with a mall, hotel and office complex had made him some enemies.

Throughout the 1970s cracks in the façade of public calm slowly opened. Speculation drove up land values and rents, deepening a chronic housing shortage. A restless youth culture emerged. Despite commercial growth, revenues couldn't keep pace with the need for services. And the next steps in the city's "urban redevelopment" would be disruptive—a highway connector into the center of the city, private waterfront development, and a pedestrian mall in the heart of downtown. The total cost was projected at more than $50 million. The local atmosphere was nervous and unsettled.

Every two years Paquette reminded voters that "he kept the taxes down." But he didn't notice that things changed by the end of the 1970s.

In January 1981, Paquette won a caucus fight for a fifth term. But afterward Richard Bove, owner of a popular local Italian restaurant, left the Democratic Party to run as an independent. Republican Party leaders decided not to oppose him and banked on his re-election. As a result, his main opponent became Bernie Sanders, the former third party radical now running as an Independent.

Sanders opposed Paquette's proposed 10 percent increase in property taxes and promised to work for tax reform. The recently formed Citizens Party, which had backed environmentalist Barry Commoner in the 1980 presidential election, ran three candidates for the City Council, also known as the Board of Aldermen. The incumbents tried to ignore them, assuming that a group of activists had no chance of upsetting the status quo. But Sanders was hard to ignore, and local leaders of both major parties underestimated the growing influence of neighborhood groups, housing and anti-redevelopment activists, young people, the disenfranchised elderly, and the city's countercultural newcomers. They also shrugged off the possibility that some of Paquette's supporters might want to send him a message.

Shown here protesting outside City Hall, Sanders had been in four statewide races by the time he ran for mayor. But he had to be convinced that seeking local office made sense.

By the time Sanders and the mayor faced each other over a folding table at the Unitarian Church tempers were hot. Sanders exploited local anger by linking the mayor with Antonio Pomerleau, then a dominant figure in Vermont shopping center development, who was leading efforts to turn Burlington's largely vacant waterfront into a site for commercial and condominium development.

"I'm not with the big money men" Paquette protested. Frustrated and desperate, he warned that if Sanders became mayor Burlington would become like Brooklyn.

He looked honestly shocked when people hissed at him.

The race began as a long shot, but Sanders turned his shoestring campaign into a serious challenge. Nevertheless, on Election Day Paquette and the Democratic old guard still predicted a decisive victory. After all, Reagan had been elected President only four months before. Sanders was no threat, they assumed, nothing more than an upstart leftist with a gift for attracting media attention.

"It's time for a change. Real change." That was his slogan. Bernie wanted open government, he said, and new development priorities. He opposed the upscale Waterfront project and Interstate access road to downtown. He supported Rent Control.

"Burlington is not for sale," he said. "I am extremely concerned about the current trend of urban development. If present trends continue, the city of Burlington will be converted into an area in which only the wealthy and upper-middle class will be able to afford to live."

On March 3, 1981, with a few thousand dollars, a handful of volunteers and a vague reform agenda, Sanders won the mayoral race by just ten votes. Burlington had a "radical" mayor, a self-described socialist who was determined to change the course of Vermont history. Terry Bouricius, a Citizens Party candidate for the City Council, became the first member of that party elected anywhere in the country. In an odd twist, Bouricius won in Ward Two, the same place that had given Paquette his first term on the City Council 23 years earlier.

Paquette often huddled with allies at Nectar's Restaurant before City Council meetings. After his defeat, they continued to meet in hopes of blocking Sanders' agenda.

The Rise of Bernie Sanders

Silk screen poster for Sanders' first mayoral campaign, created by Frank Hewitt

According to Gene Bergman, then an activist with the low-income advocacy group PACT, and later a Progressive city councilman and assistant city attorney, the victories would be "just the beginning of the efforts to bring the long neglected and exploited working class to its rightful place in the city." The next three decades proved just how much the political establishment underestimated Sanders' appeal, not to mention the potential for a progressive movement in the city and beyond.

Burlington's progressives not only consolidated their local base, affecting many aspects of city management and shaping the local debate. They challenged the accepted relationship between communities and the state, and fueled a statewide progressive surge. They also weathered the storms of succession struggle, demonstrating with Peter Clavelle's 1989 mayoral victory on the Progressive ticket that—in Bernie's words—"It's not just a one-man show, it's a movement."

Clavelle was mayor for all but two of the next 17 years, and succeeded by another Progressive, Bob Kiss. Sanders went on to become an Independent Congressman for more than a decade, and in 2006 the only independent socialist in the U.S. Senate.

By then the Queen City was nationally known for its radical mystique and "livability," transformed from a provincial town into a socially conscious cultural center.

A Race Too Far

Whether the 1986 race for governor against Vermont's first female chief executive was winnable is hard to say. Nevertheless, that's what Bernie chose to do after five years as mayor. He went up against Madeleine May Kunin, a Swiss immigrant who had come to the state with her brother in 1957 and carved out a niche in state politics as chairperson of the House Appropriations Committee.

In 1978 Kunin had defeated Peter Smith, Vermont's GOP version of Robert Redford, to become lieutenant governor. After four years in Snelling's shadow she unsuccessfully challenged him in a 1982 gubernatorial run. But Kunin excelled at building a personal organization. In the 1984 race, with Snelling temporarily retired, she squeaked into office and cracked the state's glass ceiling.

A moderate Democrat, Kunin favored social programs but fiscal conservatism. Though criticized as equivocal on feminist and labor issues, she used her success to bring more women into state government and prove, as Sanders had in Burlington, that being "different" didn't mean she was incompetent. When it came to keeping the state in sound financial shape or protecting water quality, Kunin could be as strict as Snelling.

On the other hand, she was not a world-shaker. She shied away from raising the minimum wage or demanding that corporations give notice before closing down plants. She wanted the Vermont Yankee nuclear power plant to be safe but didn't think it should be shut down overnight.

"If you ask her where she stands," said Sanders during his campaign, "she'd say, in the middle of the Democratic Party. She's never said she'd do anything. The confusion lies in the fact that many people are excited because she's the first woman governor. But after that there ain't much."

Kunin wasn't much more kind.

"I think he has messianic tendencies," she told James Ridgeway, who covered the campaign for *The Village Voice*. "That's not uncommon in politicians. But it does mean he dismisses everyone else's alternative solutions…His approach is always to tear down. But I think you can make progress and change for the better by working within the structure…A lot of what he says is rhetoric and undoable… He has to create a distinction between us, and to do that he has to push me more to the right, where I really don't think I am. I don't think it's fair. He's not running against evil, you know."

The third player in this drama, Peter Smith, had some kind words for Kunin. "She's a good person," he said. "She's got some commitment." But he also felt that she was a case of "vision without substance."

In Sanders, Smith saw passion, confusion and noise. "If Bernie were as gutsy and honest as he says he is, he'd run as a socialist. He is a socialist! That's why he went to Nicaragua. That's why he goes to Berkeley."

Smith began his own career almost 20 years before as an educational reformer, launching Community College of Vermont. But liberal tendencies didn't prevent him from joining the Republicans. In 1980 he supported George H.W. Bush and later Ronald Reagan.

Realignments

Village Voice reporter James Ridgeway saw the Sanders-Kunin race as a battle between neosocialism and neoliberalism.

Peter Freyne conferred nicknames on the three in his popular weekly column—Queen Madeleine, Preppie Peter and Lord Bernie; apt descriptions of Vermont's emerging political royalty. Each was an established political star with a proven base. But Sanders' early boast that he was "running to win" had to be revised by his campaign organizers. A July poll put the Lord at a mere 11 percent statewide, while the Queen had 53, well outdistancing Preppie.

By October the Sanders campaign, if not the candidate himself, had lowered its sights to a respectable 20 percent. Within his organization feelings were frayed. It hadn't become the grassroots uprising they expected. More than a few activists and contributors who had helped in previous campaigns felt it was the wrong race at the wrong time. Others wanted Sanders to focus on Burlington. Ellen David-Friedman, who managed the campaign for several months, compared Bernie to Jesse Jackson "in terms of focusing more on a candidacy and less on an organization." She supported him but questioned his resistance to accountability.

Anarchist thinker Murray Bookchin, who lived in Burlington, was more critical. "Bernie's running a one-man show," he charged. "The only justification for a socialist campaign at this point is to try to educate people, and Sanders isn't doing that at all. Instead, he's running on the preposterous notion that he can get elected as governor this year."

Actually, Sanders was also running on a substantive platform: less reliance on the property tax (a basis of his appeal to conservative voters), a more progressive income and corporate tax system, lower utility bills, a higher minimum wage and phasing out Vermont Yankee. But neither his program nor speaking gifts were enough to overcome the obstacles. His opponents could outspend him and his own ranks were split.

Combining forces with Leahy, who was doing well in his defense against the challenge from Snelling, Kunin staged an impressive get-out-the-vote effort, the most sophisticated voter identification program in state history. Unemployment was at a record low and there was no state deficit, so she also had economics on her side. On Election Day she didn't end up cracking the 50 percent mark. But she left her opponents well behind and was routinely confirmed by the legislature.

Sanders came away with almost 15 percent, less than he hoped yet still impressive. It wasn't simply the size of the vote that made experts and journalists take note; much of his support came from farm communities and conservative hill towns, usually Republican strongholds. In fact, he had won his highest percentage in the conservative Northeast Kingdom.

In 1986, Sanders still had time to read poetry at Maverick bookstore in the Old North End.

The campaign also reinforced an emerging division in the state's left-liberal alliance.

Going National

If a psychic had predicted in the 1970s that Sanders would someday stand on the White House lawn in support of an embattled Democratic president, enthusiastically support another Democrat for the highest office in the land, or run himself, most people would have considered it an odd joke. Even Sanders would have been skeptical.

Then he was a perennial third party candidate who, in four statewide races, had dedicated himself to broadside attacks on the two major political parties. On Dec. 19, 1998, just hours after the U.S. House voted to impeach a president for only the second time in U.S. history, there he was, lined up outside the White House with Democratic notables behind Bill Clinton.

Ten years later he backed Barack Obama for president from a seat in the Senate.

On Dec. 10, 2010, in a scene reminiscent of Jimmy Stewart in Frank Capra's *Mister Smith Goes to Washington*, Vermont's junior senator staged his own mini-filibuster on the Senate floor to protest a pending tax compromise that extended cuts for the wealthy in exchange for Republican cooperation on budget issues and repeal of the military's Don't Ask, Don't Tell policy.

After more than 40 years fighting the system Sanders' message was still the same. But his street corner had become C-Span and the viral potential of the internet.

Shortly after that speech, which quickly became a book, a "Draft Bernie Sanders for President" website was established. At first, Sanders disavowed interest. "I am very content to be where I am, but I am flattered by that kind of response," he explained. After cruising to Senate re-election in 2012 with 71 percent of the vote, however, he started to reconsider. In a March 2014 interview with *The Nation* he made it official: he was "prepared to run for president of the United States" in 2016—if he thought it was possible to win. He didn't officially announce, but by May he was making campaign-style public appearances in various states.

"Winning credibility is the first step to building a broad-based movement," Sanders explained in a 1998 interview." That meant taking on bread and butter issues. "People have got to know you are on their side."

Timing was the real issue. He didn't want to run against Barack Obama, especially since he also needed to hold onto his Senate seat and had supported Obama in 2008.

But a race against Hillary Clinton was another matter. And a 2016 race couldn't be better timing. After cruising to re-election in November 2012, he would not face another Vermont vote until 2018, six years away. That meant he could devote the next four years to building a national campaign. All he needed to do was explain why, after decades as an Independent and socialist, a caustic critic of the two-party system, it now made sense to run as a Democrat. The campaign to make the case was well underway in 2013.

"Obviously if I did not think I had a reasonable chance to win I wouldn't run," he explained coyly to Politico in one of several interviews focused on defining the choice he faced. But if other candidates weren't talking about the issues that mattered, "well, then maybe I have to do it," he would say. What issues were those? The same as ever—growing inequality and the collapse of the middle class, along with a third, "global warming."

Encouraging interviews in progressive media and constant exposure on cable news made it all but official by March 2014. Sanders was ready to run, he announced, but only if he thought that he could win, a prospect he now linked to three things—a "political revolution," raising money—not from "billionaires" but enough to be taken seriously, and getting sufficient public exposure. Visits to primary states began in May, but it took another year for the candidate to acknowledge the obvious.

To run for president, he was ready to be a Democrat. What did that actually mean? It was hard to completely define, but one implication was clear—support for the Democratic candidate if he lost, and no subsequent challenge in the general election. When asked about an Independent run by George Stephanopoulos on ABC's This Week, Sanders was unequivocal: "No, absolutely not," he said. "I've been very clear about that."

In the grueling campaign that followed, Sanders won 23 states and 13 million votes, and raised more than $220 million, mostly in donations that averaged $27 from more than a million people. It was not enough to defeat the choice of the Democratic Party's establishment,

Hillary Clinton. But within a year after her defeat by Donald Trump, he was openly discussing the possibility of another run in 2020.

Over the years this irascible outsider had become a seasoned player in the political establishment. As the longest-serving Independent, and the only open socialist in Congress, he had entered the record books. Considered an effective coalition-builder, he sometimes persuaded GOP conservatives to play ball with liberals. He also founded the Congressional Progressive Caucus, which fought for tax reform, single payer health care, military spending cuts, and control of international financial institutions. Along the way, he proved invulnerable to electoral attack.

Still, as Sanders saw it, his views "about what I believe is right and what I want to see in this country have changed very little."

As he put it during an extended, private interview in December 1998,[114] "You have two political parties that are controlled by monied interests…You have a corporate media. When you talk about consolidation, you are talking about oil and gas, banking, and perhaps most importantly, the media—where there are very few voices of dissent regarding our current position on the global economy. That gets to even the more fundamental issue—the health of American democracy."

Peter Shumlin, the fifth Democrat elected governor since 1962, and U.S. Senator Bernie Sanders, the longest-serving Independent in congressional history, held a joint press conference in 2011 to announce plans for a regional Sandia lab at the University of Vermont.

---

114 Greg Guma, Still Bernie After All These Years, *The Vermont Times*, Jan. 6, 1999.

We were meeting at the start of a mind-boggling week. Bill Clinton was two days from launching a new round of Iraq bombings—on the eve of his impeachment. Sanders had made up his mind about Clinton: Yes to censure, no to removal or resignation. He was more equivocal on foreign intervention. A critic of wasteful defense spending who voted against the first Gulf War, he nevertheless believed that military action was sometimes appropriate, for example in Yugoslavia or to get rid of a dictator like Saddam Hussein.

"Winning credibility is the first step to building a broad-based movement," he explained, and the way to do that is to take on bread and butter issues. "I don't think you can just look at the issue of war and peace. People have got to know you are on their side."

He also talked about his "friends" on the Left: "I have long been concerned that some progressive activists do not stand up and fight effectively or pay enough attention to the needs of ordinary Americans," he charged.

Sanders admitted that he had little idea of how Congress operated before he arrived. Like his early days as mayor, dealing with an unsympathetic legislature and entrenched local bureaucracy, it was a rude awakening. Years later, although he knew how the game was played, it still upset him that "what we read in the textbooks about how a bill becomes a law just ain't the case."

An unusual aspect of his early approach in Congress was to work with people whose stands on other issues he abhorred. In fact, much of Sanders' early legislative success came through forging deals with ideological opposites. An amendment to bar spending in support of defense contractor mergers, for example, was pushed through with the aid of Chris Smith, a prominent opponent of abortion. John Kasich, whose views on welfare, the minimum wage and foreign policy could hardly be more divergent from Sanders', helped him phase out risk insurance for foreign investments. And it was a "left-right coalition" he helped create that derailed the "fast track" legislation on international agreements pushed by Bill Clinton.

The power of the strategy reached its apex in May 2010 when Sanders' campaign to bring transparency to the Federal Reserve resulted in a 96–0 Senate vote on his amendment to audit the Fed and conduct a General Accounting Office audit of possible conflicts of interest in loans to unknown banks.

Having arch-conservatives as allies may sound strange for a socialist. His explanation was unapologetically pragmatic: the job is to pass legislation rather than "moralize and be virtuous and not talk to anybody.... If you are a good politician—and I use that in a positive sense—you seize the opportunity to make things happen."

Another role, perhaps closer to his heart, was provocateur. "I respect people who are in the political process," he explained. But he also enjoyed flushing them out. "As a result of the role I and others have played, there may be more transparency," he concluded. "But obviously the issue goes beyond that."

We were getting to the core of his analysis: international financial groups protecting the interests of speculators and banks at the expense of the poor and working people—not to mention the environment—behind a veil of secrecy. Governments reduced to the status of figureheads under international capitalist management. Both political parties kowtowing to big money flaks. And media myopia fueling public ignorance. His task, he said, was to raise consciousness and, when possible, expose the real agendas of the powerful.

"I think it's imperative that people keep working on what is a very difficult task; that is, creating a third party in America," he said. Despite that view, he had no plans to help develop one: "I am very much preoccupied and work very hard being Vermont's congressman. I am not going to play an active role in building a third party."

It sounded like a contradiction. But active involvement in party-building would inevitably mean supporting statewide candidates against people like Howard Dean, who was governor at the time, as well as strain his personal détente with other Democrats.

Forced to choose between being virtuous and effective, he opted for success—as long as it didn't violate his long-held beliefs. On the other hand, "There are not very many members of congress who hold my views," he claimed. "The president does not hold my views. The corporate media does not hold my views. That is the reality I have to deal with every single day."

Sanders' job, as he defined it, was to understand the constraints and "do the best you can with the powers you have. You don't just stand on a street corner giving a speech."

Vermont's sense of community is linked to its size and traditions like Town Meeting. Research indicates that almost half of those who attend actually speak, a high percentage, and women fare better than in any other part of the political system.

24

Local Democracy and State Power

In the late 20th century Vermont's Town Meetings gained some fresh traction, becoming the main way for local communities to exercise a measure of control over an increasingly broad range of public affairs. At their best, these annual public meetings epitomized the value of equalitarian democracy. On the other hand, attendance was 20 percent or less in many places, and business was often decided by local bosses before the formal session began.

Over time growth brought increased complexity, while the state and federal government assumed more responsibilities, leaving a largely ceremonial shell in which the purchase of a truck could become "major" business.

Political scientist Frank Bryan began observing town meetings in the late 1960s. In early analysis, he noticed that participation was relatively greater in smaller towns, educational level didn't influence the level of involvement, and increased use of the Australian ballot threatened to kill the tradition. He also talked about the "atomizing" of local authority; basically, the shifting of local functions to various regional groups and the state were leaving towns with little to draw residents each year.[115]

---

115 Bryan Interview, Feb. 1983

Realignments

In the 1970s, however, a new type of business began to appear on Town Meeting agendas—resolutions that dealt with issues beyond the usual boundaries of local government. In 1976 anti-nuclear activists brought up items that called for the banning of nuclear power plants or the transportation and storage of nuclear waste. People knew the towns had no way to enforce such a decision, and yet by 1977 more than 40 communities took such a stand. In subsequent years more Vermont communities voted to end the production and deployment of nuclear weapons—a campaign that gained national recognition when 162 town meetings endorsed resolutions in March 1982—basically issuing instructions to the president and the state's congressional delegation to help lead the charge. Federal officials eventually took their advice.

At the time Bryan and other Town Meeting boosters were concerned that "larger" issues might begin to dominate the annual gatherings and reduce attendance in the long run. In 1974 he predicted "the functional death of the Vermont town" as rural political systems became "more closed than open, more individualistic than communal, and politically more passive than active."

Burlington's multi-party system expanded participation and produced innovative programs. City Council meetings are well-attended, and Neighborhood Planning Assemblies, part of local government since 1983, sometimes challenge traditional relationships between citizens and their representatives.

But in a 2004 book, *All Those in Favor*,[116] Bryan was more optimistic, praising the global impact of local votes on the Nuclear Freeze "because the world knows that town meetings are authentic, democratic governments and Vermont has the healthiest system of this kind of government anywhere."

Pointing to a series of social innovations—from challenging slavery and McCarthyism to leading the national debate on environmental protection and gay marriage in more recent times—Bryan and co-author Susan Clark argued that town meeting is the reason Vermont "consistently places better on indices of achievement in the areas of good government, civil society, social capital, collective generosity, and political tolerance." Among their observations:

- An average 20 percent of eligible voters attend Vermont town meetings, a more significant figure when you consider the amount of time involved and the fact that voter turnout for local elections across the U.S. is only 25 percent.

- Forty-four percent of those who attend actually speak, a high number for any legislative process.

- Women fare better than in any other part of the U.S. political system. Less than 20 percent of the Congress is female; in the Vermont state legislature it is around 30 percent. But according to a 2003 study of 44 town meetings, 48 percent of those involved in passing local budgets and setting the tax rate were women.

- The level of participation varies widely. Small towns average more than 30 percent attendance, while only about 5 percent show up in larger communities. Bryan and Clark suggested that town meetings aren't that effective in participatory terms when the community grows beyond 5,000 people, and recommended that larger places consider either a representative town meeting or division into neighborhood meetings.

---

116 Susan Clark and Frank Bryan, *All Those in Favor: Rediscovering the Secrets of Town Meeting and Community*, RavenMark, 2005

Aside from the Australian ballot, which lets voters avoid discussion and instead use pre-printed forms, the largest threat they saw was the long-term loss of decision-making power to other levels of government. Until 1947, Vermont towns conducted their own business on Town Meeting Day without much state interference. Since then, however, the legislature had been tinkering with the process, gradually usurping local power in more areas. In response to town meeting initiatives like the nuclear freeze votes, for example, there was an attempt in 1983 to raise the petition requirement for placing items on local ballots. It didn't happen, but the intention was clear—to make it harder for people to raise issues not in favor with elected leaders.

This dynamic illustrates an inconvenient reality. Although the state has a tradition of local democracy and an accessible citizen legislature, it also has one of the nation's most centralized governments, due in part to the weakness of county structures.

Beyond that—and also contrary to myth—both citizens and leaders, progressives and conservatives alike, have repeatedly opted to expand the state's authority in areas ranging from roads and the environment to health and education. Much of what makes Vermont attractive to those bewitched by its image can be traced to the use of state power.

State government places restrictions on local autonomy. As one Vermont legislator bluntly explained, "The towns are creatures of the state." But most lawmakers are not professional politicians and many remain responsive.

Based on Vermont's contemporary image as a liberal stronghold, it is easy to forget that Republicans largely made it what it is today. GOP governors were among the most ardent early proponents of a statewide tax to fund education. Gov. Ernest Gibson Jr. said, as early as the late 1940s, that the greatest problem facing Vermont was "equalizing educational opportunity and distributing the costs as equally as possible among the towns and school districts."

Thirty years later, another Republican, Richard Snelling, called for a state-administered property tax to spread the burden between rich and poor towns. The proposal failed when wealthy towns squealed, while communities that would have come out ahead worried instead about a loss of local control.

Despite such occasional setbacks, Republican leaders had little difficulty embracing centralization and for most of the century they dominated state politics. After the Civil War, the issue was state aid to highway programs, designed to help businesses compete and farmers transport milk. In the early 20th century, under Fletcher Proctor, it was centralization of rural schools and industrial education. Far from being a libertarian, Proctor also supported prohibition, only relenting when a "local option" movement for liquor licensing threatened to overturn GOP rule. Subsequently, he struck a deal with liquor distributors and managed to maintain state control of local license committees.

Republicans were firmly in command when the state stepped into education management, passed and increased the income tax, and established the state highway system after the flood of 1927. In each case, they were accepting reality; namely, that local communities needed outside help. By the 1940s, it was common knowledge that individual towns couldn't handle all the necessary services properly on their own.

Although Phil Hoff was both praised and blamed for expanding state services and power in the 1960s, the stage was set by yet another Republican. In the late 1950s, insurance executive Deane Davis chaired the Little Hoover Commission, a reorganization study that called for agency consolidation and more control by the governor. The buzzwords then were simplification and efficiency. A decade later, Davis presided over the formation of what became known as "super agencies." It was precisely the type of bureaucratic centralization that Republicans today view as a threat to personal rights and local autonomy.

Davis, who succeeded Hoff as governor in 1968, was also "godfather" to the first major land development control law in the country, Act 250.

Like Hoff, he wanted a statewide land use plan, but was blocked by large landowners and conservatives in his own party. Though he euphemistically labeled the approach "creative localism," the main objectives were to regulate development and protect the environment through consistent statewide policies. In more optimistic and trusting times, these sounded like common sense notions that might help local areas cope with development pressures.

When Snelling proposed a statewide property tax he was building on an established Republican stance, the moderate centralism of the Vermont party's Aiken-Gibson wing, a combination of populist rhetoric and policy pragmatism.

In more recent times, state government has often regulated, and sometimes even negated, changes in local policies and practices. The legislature's 1989 attempt to strip local communities of the power to choose alternatives to the property tax is one episode in that struggle. On the other hand, people have continued to use town meeting—in many cases the only forum open to them—to influence the policies and decisions of "higher" levels of government.

25

Howard Dean's Moment

The quest for the nation's highest office is a body-and-soul-challenging job. Campaigns begin years before Election Day, and hopefuls are locked in an endless race around the country, repeating the same arguments as they fight to out-fundraise and out-spend one another. It was therefore no surprise that, on the eve of the Iowa caucuses in January 2004, Howard Dean looked squeezed out on the campaign trail.

After more than a decade as Vermont governor he was running as a feisty outsider, challenging the Bush administration about the conduct of the Iraq War while riding an internet-driven wave of anti-incumbent anger.

In the late 1930s Republican George Aiken toyed with the possibility of challenging Franklin D. Roosevelt. Thirty years later, Phil Hoff briefly leapt into the national spotlight as the first Democratic governor to break with Pres. Johnson over the Vietnam War. In 1968, Hoff delivered a moving speech to the Vermont General Assembly eulogizing Robert Kennedy, who was assassinated that June. When the Democrats gathered in Chicago, his name circulated as a "protest" candidate for vice president. But Hoff was worn down by a decade of political struggle at home and did not pursue it.

Howard Dean had fewer doubts or personal issues to consider. The son of a Republican Wall Street executive, he grew up in affluent surroundings and attended an exclusive boarding school. At Yale he opposed the Vietnam War but wasn't a protester, then drifted briefly before becoming a stockbroker. But that didn't satisfy his desire to help people, so Dean enrolled at Albert Einstein College of Medicine, a school in the Bronx famous for its community-based approach.

After medical school, the challenge was finding a place for his residency. Burlington wasn't his first choice, but it offered a way to combine practicing medicine with political engagement. His first significant local move was to help launch the Citizens Waterfront Group, which fought for a bike path along the shore of Lake Champlain and locked horns with the administration of Bernie Sanders. The campaign took several years but ultimately succeeded.

In the meantime, Dean learned the ropes from established Vermont politicians. "They shaped me into a pragmatic Democrat," he wrote in a political autobiography. "I was friendly with the younger, more liberal Democrats because they were my age, but I didn't vote with them. I didn't relate to their political sensibilities."[117] By 1982 he was chairing the Chittenden County Democratic Committee and running for the state House of Representatives.

"The district was in Burlington, and it was the most liberal, working-class district in the state," he wrote. "There was a very strong Progressive Party in the ward and no Republican Party whatsoever. So, interestingly, I ended up running against a candidate to my left in my first election."

In the legislature he joined a group of young, moderate Democrats and Republicans known as the "blue shirts," focused on education, and became minority leader in just two years. By 1986 he was ready to go statewide. Looking at the options—lieutenant governor or a race for Congress against moderate Republican James Jeffords—he chose the former. Fortunately for Dean, the current lieutenant governor, Peter Smith, had decided to run for governor.

In 1990, he passed up an opportunity to run for governor himself, but ended up in office due to the unexpected death of Richard Snelling. Reviewing his accomplishments over the next decade, Dean stressed balancing the budget, building a surplus, land conservation, health care for almost all children under 18, and an early intervention program that reduced childhood abuse. On some issues he resisted demands from the left, however, and was generally known as a centrist.

---

117 Howard Dean, *Winning Back America*, Simon & Schuster, 2003

Time and *Newsweek* published Dean cover stories on the same day.

His response to calls for same-sex marriage was indicative. On Dec. 10, 1999 the Vermont Supreme Court ruled in *Baker v. Vermont* that gay couples had a right to the same benefits provided to straight couples and told the legislature to deal with implementation.

At the time same-sex couples could not be legally married anywhere in the U.S. Some states had passed laws forbidding or declining to recognize such marriages. The federal government had enacted the Defense of Marriage Act (DOMA), which said states need not recognize same-sex unions from other places.

Sensing political risk, Dean initially expressed some discomfort with the idea of gay marriage.[118] But the legislature moved forward and made Vermont the first state to legalize civil unions. Dean signed the bill—but without a public ceremony, apparently in the hope of cooling down the atmosphere.

It didn't happen. Gay rights activists felt cheated and an anti-gay backlash almost cost him re-election in 2000.

---

118 John Cloud, The Cool Passion of Dr. Dean, *Time*, Aug. 11, 2003

In retrospect, Dean insists that he was committed to marriage equality for all. "That's why I knew I had to work for civil unions," he wrote in 2003, in the midst of his presidential race. "I never viewed the bill as a gay rights issue. I signed it out of a commitment to human rights, and because every single American has the same right to equality and justice under the law that I have."

Whatever the reasons, he benefited in the long run. Wealthy gay supporters, especially in the Fire Island beach community, were early and generous contributors to his presidential campaign.

By the time civil unions became Vermont law in 2000, Dean was already considering a presidential race. But he held back, instead waiting until the end of his last term as governor two year later to begin building an organization. He also made sure Al Gore wasn't running again.

Early on, Dean tapped into an internet-based strategy, meetups, and used the concept to organize supporters across the country. "We were seeing a phenomenon where the effort was owned and directed by the people who supported it," he explained. He was also discovering a new way to raise money. By June 30, 2003, he had raised almost $8 million, beating his rivals and advancing to the top candidate tier. A week before that, he officially announced in front of a standing room only crowd on Church Street.

"On that stunning early summer day," he recalled, "I stood in front of more than thirty thousand Americans who had gathered in Burlington and, via the internet, across the country...In many ways, that speech on June 23 was the culmination of what I had learned in a year of listening to the American people."

By August Dean was the hottest political story in the country, the wild card of the presidential race. In cover features published simultaneously on August 11, both *Time* and *Newsweek* declared him the candidate to watch. *Time* was circumspect, titling its cover "The Dean Factor" and inside headlining his "cool passion" as an "unlikely spokesman for the anti-Bush left." *Newsweek* was more provocative. Dean pointed angrily at an unseen audience as the cover headline asked, "Howard Dean: Destiny or Disaster?" Inside, Jonathan Alter's coverage telegraphed the fear among establishment Democrats that "if Dean does win the nomination, his liberal supporters will put their

Birkenstocks on the gas pedal and drive the party right over the cliff, a la George McGovern in 1972."[119]

Back in Vermont, people were perplexed. This was another Howard Dean, no longer the moderate who often frustrated progressives. Now he was, as Alter described him, "the fire-breathing neopopulist" calling on liberals to "Take your country back."

In Dean's book, released a few months later, he chided fellow Democrats for "actually empowering the radical right" by being afraid to "stand up to the Republicans and their radical agenda." He defined his cause as "the Great American Restoration—the restoration of our ideals, of our communities, and of our nation's traditional role as a beacon of hope in the world."

Dean had become governor by accident, but he was running for president with gusto and purpose.

Dean for President campaign mailer

Six months later, on the weekend before the Iowa caucuses in 2004, he was still pushing hard, and pulling out the stops by spending Sunday with Pres. Jimmy Carter in Georgia. Then he flew back to caucus-land for a rare appearance with his wife. He had focused on Iowa early, risking $300,000 to air the first TV ads. Everything looked set for an early victory.

But groups like the Club for Growth had something else in mind. In an ad released by the conservative anti-tax group shortly before the crucial caucuses, two actors, playing an elderly couple, were asked to describe the threat looming over the country.

---

119 Jonathan Alter, The Left's Mister Right, *Newsweek*, Aug. 11, 2003

Responding directly to the camera, the "husband" said, "Howard Dean should take his tax-hiking, government-expanding, latte-drinking, sushi-eating, Volvo-driving, New York Times reading..." Then the "wife" jumped in with, "body-piercing, Hollywood-loving, left-wing freak show back to Vermont where it belongs."

It was a brilliant blend of dark comedy and cultural hate speech, a harbinger of the culture warfare to come, so effective that the club didn't have to pay much for airtime. The news networks were more than willing to provide free play. As CNN's Judy Woodruff explained on Jan. 9, 2004, "This is so catchy, we love to run it over and over again."

Club for Growth's president Steve Moore readily admitted that the goal was to re-brand Dean as a tax-hiking elitist. The theme would have been developed further if he had become the nominee, and was cleverly recycled in 2008 to fit Barack Obama. Dean endured such assaults throughout his campaign, and not just from other candidates and columnists. In addition to a barrage of negative campaign ads, a majority of nightly network newscast evaluations of Dean were negative, while three-quarters of the coverage given to the other candidates was favorable, according to research conducted by the Center for Media and Public Affairs.

In 2003, only 49 percent of all on-air evaluations of Dean were positive, while the rest of the democratic field collectively received 78 percent favorable.

By Jan. 19, 2004, most candidates were ready to say and do anything to survive. A few hours before the caucuses, John Kerry wondered aloud whether John Edwards was "out of diapers" when he (Kerry) came back from Vietnam. He had to apologize, since Edwards was 16 at the time.

In frigid weather, steelworkers were showing painted chests for Dick Gephardt. Wesley Clark, not in the caucus but gaining ground at the time, was hugging George McGovern in New Hampshire, while Edwards and Dennis Kucinich struck a deal to pool delegates.

CNN analysts issued a forecast for Iowa hours before anyone voted. On *Crossfire*, Democratic insiders Paul Begala and James Carville, as well as conservative Robert Novak, predicted that Kerry's late surge would make the difference. Dean sounded over-confident, but there was uncertainty among his supporters, nicknamed the Deaniacs.

Volunteers in at least three cities were handing out flyers that charged Kerry wasn't electable, his wife was too rich, and Ralph Nader wouldn't step aside if he was the nominee. It sounded desperate.

Waiting for the numbers, Tom Brokaw noted that politics at that moment was about cultural values, and Dean's message had become confused. He was an "outsider" with more key endorsements than anyone else, an angry guy whose wife didn't want much to do with his campaign. According to a focus group led by Frank Luntz, Dean's support had tanked, largely because people found him testy, even mean—partially based on a last-minute shouting match with a critic that made Iowa TV news.

Becoming the frontrunner had allowed Dean to launch and fund a national campaign. Thus, losing in Iowa didn't have to spell doom. But it did allow the media to question his claims to be leading a broad-based movement, and set the stage for Kerry to beat him in New Hampshire.

And then, when he could have been humble, Dean went on TV to thank his supporters and unexpectedly turned into a wild-eyed firebrand who rasped out his fierce determination to beat any rivals, shouting out state names with a frightening sneer.

Columnist Howard Fineman was subdued when he called it "a little nutty." CNN's senior analyst Bill Schneider concluded that "people looked at Howard Dean, and they didn't see a President." But Boston's Mike Barnacle was the bluntest, saying "that guy's not going to the White House."

Like the outbursts of Barack Obama's former minister Jeremiah Wright in 2008, Dean's so-called "rant" after the 2004 Iowa caucuses—instantly infamous as the "I have a scream" speech—was the hot clip on TV and the internet for weeks, the focus of endless late night jokes. Within five days, the "scream heard round the world" was played almost 700 times on U.S. television networks.

As Dean's poll numbers tanked, critics concluded that he simply didn't have the "temperament" to be president. The emphasis shifted from which candidate had the most compelling message to which would be more "electable."

Kerry seized the moment, stressing his "gravitas" and showcasing manly skills by playing Hockey and piloting a helicopter. When New Hampshire primary votes were tallied, the strategy paid off. Kerry repeated his Iowa performance, pulling in 39 percent. Dean made a partial comeback with a decent second place finish. His speech that night was more controlled, but still defiant.

On Feb. 18, after coming in third in Wisconsin, he finally acknowledged that the campaign had "come to an end." Yet he urged people to keep voting for him. The notion was that Dean delegates might yet influence the party platform.

On March 2 he won the Vermont primary but it was already over.

After the 2004 election Dean became chairman of the Democratic National Committee, creating a "50 State Strategy," designed to make Democratic congressional candidates competitive in normally conservative states. The approach bore fruit in the 2006 midterms; Democrats took back the House and picked up seats in the Senate from normally Republican states. In 2008 Barack Obama made Dean's strategy the backbone of his campaign.

Back in Vermont, over a veto from Dean's Republican successor James Douglas, the state legislature became the first in the country to allow marriage for same-sex couples on April 7, 2009. Rather than sparking a backlash, a UCLA study concluded that the decision would actually boost the state's economy by more than $30 million over three years. That, in turn, would generate $3.3 million more in fees and sales taxes and create 700 new jobs.

26

Re-imagining Independence

The idea of defying the forces of centralized power and wealth can be seductive, especially if you live in a small, isolated place with a reputation for being contrary and the sense that it's different, even exceptional.

In Congress and his historic presidential races, Bernie Sanders has reflected this perspective, challenging corporate secrecy and the powers of financial institutions by forging coalitions that cross traditional lines. So did Howard Dean in 2003-2004, the same time that former Duke University professor Thomas Naylor launched a related but even more ambitious crusade, the Second Vermont Republic. The aim was to dissolve the United States and, in particular, return Vermont "to its status as an independent republic."

Abraham Lincoln persuaded the public that secession was unconstitutional and immoral, Naylor argued. "It's one of the few things that the left and right agree on. We say it's constitutional—and ultimately it is a question of political will: the will of the people of Vermont versus the will of the government to stop us."

Historian Frank Bryan, whose 1989 book with Republican thinker John McClaughry called for restructuring the state's democracy along decentralist lines, has argued that "the cachet of secession would make the new republic a magnet" and "people would obviously relish coming to the Republic of Vermont, the Switzerland of North America."

Naylor replied that the question wasn't if but when.

Vermont attorney and historian Paul Gillies respectfully disagreed. "It doesn't make economic sense, it doesn't make political sense, it doesn't make historical sense," he replied. "Other than that, it's a good idea."

Archivist Gregory Sanford claimed that some of the arguments for secession, in Vermont at least, were based on "historical facts of dubious reputation." The State Archives often received requests for copies of an "escape clause" in the Vermont Constitution, which supposedly allows Vermont to withdraw from the U.S. "The truth, drawn from documents, is less satisfying," he confided. "There is no, nor has there ever been, such an escape clause."

Passports assert the human right to enter and leave a place, argued Garry Davis, a Vermonter who distributed World Citizen passports for decades. Although the state doesn't issue them, it might. Like nullification or the right to secede, it is largely a question of political will.

Still, some people have considered it an attractive idea. In 2008, a Zogby poll commissioned by the Middlebury Institute, a think tank studying "separatism, secession, and self-determination," indicated that that 20 percent of Americans thought "any state or region has the right to peaceably secede from the United States and become an independent republic."

More than 18 percent told pollsters that they would support a secessionist effort in their state.

Leaving the Empire

In Vermont, the argument is that "the U.S. has become an empire that is essentially ungovernable—it's too big, it's too corrupt and it no longer serves the needs of its citizens," summarized Rob Williams, editor of *Vermont Commons*, a publication that emerged to cover secession-related issues. "Congress and the executive branch are being run by the multinationals. We have electoral fraud, rampant corporate corruption, a culture of militarism and war. If you care about democracy and self-governance and any kind of representative system," Williams and Naylor argued, "the only constitutional way to preserve what's left of the Republic is to peaceably take apart the empire."

As history demonstrates, the state has been fertile ground for such outside-the-box thinking in the past. It didn't immediately join the United States. It was the first state to ban slavery. Explicit constitutional authority aside, it also came close to separating from the new union before and during the War of 1812.

Between 1809 and 1812, Federalists and other opponents defied national policies, flirting with secret societies, secession and other forms of dissent. In 1813 it elected a governor who rejected the necessity of war. Martin Chittenden's refusal to let Vermont troops defend the lake became a factor that emboldened the British.

In October 1814, although Chittenden stopped short of supporting secession, Vermont delegates were among those who responded to a call by the Massachusetts legislature for a convention in Hartford to consider more extreme options. Seventeen years later it was the first state to elect an Anti-Mason governor during a period when opposition to elites and secret societies was growing.

Assessing whether Vermont could "go it alone," environmentalist Bill McKibben once argued that "functional independence would be the proper first step, and useful in its own right." He also provided a list of practical projects to help create more food self-sufficiency, energy independence, and local economic power.

However, the 2008 election of Barack Obama and the global nature of many problems convinced him that "any political independence movement is going nowhere now." Therefore, McKibben's advice became more modest: build affection and trust by sharing information and making small but effective moves in the right direction.

Secession activist Rob Williams argued that the U.S. has become ungovernable and "no longer serves the needs of its citizens."

Before he died, Second Vermont Republic founder Tom Naylor defined secession—or independence, as some supporters prefer—in idealistic terms. It is a rebellion against empire, he contended, designed to retake control from big institutions and help people care for themselves and others by "decentralizing, downsizing, localizing, demilitarizing, simplifying, and humanizing our lives."

The Urge to Nullify

By 2012 secession groups were organizing across the United States and a dozen states had active movements. Even more legislatures were debating laws designed to "nullify" federal actions in areas from gun control and health care reform to marijuana possession and overseas troop deployments.

If the federal government fails to check itself, goes the argument, it's up to the states to call a halt. Nullification rests on the theory that the states created the national government. Therefore, they have the right to judge the constitutionality of federal laws and potentially refuse to enforce them. It was used when American colonists nullified laws imposed by the British. Since then states have used it to limit federal actions, from the Fugitive Slave Act to unpopular tariffs.

Vermont had direct, dramatic experience with nullification early in its history. In November 1850 the state legislature approved a so-called Habeas Corpus Law that required officials to assist slaves who made it to the state. The law rendered the Fugitive Slave Act effectively unenforceable. It was a clear case of nullification, a highly controversial concept even then. Poet John Greenleaf Whittier suggested such tactics, while Virginia Gov. John B. Floyd warned that this form of resistance could push the South toward secession. President Millard Fillmore threatened to enforce federal law in Vermont through military action if necessary—but nothing happened.

Even earlier, support for nullification emerged in reaction to the Sedition Act and the jailing of Matthew Lyon. These two events prompted the Kentucky Resolve of 1798, written by Thomas Jefferson, and the almost identical Virginia Resolve penned by James Madison.

In the first section of his version, Jefferson stated that federal authority wasn't unlimited, and, if it went too far, need not be obeyed. The national government wasn't the "final judge" of its own powers, he suggested, and therefore various states had a right to decide how to handle federal overreach. Madison's Virginia version declared that, in the case of a deliberate and dangerous abuse of power, states not only had a right to object, they were duty bound to stop the "progress of the evil" and maintain their "authorities, rights and liberties."

Ten years later, after Jefferson enacted a trade embargo as president in response to British maritime theft and kidnapping of sailors, legislatures nullified the law using his own words and arguments. On Feb. 5, 1809, the Massachusetts legislature declared that the embargo was "not legally binding on the citizens of the state" and denounced it as "unjust, oppressive, and unconstitutional." Eventually every New England state, and Delaware, voted to nullify the Embargo Act.

Although nullification has clearly exerted an influence on federal policies at times, secession is another matter. Could it ever happen? Not according to at least one U.S. Supreme Court Justice, the conservative Antonin Scalia. In 2006, he responded to a letter from screenwriter Daniel Turkewitz, who was developing a script about a secessionist movement in Maine. He wrote to all of the justices but only Scalia replied. And the message was that a legal showdown in the Supreme Court will never happen.

"If there was any constitutional issue resolved by the Civil War," Scalia said, "it is that there is no right to secede."

Assuming that is true, the court's refusal to revisit the issue hasn't stopped some Vermonters from pursuing it. Part of what has driven the movement is clearly anger, but another element is distrust and disbelief, a general loss of faith in political institutions, especially "big government."

The left and right have been culturally polarized for generations, disagreeing passionately over moral issues, racism, abortion, immigration, climate change, and how to control the distribution of wealth as well as power. Yet there is some common ground, beginning with the idea that in the face of oppression (however you define it) withdrawal of consent can make a difference. For a growing number of people, disengagement, whether gradual or sudden, is preferable to sticking with a system in which you no longer believe.

And if any place does ever take the road less traveled, why not Vermont, the "reluctant republic," fertile ground for original thinkers, common sense tolerance and independent idealism, a cantankerous maverick that wasn't sure it wanted in from the start?

There's even a bumper sticker: Most Likely to Secede.

27

Power Struggles

Running for Senate in 2010, Anthony Pollina joined Tim Ashe as the second Vermont Progressive Party leader to be elected as a fusion candidate with both Democratic and Progressive nominations. But he had entered statewide politics with a splash many years earlier.

In 1984, Pollina won an insurgent victory in the Democratic primary for US Congress, then decisively lost in the general election to James Jeffords, the popular incumbent. He didn't try again for 16 years.

In between, Pollina instead served during the 1990s as senior policy advisor to then-Rep. Bernie Sanders. He also fought for campaign finance reform legislation that established public funding for statewide political campaigns. In 2002, however, when his own campaign for lieutenant governor failed to qualify for public funding Pollina filed a lawsuit in federal court to challenge the law.

Running for governor as a Progressive in 2000 Pollina received 9.5 percent of the vote in a crowded field with Republican Ruth Dwyer, leader of the conservative Take Back Vermont movement, who got 37.9 percent in her second gubernatorial race. Incumbent Gov. Howard Dean won with 50.4 percent. Two years later, in the race for lieutenant governor, Pollina received 24.8 percent in a three way race, this time behind Democrat Peter Shumlin, with 32.1 percent, and Republican Brian Dubie, who won with 41.2.

Howard Dean had just retired, and was planning his presidential race.

The Democratic candidate for governor that year was Doug Racine, a former senator and three-term lieutenant governor. The Progressive candidate was Michael Badamo, who ran without much support from his party, and received just 0.6 percent. Republican James Douglas, previously House Majority Leader, Secretary of State and State Treasurer, was elected.

In 2004, Peter Clavelle, a Progressive in the midst of his last term as Burlington mayor, returned to the Democratic Party and challenged Douglas's re-election bid. Douglas won again, this time with 57.8 percent. Clavelle received 37.9. The Progressive Party didn't field a candidate for governor in that cycle, or in 2006.

"What gets me excited is to bring people together," said Peter Clavelle during his 2004 campaign for governor. "The truth is that most Progressives are Democrats. And unless we find common ground, the only winners will be Republicans."

Then Pollina announced again for governor in 2008. At a July press conference, however, the Progressive Party leader explained that he would appear on the ballot this time as an Independent. It was "by far the best way" to build a coalition, he claimed.

The decision raised questions about his party's future. Both Sen. Sanders and his predecessor Jeffords had been embraced as

Independents, Pollina argued. But Sanders became an Independent in the late 1970s after several disappointing runs as a Liberty Union candidate. At the time he publicly announced that the timing wasn't right for a new party. He had since served four terms as Burlington mayor and eight in Congress, before successfully running for U.S. Senate in 2006. In every one of those races he ran as an Independent.

Jeffords, on the other hand, was a life-long Republican, serving in the U.S. House and Senate for decades. But he left the GOP in 2001, citing deep differences with the Republican leadership and the Bush administration. It turned out to be his last term, and there was no way to know how Vermont voters might have responded had he attempted to seek re-election as an Independent.

Pollina's reasons were different. He had devoted years to building the Vermont Progressive Party, and had declined to enter the Democratic primary earlier the same year, claiming he had no intention of running as anything but a Progressive.

"You know, I'm a Progressive," he told columnist Peter Freyne. "I'm not going to leave the Progressive Party to become a candidate of another party." Doing so "would undermine people's faith in me and also in the process," he said. "I wouldn't be too surprised if there were Democrats who would accuse me of being opportunistic in switching parties."

Once he announced his status change to Independent, Democrats did exactly that. "This is about opportunistic decision-making," Democratic Party Chair Ian Carlton told *The Burlington Free Press*.

Thirty years earlier Sanders faced such a choice, made it, and held various offices almost continuously since 1981—always as an Independent. Although the de facto leader of the state's progressive movement, he never actually joined the party and didn't feel accountable to any partisan line. At times he was criticized for not doing enough to build an alternative to the Republicans and Democrats. He simply ignored the issue.

In the end, Pollina's 2008 campaign won the backing of the three largest unions in the state. The Vermont-National Education Association backed an independent candidate for governor for the first time. He also received support from the Gun Owners of Vermont, a "libertarian" connection Sanders also made in some campaigns.

When the votes were counted, however, he had 21.8 percent, only one tenth of a percent ahead of the Democrat.

Douglas won again, this time with 53.4 percent.

In the same election cycle Tim Ashe was elected to the state Senate, and eventually became President Pro Tempore. He had been endorsed by Bernie Sanders and ran as a Democratic/Progressive fusion candidate.

Ashe had already been on the City Council. In October 2011 he proposed fusion as a candidate for mayor. It was time "to bring Progressives and Democrats together to stop this crazy infighting that is so counter-productive," he explained in an interview.

His pitch was that looming threats and Burlington's unique political dynamics called for someone who could unite a "new majority." But fusion was still an unfamiliar concept to most voters, despite the attempt a century earlier by James Burke and Pervical Clement.

It also had been used in New York City, the only way a Republican could become mayor in the early 20th century, bringing together clean government supporters across party lines. The most famous fusion politician in the Big Apple was Fiorello LaGuardia. Although a Republican, nearly half his votes for New York mayor in 1933 came from Progressives and Fusionists.

And the tactic almost succeeded in Burlington. On Nov. 13, 2011, Ashe ended up tied with Miro Weinberger at the largest Democratic Party caucus in recent city history. Many stalwart Progressives attended, and each candidate had 540 votes after three rounds of voting. At a second caucus four weeks later, however, Weinberger prevailed, 655–533, and went on to win the general election. The local Progressive Party didn't nominate a candidate that year.

By then, Pollina had run for the state Senate, as a Progressive and Democrat, and won. The fusion approach was finally working. State Auditor Doug Hoffer and Lt. Gov. David Zuckerman subsequently took a similar path to statewide victories.

In 2020 Zuckerman became the Democratic candidate for governor, but lost to incumbent Phil Scott, another Republican prepared to break with his party's national leaders. Ashe ran for lieutenant governor, but lost in the Democratic primary to Molly Gray. In April 2021, Hoffer hired him as deputy auditor.

Power Struggles

Bottom: Burlington's 2011 Democratic caucus attracted more than 1000 residents. Top: Finalists Miro Weinberger and Tim Ashe waited hours, but had to return weeks later for the results. In March 2012, Weinberger became the city's first Democratic mayor in 31 years.

Progressive Predicaments

For most Vermonters the big stories of 2011 were the state's response to Tropical Storm Irene, which produced the state's worst natural disaster since 1927, the struggle over closure of Vermont Yankee, and passage of the first-in-the-nation universal health care system.

After almost a decade the state again had a Democratic governor, Peter Shumlin, who pledged to usher in single-payer health insurance and usher out Yankee.

Around the country people were rallying to the economic critique of Bernie Sanders, who was in the early stage of planning his first presidential run. Yet in Burlington, where Sanders had made his political breakthrough three decades earlier, both financial trouble at Burlington Telecom (BT), a city-owned enterprise, and a deal with military contractor Lockheed Martin forged by Progressive Mayor Bob Kiss, had sparked local outrage. By spring there were clear signs of political upheaval ahead.

Five candidates to replace Mayor Kiss had announced by early October. The list included three Democrats—Airport Commissioner Miro Weinberger, State Representative Jason Lorber, and City Councilor Bram Kranichfeld—plus Progressive Tim Ashe, and Republican Kurt Wright, a council member and state lawmaker who had come close to beating Kiss three years earlier. Later in that long campaign season, Wanda Hines, a Black activist and former director of the city's Social Equity Investment Project targeting nonwhite communities, entered the race as an Independent.

All of them were hammering Kiss about BT finances and other examples of what they considered the administration's mismanagement and failure to communicate.

Mayor Kiss was mum about his plans until the last minute, even at party meetings. But the push for someone to replace him, along with an upsurge in local activism on issues like his attempt to forge a climate change partnership with Lockheed Martin, pointed to a fractious transition. The discussion also highlighted the unique nature of Burlington's political landscape, three political parties sharing legislative power, and an executive branch run by Progressives for all but two of the last 30 years.

From Vermont to San Francisco, millions of people were protesting the growing wealth disparity between the rich and almost everyone else. In Burlington, Montpelier and other Vermont communities, thousands began gathering to express themselves and organize. Using social networks and a collective (aka leaderless) approach, the emerging Occupy movement spread rapidly to hundreds of cities, gaining momentum as unions and politicians offered support.

According to a Gallup poll, 44 percent of Americans felt that the economic system was personally unfair to them. More to the point, the top 1 percent had greater net worth than the bottom 90 percent. And, in an unusual generational twist, more people under 30 viewed the general concept of socialism in a positive light than capitalism. The movement's objective was nevertheless ambitious—to occupy parks, schools, corporate offices, streets, anywhere and everywhere—until something real was done about what the new movement defined as economic tyranny.

As protesters chanted "We are the 99%" Burlington's local elections shifted into high gear. At a Democratic debate two days after declaring his run for mayor, Ashe, once a Progressive member of the City Council, proposed fusion with Democrats to defeat the Republican challenge. But there were other viable candidates, especially Weinberger, a housing developer upset about how the city had been managed under Progressives. Well-funded and confident, he pitched a "fresh start" for the city as he planned for financial and development challenges ahead.

In late October, as the mayoral race heated up, Occupy activists launched an encampment at City Hall Park. As long as some basic rules were followed, Mayor Kiss signaled, he was prepared to be flexible.

Things went fairly well at first, in contrast with violent confrontations between police and protesters elsewhere. But an impromptu concert one night sparked the relaxation of normal restrictions, and the next morning some revelers were still intoxicated, including 35-year-old Joshua Pfenning. His death that day from a self-inflicted gunshot wound was traumatic, especially for those who knew him and tried to help. It also abruptly ended the encampment. Still, general assemblies continued for a while, as local working groups tried to develop the movement's next phase.

In 2011 and 2012, thousands converged on Burlington for Occupy and globalization mobilizations to protest economic inequality, legal repression, climate change, financial schemes, and human rights abuses.

By Thanksgiving almost everyone had an opinion about the one percent (or 1%, as some preferred), the very few with most of the wealth—bankers, oil tycoons, hedge fund managers and the like. But as filmmaker Robert Greenwald pointed out, there was an even smaller elite—the top 0.01 percent, wealthy military contractor CEOs. And that made the embrace of Sandia Laboratories and Lockheed Martin by Vermont's progressive leaders, including Sanders, somewhat perplexing. On military funding and partnerships with defense corporations, otherwise vocal critics of the 1% and military-industrial complex were making much the same arguments as other members of Congress.

Although Lockheed ultimately backed out of its climate change agreement with the city—at least partly in reaction to public pressure—Sanders succeeded in attracting Sandia, which is managed by Lockheed for the Department of Defense. One short-term result was a multi-million-dollar satellite lab at UVM to usher in Smart Grid metering, announced at a December 2011 press conference with Gov. Shumlin. Along with Sen. Patrick Leahy and Rep. Peter Welch, Sanders also endorsed the bedding of Lockheed-built F-35 fighter jets at the Burlington International Airport. If the plane was going to be built and deployed anyway, he argued, Vermont should get a fair share of the manufacturing jobs and support for its National Guard.

On the other hand, Sanders continued to fight for working people and speak out strongly against economic inequality and corporate personhood. Momentum grew for town meeting and legislative action on a Constitutional amendment to declare that money isn't speech and corporations aren't people, in reaction to the US Supreme Court's Citizens United ruling. A state legislative resolution introduced by Sen. Virginia Lyons, the first of its kind in the country, proposed "an amendment to the United States Constitution that provides that corporations are not persons under the laws of the United States."

In December, local Democrats reconvened their caucus, after the historic tie in November, and nominated Weinberger, the political newcomer. Two days later Republican Kurt Wright, a state legislator with more than a decade of experience on the city council, officially launched his campaign. The emerging dynamic pitted an experienced insider downplaying his conservative approach against a neophyte outsider with business expertise—at a time when the city faced tough choices.

The following March, Weinberger won decisively, beginning the first of four three-year terms. But Progressives rebuilt a strong presence on the council, and fielded candidates in subsequent mayoral races. In 2015, a local caucus chose former Director of Public Works Steve Goodkind, originally appointed by Sanders in the 1980s. In 2018, the Party endorsed Sanders' step-daughter Carina Driscoll.

In 2021, virtual Progressive caucus-goers picked City Council President Max Tracy, a long-time Prog who ran a media-savvy campaign and forged a radical agenda emphasizing class and racial justice issues. He raised more than $63,000, half what Weinberger brought in, and lost by just 129 votes.

Campaign postcard for Max Tracy

Weird Energy

A year after the Occupy movement swept the nation, author and '60s activist Todd Gitlin assessed the mobilization and called it a "qualified but real success." It was quixotic, he told a standing-room-only crowd in the Sugar Maple Ballroom of the Davis Center at UVM.

"And it worked," he said, but its success also pointed to problems, and "you could also say it failed."

Gitlin defined Occupy as the first U.S. social movement in modern history "to begin with the benefit of majority support for its main thrust." Early unions didn't experience "unadulterated" support, he noted. Neither the civil rights nor women's movements were especially popular at the start, and the Vietnam War had 60 percent public support in the mid-1960s.

At its core, however, the Occupy movement's identity was closely tied to its famously "horizontal," cooperative style, most visible at general assemblies. It expressed an "intense existential affirmation of itself," a desire to evolve a new way of life.

In Vermont and elsewhere, however, the movement's broad scope and "leaderless" approach made it difficult to sustain momentum. There were organizational problems and internal disagreements about process and tactics. Most encampments, fundamentally expressions of the constitutional right of assembly to redress grievances, were broken up—often violently—during a coordinated response by local officials across the country. That said, many Occupy supporters also displayed a tendency to be "phobic" about cooptation and thought unions and moveon.org were political "Trojan horses."

In Burlington, the flashpoint was the suicide of Pfenning, who was unhoused at the time, in a tent at the Burlington encampment.

Occupy combined 18th century democratic principles with 21st century methods, Gitlin concluded. As a result, the focus on debt and deficits that had been dominating political debate gave way to a debate about wealth inequality. But the core of the movement wanted much more.

"They wanted to produce a society of their own, and half believed they were producing it," he explained.

More than a year after the launch, in December 2012, Occupy still had a membership in the tens of thousands, largely young and "dis-embedded." Gitlin compared it to the wing of the civil rights movement that was prepared to engage in civil disobedience. He also pointed to promising spinoffs like a Jubilee movement to cancel debt and an anti-foreclosure campaign. Yet he questioned whether Occupy itself would have staying power. Its focus on encampments was "inspiring but self-limiting," he opined, and added that it could not be run "horizontally."

The basic problem is that "there aren't enough saints," he sighed. There is little potential in trying to convince people committed to a prophetic vision of a radically different society to simply give it up. A decade later, much the same could be said about dealing with die-hard Trump supporters.

But it will be "a weird movement," Gitlin predicted, "if it's restricted to people who can show up for general assemblies." Or those who enjoy angry mass rallies fueled by grievance and blame.

28

Land, Politics and People

Ethan Allen, the unpredictable frontier rebel who rallied resistance to any person or power threatening the property rights of settlers and his fellow land speculators, has exerted a powerful influence over Vermont's image as a home for rugged individualists and defiant outsiders.

His story, both the factual and mythical aspects, has nurtured an affinity with rebels and independent thinkers. Nevertheless, political values that have more fundamentally influenced Vermont are accountability, local control and autonomy. Frequently crossing ideological lines, they persisted through a century in which the state was known as reliably Republican, a place where not even Franklin D. Roosevelt could win an election, and have continued to exert an influence in the decades since 1988, a period in which Vermonters have voted for every Democratic presidential candidate.

By 2020 the state was as identified with liberal social causes and political mavericks like Bernie Sanders and Howard Dean as it once was with progressive Republican thinking. Beneath the labels is a similar approach to governance. Despite a centralized administrative structure, Vermont's state government has been kept more accountable than most by the retention of short terms of office, a citizen legislature, and the rhetoric of local control.

Even when Gov. Deane Davis was backing a state land use law in the late 1960s, he called it "creative localism."

Town meeting has a powerful image as the last vestige of direct democracy, holding out hope that self-government remains possible in the age of powerful administrative states. Of course, the image is somewhat overstated, but it can be a form of self-empowerment reminiscent of the early Jeffersonian impulse.

Vermont's "citizen legislature" meets four days a week for up to five months, and House and Senate members often return to other jobs. Because of the size of the state, many drive home at night during sessions. The pay is modest, and the Legislature functions much like a graduate school for motivated students. Some are in training for higher office, but most stay in touch with home base.

The state's political establishment has repeatedly advocated a constitutional amendment to extend the terms of some or all statewide offices to four years. In the late 1950s a Commission to Study State Government—known as the "Little Hoover Commission" for its similarity to a federal effort in the 1940s led by the former president—concluded that forcing candidates to campaign for re-election so often was a waste of money and detrimental to the state's welfare. The necessary amendment failed in the legislature, but was brought back repeatedly over the next decades.

In 1974, at the height of the Watergate scandal, it was voted down on Town Meeting Day.

Gov. Snelling recommended four-year terms for the governor and lieutenant governor "as a team" in his 1983 inaugural address. His rationale was that the "structure and complexity of our society and the value of experienced administrative leadership" had increased. Leaders of both the Republican and Democratic Party supported the proposal, citing the increased expense of campaigns and the need for more continuity in program implementation.

The proposal failed again.

Most other states extended terms of office long ago. Beyond a suspicion of politicians and the power of Vermont traditions, the main reason it has not happened here can be traced directly back to the last of the conventions called by the old Council of Censors. When terms of office were doubled to two years in 1870, the amendment process was also altered. The Legislature would henceforth initiate any constitutional changes, but only once every ten years. This "time lock" provision was later shortened to five-year intervals, but remained a conservative deterrent to rapid changes in the structure and processes of government.

Vermont does not have a provision for referendum by public petition. But the state has played an active role in local politics since 1890, when legislation permitted Australian ballots printed by state government to be used at town meetings. Lawmakers can also request endorsement of a decision in a town meeting referendum. Exercising this authority to seek local opinion led to the enactment of the local option for alcohol in 1902 and death of the proposed Green Mountain Parkway in 1936.

All these traditions—local control, short terms, a citizen legislature—and impulses toward decentralism and even secession reflect a fundamental commitment to autonomy. The original Greek idea is self-rule. Valued for its contribution to the search for truth and the functioning of a self-governing society, autonomy involves making conscious choices.

According to anarchist philosopher Murray Bookchin, who lived in Vermont for three decades, "Self-rule applies to society as a whole. Self-management is the management of villages, neighborhoods, towns, and cities. The technical sphere of life is conspicuously secondary to the social. In the two revolutions that open the modern era of secular politics—the American and French—self-management emerges in the libertarian town meetings that swept from Boston to Charleston and the popular sections that assembled in Parisian quatiers."

In Vermont, the quest for autonomy underpinned the struggle of settlers against outside control during the revolutionary period. Since then, it has fueled campaigns of resistance and sometimes direct challenges to state and federal policies—from the rejection of the Masons, abolition movement and development of new political parties to campaigns for a nuclear freeze and same-sex marriage.

A less progressive aspect is the enduring tension between the desire for local control and the state's authority over education. The Vermont Constitution called for a system of public schools, but education remained uneven and chaotic for years as independent school districts of varying quality popped up across the state. The autonomy of local schools remained the rule until the legislature mandated reforms such as compulsory attendance, effective training of teachers, free textbooks and a fair school tax system. School district autonomy persisted until 1892, when the state turned over power to the towns. But local resistance to state education plans and mandates continued throughout the 20th century.

> "Vermont is a country which abounds in the most active and rebellious race on the continent and hangs like a gathering storm on my left."
>
> – General John Burgoyne, after losing the Battle of Bennington in 1777

Whether or not a tiny state can become a political "David," one that either brings an arrogant power to heel or successfully withdraws, Vermont's past, geography and image suggest qualities and values that have found special expression. Vermont's location, for example, led to tensions with acquisitive neighbors in New York before 1776, and an ambivalent early relationship with the United States.

Harsh weather and small farms made slavery impractical, and many Vermonters opposed it on moral grounds. Its size made it a natural place for enterprises and policies that took advantage of small scale. As Joe Sherman put it, "Here you could simply see the issues more clearly, identify the key players, and still enjoy the view."[120] The largest city still has less than 50,000 people, and even in the 21st century the tallest building is less than 12 stories.

The importance of balance also became apparent early, first in the distribution of state offices between post-revolutionary factions and, after the Republican Party assumed control, in an unofficial system for distributing patronage and electoral power known as the "Mountain Rule." The idea was that occupancy of top state offices should alternate between the east and west sides of the mountains. It started with U.S. Senate seats as soon as Vermont joined the union, and after expanding to include governor and lieutenant governor in 1870, served a purpose for the next 70 plus years. The tradition was combined with another practice, rotation out of office after two terms. Once Vermont adopted two-year terms for statewide offices, also in 1870, no governor served more than two terms until Phil Hoff in the 1960s.

---

120 Joe Sherman, *Fast Track on a Dirt Road*

Vermont gained national notice as an environmentally conscious place during the Hoff years, particularly after the banning of billboards from roads and highways. Even before that, Hoff supported legislation to preserve the scenery, regulate dumps, and increase state oversight. His successor Deane Davis created a Commission on Environmental Control and supported passage of a landmark land-use law. But the state's environmental ethic goes deeper and farther back.

By the 1840s George Perkins Marsh, a scholar, congressman and railroad commissioner, had come to view much of human development as a threat to the natural world. Humanity and nature were interrelated, he said, but wherever men went, the "harmonies of nature" were disturbed. His thinking and book, *Man and Nature*, inspired forest conservation efforts in the late nineteenth century and provided a philosophical foundation for the state's environmental movement in the 1960s and 70s.

As Marsh warned, Vermont's forests began to shrink as the timber industry grew, affecting runoff, wildlife and the basic abundance of the land. In response big landowners began to experiment with a more scientific approach to forest management. A key figure in that effort was Joseph Battell, a wealthy eccentric, legislator, and the state's largest landholder by the 1880s. He deeply appreciated Vermont's natural beauty and pushed for a larger state role in preserving it.

As Gov. Urban Woodbury pressed for conservation in the 1890s, Battell bought up as much forest land as possible, including Camel's Hump and the ridge of the Green Mountains. But it took forest fires and a serious loss of trout to launch a concerted campaign for serious state involvement. Battell and others began granting land to the state, sometimes under the condition that places like Camel's Hump and Mt Mansfield remain open to the public and free from development in perpetuity. A decade before Theodore Roosevelt made conservation a priority, the state had begun buying tracts and taking more responsibility for conserving state resources.

Finding the Way

In a tongue-in-cheek guide to being an authentic Vermonter released in 1983, Frank Bryan and Bill Mares joked that most people would agree "Vermont, like Texas, is more than just a place—it's a state of mind. Vermonters are committed to a certain creed and live by certain values that set them apart. Some people have them. Others do not. Most are somewhat in between. Yet social critics often are content to divide the world into two classes—Real Vermonters and Flatlanders."[121]

The writers acknowledged at the time that the distinctions were already narrowing as the fence between the two types grew "more rickety." In the 21st century those categories have become outdated. Yet mention of Vermont still suggests certain attitudes and sensibilities—community involvement, civil discourse, social concern and tolerance, a shifting mixture of libertarian and egalitarian tendencies.

Even conservative writer David Brooks, who tried to stereotype Burlington as a "Latte Town," admitted it had "a phenomenally busy public square—arts councils, school-to-work collaborations, environmental groups, preservation groups, community-supported agriculture, anti-development groups, and ad-hoc activist groups… The result is an interesting mixture of liberal social concern and paleoconservative effort to ward off encroaching modernism."[122]

Since the 1970s the state has been a testing ground for alternative approaches to politics, but the many ex-urbanite professionals and members of the counterculture who have helped to make that possible were building on a solid foundation. Active dissent began before the American Revolution, as early settlers organized to declare themselves free of British rule and exploitation by land speculators. It continued with the re-election of Matthew Lyon in defiance of the Alien and Sedition Acts, resistance to an embargo of Britain and the War of 1812, rejection of Masonic secrecy and Town Meeting defeat of the Green Mountain Parkway during the New Deal. This pattern reflects a libertarian streak that has resisted the pull of modern liberalism.

---

121 Frank Bryan and Bill Mares, *Real Vermonters Don't Milk Goats*, New England Press, 1983
122 David Brooks, The Rise of the Latte Town, *The Weekly Standard*, September 15, 1997

The Volkswagen bus was one of the favorite vehicles for young Vermont progressives in the 1960s. After buying this one and moving to Shaftsbury, artist Greg Winterhalter learned that it had previously been used in the film adaptation of Arlo Guthrie's *Alice's Restaurant*.

Despite relative isolation before the arrival of railroads, telephones, highways and instantaneous global communication, many Vermonters also expressed an egalitarian belief in equality and tolerance that made it fertile ground for revival-era religious experiments and persistent leadership in the fight to end slavery. Although the state was sometimes slow to respond, as with the decision to extend voting rights to women, or even reactionary when handling union activism, the tradition re-asserted itself in Ernest Gibson's expansion of social services in the 1940s, the peaceful assimilation of counterculture immigrants in the late 1960s and the landmark legislative decision in 2009 to legalize same-sex marriage.

Concern has frequently extended beyond the protection and defense of state residents and resources. Ecological consciousness, rooted in Vermont's rural character and a practical understanding of interdependence, has made it an advocate for national and global action to reduce pollution, conserve limited resources, and protect endangered habitats. Skepticism about wasteful military spending and the logic of war, combined with the symbolic power of Town Meeting, helped it to spur national reconsideration of the nation's nuclear weapons stockpiles and intentions.

In 2012, despite winning a legal battle to stay open, the owners of the Vermont Yankee nuclear plant, one of the country's oldest reactors, finally accepted what critics and protesters had demanded for decades and the Senate finally voted in 2010: the plant should close.

In a long-shot 2008 campaign for state attorney general, writer and lawyer Charlotte Dennett promised to prosecute Pres. George W. Bush for murder if she was elected. Dennett was running as a Progressive Party candidate against William Sorrell, a popular incumbent who had held the job since 1997.

The previous year Vermont's Senate agreed that the actions of Bush and Vice President Dick Cheney in taking the country to war in Iraq raised "serious questions of constitutionality," and passed a resolution calling on the U.S. Congress to impeach them. "There is no better state to bring this forward," Dennett said, pointing to the facts that, as in the Civil War, Vermont had again lost more soldiers per capita than any other state, while voters at 36 Town Meetings had called for Bush's impeachment.

Dennett's electoral campaign wasn't successful. But it made a point and, like past challenges to prevailing national policies, served as an act of conscience in keeping with long-standing Vermont values.

The following winter, on March 4, 2009, voters in Brattleboro and Marlboro backed her up, passing a symbolic resolution that instructed their town police to arrest Bush and Cheney for "crimes against our Constitution" if they ever stepped foot in either town, and then "extradite them to other authorities that may reasonably contend to prosecute them."

It sounded like Ethan Allen—and another apt example of the Vermont Way.

And what is that Way? Based on Vermont's unusual history and remarkable leaders, it looks like a delicate dance of sovereignty and solidarity, independence and mutual aid, or as the motto adopted as part of Vermont's Great Seal in 1788 says, "Freedom and Unity."

It has evolved and adapted when necessary. Frequently a laboratory for autonomy, citizen government and local democracy,

Vermont has become a mixture of pragmatism and idealism, tolerant, concerned and yet sometimes wary of newcomers or higher authorities, and naturally drawn to solutions that stress conservation and balance, civil liberties and human scale.

Epilogue

So, Vermont is different from other places. But that doesn't confer immunity from the forces that have often shaped American history or continue to fuel its divisions. While movements like the Tea Party and white nationalism haven't gained a big enough foothold in the state to put leaders in power, systemic racism and class conflict have underpinned many of its debates. The political balance of power has shifted from Republican to Democrat, but in many communities concerns about injustice and inequality have deepened at the same time.

Key events in 2020 underline this dynamic, a year in which the COVID-19 crisis, economic instability and rising demands for racial justice impacted daily life. Bernie Sanders was running for president again, but his campaign hit an electoral roadblock by March. In truth, the barriers went up much earlier, when some Democratic thought leaders made up their minds that he was too risky to be the party's nominee. Many defensively declared themselves capitalists, or at least deeply skeptical about socialism.

A notable exception was Pete Buttigieg, the Indiana mayor who was also running for president. In a high school essay he once praised Sanders for his courage in describing himself as a socialist. At the time, he noted, most Democrats even shied away from the word liberal. "Even though he has lived through a time in which an admitted socialist could not act in a film, let alone hold a congressional seat," he wrote, "Sanders is not afraid to be candid about his political persuasion."[123]

---

[123] Greg Guma, Poisoned Press: The Original Plot to Stop Bernie Sanders… and Why It Didn't Work, *VTDigger.com*, April 14, 2019

In 2000, that argument won Buttigieg the Profiles in Courage Essay contest, sponsored by the John F. Kennedy Library in Boston. But in 2020 there was another insurmountable obstacle—the preference of Black thought leaders and voters for Joe Biden in too many primary races. Not such a shock, with Sanders' preference for class analysis and his home state still one of the whitest.

At about the same moment Gov. Phil Scott declared a state of emergency in response to what had become a global pandemic. People became angry or frightened about the severe impacts on the economy and their personal lives. But unlike in some states, most Vermonters managed to stay calm, and maintained a balance that produced the lowest COVID-19 case rate in the country by summer.

After the police murder of George Floyd, a Black man from Minneapolis, thousands of Black, white, Indigenous and people of color gathered in communities across the nation and the state, calling out the names of those killed by police. Over the summer, more than a thousand people rallied in Burlington to demand changes in law enforcement. That led to a 30 percent cut in the police budget, with money redirected to social services.

Burlington's city council also declared racism a public health emergency. A proposed state legislative resolution echoed that conclusion, noting that Black, Indigenous and people of color accounted for a disproportionate number of Vermont's COVID-19 cases.

According to J.H. R, 6, introduced in 2021, people in those communities were also less likely than other Vermonters to have a primary care doctor, and more likely to have poor mental health, experience homelessness and live in poverty. But in response, a Black Lives Matter mural in Montpelier was defaced. In Bennington, four people—one a white supremacist— were arrested for harassing peaceful protesters.

Polarization, inequality, and distrust had built up for decades, but intensified and metastasized after the presidential election of Donald Trump. As Adam Server put it in *The Cruelty Is the Point*, his book on Trump's impact, "Once malice is embraced as a virtue, it is impossible to contain."[124]

---

[124] Adam Serwer, *The Cruelty Is the Point: The Past, Present, and Future of Trump's America*, One World, 2021

"He says what we're thinking and what we want to say," acknowledged one supporter at a 2018 Trump rally. The sentiment echoed what followers of fascist, authoritarian and white supremacist leaders have felt for a century. But Max Misch, a transplant to Bennington from Queens, N.Y., didn't need encouragement in 2016 when he first launched a relentless campaign of racist trolling and harassment against another recent newcomer, Kiah Morris.

From Chicago, Morris had come to town around the same time as Misch. In 2014 she ran for a seat in Vermont's House of Representatives and won. Her victory made her the only Black woman lawmaker in the Statehouse, and one of only about 285 Black people in Bennington County.

It apparently also made her a target.

In August 2018, Morris announced that she was dropping her reelection campaign, and cited the harassment by Misch as a reason. It had resumed after a stalking order expired, she explained, and didn't stop even after she decided not to seek re-election. In September, Morris and her husband also reported that a group of young people knocked on their windows and banged on doors. When police downplayed their complaint, the couple's distrust of law enforcement deepened.

At this point Attorney General T.J. Donovan entered the picture, announcing that his office would conduct a review to see if criminal laws had been broken. In January 2019, he announced the results to an overflow crowd at Bennington's Beth El Synagogue. Unfortunately, the decision was that the state would not bring criminal charges against Misch, but instead create a Bias Incident Reporting System. The initiative's goal was to develop a process for police to work with groups like the Human Rights Commission and the civil rights divisions of state and federal prosecutorial offices on bias-related incidents.

Many racial justice leaders were not impressed, saying it failed to address the underlying problems.

Donovan had barely finished explaining the report's findings when Misch entered. He was wearing a T-shirt that prominently displayed Pepe the Frog, a cartoon character used by right-wing extremists as a symbol of anti-Semitism and racism.

In April 2021, a local settlement was reached on the harassment case requiring the town of Bennington to pay $137,500 to Kiah

Morris's family. Despite the attention the case attracted, however, little changed in Bennington or Vermont.

Likewise, despite Trump's defeat in November 2020, the prospects for racial justice and the viability of democracy remained in doubt. Much of the blame was placed on disinformation and the chaotic power of populism, the latter identified with the rise of both Trump and Sanders, as well as the European movement "Brexit" and even the attraction to authoritarian leaders.

But the common description of populism is a semantic fiction, a set of mistaken assumptions, stereotypes, and false narratives that ignore the movement's real history, confuse it with political sectarianism, and betray a contempt for the public's discontent with elites and the status quo. Much opposition to populist movements is rooted in an underlying pessimism about popular sovereignty, the "dangerous" power of the masses. It's easier to dismiss them as a mindless mob.

In 1891, the first populist movement in the United States began with the rise of the People's Party, an electoral revolt that sought "equal rights to all, special privileges to none." It was the last serious third-party movement in the U.S., an alliance of farmers and the labor movement that called for class solidarity and the end of poverty and debt, and envisioned working people coming together against monopolies and corrupt political regimes. Contrary to misinformation, it also favored human and women's rights and open immigration, and opposed imperialism.

Sounding radical at first, many populist ideas ultimately became mainstream. Several became laws, including direct election of senators, railroad regulation, price supports for farmers, and a progressive income tax. As Thomas Frank writes in *The People, No: A Brief History of Anti-Populism*, the movement reached its peak during the presidency of Franklin D. Roosevelt.

"Populism is what strengthened the unions and built middle-class democracy," Frank writes. It helped Roosevelt win four presidential terms and gave Democrats a long-running Congressional majority.[125] It also inspired Bernie Sanders' updated vision of a working-class alliance that could confront the power of billionaires and big corporations.

---

125 Thomas Frank, *The People, No: A Brief History of Anti-Populism*, Metropolitan, 2020

By the time Sanders ran for president many white working-class voters had given up on both the Democratic and Republican Parties. Instead, they turned against their own economic interests, embracing a false media messiah and a toxic cultural conservatism: a mixture of guns and God, combined with fear of "the others"—gay people, immigrants, people of color, basically anyone who seemed "different" than them. A defensive narrative, often misleading, triumphed over facts and reason. It didn't help that Democrats had failed to deliver on economic issues.

As I write, there are early signs that building a new progressive majority is possible. But certainly not inevitable. And it will have to be multiracial, while also addressing both class and systemic racism. According to Heather McGhee, although racism disproportionally hurts Black people, it also affects white folks. "Black people and other people of color certainly lost out when we weren't able to invest more in the aftermath of the Great Recession," she writes. "But did white people win? No, for the most part they lost right along with the rest of us."[126]

Her prescription is cross-racial organizing around raising the minimum wage and other issues: union organizing of service and assembly line workers, even in the south; welcoming refugees who can reopen businesses and re-energize depressed communities; and fighting for a "solidarity dividend" in the form of better social protections for all races.

In 2017, McGhee and others launched the Race-Class Narrative Project, which examines and tests the language used to discuss such matters. Researchers have concluded that presenting ideas with the recognition of both race and class is more effective than either a "racial fear message" or "colorblind economic populism." But it won't be easy. Many white people will adamantly resist or retreat into denialism; so may some Black activists and others who are directly and deeply focused on racial justice.

Ian Haney-Lopez, author of *Dog Whistle Politics* and *Merge Left*, looks toward transracial unity strategies and new language that can persuade both groups that they actually need each other. For centuries, he explains, "our greatest heroes—radicals like W.E.B. Du

---

[126] Heather McGhee, *The Sum of Us: What Racism Costs Everyone and How We Can Prosper Together*, One World, 2021

Bois, Martin Luther King Jr. and Cesar Chavez—have insisted that American salvation requires cross-racial alliances."[127]

Such insights could be keys to creating the next progressive era.

---

127 Ian Haney-Lopez, *Merge Left: Fusing Race and Class, Winning Elections and Saving America*, New Press, 2019

Bibliography

Jonathan Alter, *The Left's Mister Right*, Newsweek, Aug. 11, 2003.

Consuelo Northrup Bailey, *Leaves Before the Wind: The Autobiography of Vermont's Own Daughter*, George Little Press, 1976.

T. D. Seymour Bassett, *The Leading Villages of Vermont in 1840*, Vermont History, Vol. 26, No. 3, 1958.

T. D. Seymour Bassett, *Nature's Nobleman: Justin Morrill, A Victorian Politician*, Vermont History, Vol. 30, No. 1, 1962.

Cynthia D. Bittinger, *Vermont Women, Native American & African Americans: Out of the Shadows of History*, History Press, 2012.

David Brooks, *The Rise of the Latte Town*, The Weekly Standard, Sept. 15, 1997.

Frank Bryan, *Yankee Politics in Rural Vermont*, University Press of New England, 1974

Frank Bryan and Bill Mares, *Real Vermonters Don't Milk Goats*, New England Press, 1983.

Frank Bryan and John McClaughry, *The Vermont Papers: Recreating Democracy on a Human Scale*, Chelsea Green, 1990.

Edward Brynn, *Patterns of Dissent: Vermont Opposition to the War of 1812*, Vermont History, Vol. 40. No. 1, 1972.

Susan Clark and Frank Bryan, *All Those in Favor: Rediscovering the Secrets of Town Meeting and Community*, RavenMark, 2005.

John Cloud, *The Cool Passion of Dr. Dean*, Time, Aug. 11, 2003.

Roby Colodny, *Labor in Barre, 1900–1941*, Vermont's Untold History, Public Occurrence, 1976.

Howard Dean, *Winning Back America*, Simon and Schuster, 2003.

Albert R. Dowden, *John Gregory Smith*, Vermont History, Vol. 32, No. 2, 1964.

William Doyle, *The Vermont Political Tradition*, Northlight Studio Press, 1984.

Denise Helen Dunbar, *Black Males in the Green Mountains*, Peter Lang, 2013.

Richard Eder, *Aiken Suggests U.S. Say It Has Won the War*, New York Times, Oct. 20, 1966.

Thomas Frank, *The People, No: A Brief History of Anti-Populism*, Metropolitan, 2020.

David Hackett Fischer, *Champlain's Dream*, Simon and Schuster, 2008.

Robert C. Gilmore, *The Vermont Marble Company: An Entrepreneurial Study, 1869–1939*, New England Social Studies Bulletin, Vol. 14, No. 2, 1956.

Hal Goldman, *James Taylor's Progressive Vision: The Green Mountain Parkway*, Vermont History, Vol. 63, 1995.

Greg Guma, *Mayor James Burke*, Burlington Free Press, Vermonter, Sunday, Jan. 8, 1984.

Greg Guma, *Poisoned Press: The Original Plot to Stop Bernie Sanders . . . and Why It Didn't Work*, VTDigger.com, April 14, 2019.

Greg Guma, *Spirits of Desire*, Maverick Books, 2005.

Samuel B. Hand and D. Gregory Sanford, *Carrying Water on Both Shoulders: George D. Aiken's 1936 Gubernatorial Campaign in Vermont*, Vermont History, Vol. 43, No. 4, 1975.

Ian Haney-Lopez, *Merge Left: Fusing Race and Class, Winning Elections and Saving America*, New Press, 2019.

William Haviland and Marjory Power, *The Original Vermonters: Native Inhabitants, Past and Present*, University of New England Press, 1981.

Phil Hoff and Greg Guma, *A Clash of Giants*, Vermont Affairs, 1987.

Edward Swift Isham, *Ethan Allen: A Study in Civic Authority*, Address to the Vermont Historical Society, Vermont House Chamber, November 2, 1898.

Otto T. Johnson, *Nineteen-Six in Vermont*, privately printed, May 1944.

Richard M. Judd, *The New Deal in Vermont: Its Impacts and Aftermath*, Garland Publishing, 1979.

Bruce Levine, *Thaddeus Stevens: Civil War Revolutionary, Fighter for Racial Justice*, Simon & Schuster, 2021.

David McCullough, *John Adams*, Simon & Schuster, 2001.

Heather McGhee, *The Sum of Us: What Racism Costs Everyone and How We Can Prosper Together*, One World, 2021.

Walter Russell Mead, *The Tea Party and American Foreign Policy*, Foreign Affairs, March/April 2011.

Lewis H. Meader, *The Council of Censors in Vermont*, address to the Vermont Historical Society, Vermont House Chamber, Nov. 2, 1898.

Messages and Papers of the Presidents, Bureau of National Literature, 1911.

H. Nicholas Muller and John Duffy, *Jedidiah Burchard and Vermont's "New Measure" Revivals*, Vermont History, Vol. 46, No. 1, 1978.

H. Nicholas Muller III, *Early Vermont State Government: Oligarchy or Democracy?, 1778–1815*. From *Growth and Development of Government in Vermont*, Vermont Academy of Arts and Sciences, Occasional Paper #5, 1970.

Andrew and Edith Nuquist, *Vermont State Government and Administration*, University of Vermont, 1966.

Daniel Okrent, *Last Call: The Rise and Fall of Prohibition*, Scribner, 2010.

Neal R. Pierce, *The New England States*, W.W. Norton, 1976.

Proceedings of the Anti-Masonic State Convention, Montpelier, June 26–27, 1833, Knapp & Jewett Printers.

Edwin C. Rozwenc, *Agriculture and Politics in the Vermont Tradition*, Vermont Quarterly, Vol. 17, No. 4, 1949.

Jo Schneiderman, *Beyond Midwifery and Motherhood*, Vermont's Untold History, Public Occurrence, 1976.

Jo Scheiderman, *Clarina Nichols: Rediscovering Vermont's Common Sense Feminist*, Inroads, 1982.

Adam Serwer, *The Cruelty Is the Point: The Past, Present, and Future of Trump's America*, One World, 2021.

Joe Sherman, *Fast Track on a Dirt Road, Vermont Transformed 1945–1990*, Countryman Press, 1991.

Michael Sherman, Gene Sessions and P. Jeffrey Potash, *Freedom and Unity: A History of Vermont*, Vermont Historical Society, 2004.

Hannah Silverstein, *No Parking: Vermont Rejects the Green Mountain Parkway*, Vermont History, Vol. 63, 1995.

Sustainability and Growth Center Team, *The History of Sprawl in Chittenden County*, Champlain Initiative, 1999.

Stephen C. Terry, *Say We Won and Get Out: George D. Aiken and the Vietnam War*, Center for Research on Vermont/ White River Press, 2020.

Hunter S. Thompson, *Fear and Loathing at Rolling Stone*, Simon & Schuster, 2011.

David Wallechinsky and Irving Wallace, *The People's Almanac*, Doubleday, 1975.

Harold Fisher Wilson, *The Hill Country of Northern New England: Its Social and Economic History, 1790–1930*, AMS Press, 1967.

Rick Winston, *A Sinister Poison: The Red Scare Comes to Bethel*, Vermont History, Vol. 40, No. 1, 2012.

Rick Winston, *Red Scare in the Green Mountains: Vermont in the McCarthy Era, 1946–1960*, Rootstock Publishing, 2018.

Frederick Wiseman, *The Abenaki and the Winooski*, from The Mills at Winooski Falls, Onion River Press, 2000.

Illustrations

Photos by Greg Guma appear on the cover and the following pages:
viii, 6, 8, 18, 45, 71, 82, 112, 166, 176, 179, 181, 189, 196, 199, 218, 217, 220, 222, 224, 229, 236, 242, 245, 248, 259, 262

Other illustration sources and the pages on which they appear:
Anarchist Agency — 125
Courtesy of Bill Barton — 188
Courtesy of Paul Boisvert — 76
Bureau of National Literature — 12, 16, 40, 52, 54, 69, 86, 88, 94
Courtesy of Mrs. Karl Cask — 114, 117, 127, 129, 130
Church of Jesus Christ of Latter-Day Saints — 90
Collection of Greg Guma — 56, 104, 136, 208, 209
Harper's — 36
Courtesy of Phil Hoff — 163
Inroads — 35, 75
Library of Congress — 60, 92, 96
Courtesy of George Little — 73
New York Herald — 154
Courtesy of the Oneida Community Mansion House — 48, 49
Public Occurrence — 14, 22, 31, 98, 134
Courtesy of Rob Swanson — 207
University of Vermont — 43, 62, 118, 149, 156
Collection of U.S. House — 10
Vanguard Press — 168, 179, 203

Vermont Historical Society — 28, 67, 106
The Vermont Movie — 142, 144
Vermont Public Radio — 158
Vermont Times — 215
Courtesy of David Wasco — 183

About the Author

Greg Guma grew up in New York City, and moved to Vermont in 1968. He has a B.S. from Syracuse University and an M.Ed. from the University of Vermont. He has been a journalist, editor, educator and administrator, a community organizer, bookstore owner, novelist and CEO of a national broadcast network.

Also by Greg Guma

Fiction
Spirits of Desire
Dons of Time
Inquisitions (and Other Un-American Activities)

Non-Fiction
The People's Republic: Vermont and the Sanders Revolution
Uneasy Empire: Repression, Globalization, and What We Can Do
Fake News: Journalism in the Age of Deceptions
Planet Pacifica: Progressive Media's Fragile Democracy

Digital
Progressive Eclipse: Bernie, Burlington and the Movement That Changed Vermont
Big Lies: Warping Reality and Undermining Democracy
Green Mountain Politics

As editor/writer/producer

If It Makes You Want to Learn (film)

Bread & Puppet: Stories of Struggle and Faith (photo book, with Susan Green)

Nonviolent Warriors: Dave Dellinger and the Power of the People (CD set)

Journey Home: Accompaniment in Guatemala (script & narration, with Robin Lloyd)

Passport to Freedom: A Guide for World Citizens (with Garry Davis)

Reign of Error (illustrations & quotations, with Dan Florentino)

Celia's Land (novel, with Georgia Davis Powers)

Informed Dissent (Pacifica radio series)

Fragile Paradise (film)

Index

Abenaki, 19–27
    epidemics, 23
    hunting and fishing licenses, 27
    petition to legislature, 24
    recognition, 26–27
accountability, 63, 160, 212, 253
Act 250, 201, 204, 226
Adams, Abigail, 12
Adams, John, 12–17
Adams, John Quincy, 58
Advent Herald, The, 50
agriculture, 68, 82, 99,
    abandoned farms, 105
    commercial farming, 69
    dairy production, 107–108
Aiken, George, 141, 147–149
    as governor, 148
    in Senate, 151–152
    political alliance, 150
    race for governor, 147
alcohol, 48, 50–51, 66, 77, 160, 255
    abstinence, 49
    local option, 45, 118, 119, 225, 254
Alien and Sedition Acts, 13, 15
All Those in Favor, 223
Allen, Ethan, 14, 29, 32, 37–38, 44, 253
Allen, Heman, 30, 36, 44
Allen, Ira, 30, 39, 43, 44
Alling Enterprises, 171
Alter, Jonathan, 230
American Party, 86
American Plan, 136–137
Anthony, Susan B., 77

anti-communism, 156
Anti-Masons, 56–64
    and secret oaths, 58, 63
    decline of, 64
    elected in Vermont, 61-62
    John Quincy Adams, 58
anti-nuclear activism, 188-189
Anti-Slavery Society, 51
Arkansas, 17
Army-McCarthy hearings, 157-158
Arthur, Chester, 88, 93–95
    Mormon attacks, 95
    Vice President, 93
Association of General Contractors, 198
Ashe, Tim, 244–245, 246
Australian ballot, 221, 224, 255
autonomy, 30, 39, 165, 225, 253–254

Bailey, Consuelo Northrup, 5, 80
Baker v. Vermont, 229
Baltimore, 35, 61
Barre, 101–101, 119, 124, 133–137,
    agitation, 136–139
    socialist mayor, 133
Barre Opera House, 135
Battell, Joseph, 257
Beard, Edna L., 80
Bennington, 20, 29, 32, 42, 51, 73,
    119, 176–184, 185–187, 265
Bennington Banner, iv, v, 178–179
Bennington College, 178, 184

resentment of, 180
Bennington School of Dance, 177
Bergman, Gene, 210
Bible Communism, 49
Bigelow, Walter, 118, 120, 121, 127
bike path, 228
Billings, Franklin, 163
    House Speaker, 164
Bischof, John, 184
Blanchard, Jane, 78
Bloomer, Amelia, 79
Board of Agriculture, 105
Bookchin, Murray, v, 212, 255
Boston Chamber of Commerce, 107
Boston Tea Party, 34
Bouricius, Terry, 208
Bove, Richard, 206
Branon, Frank, 162
Brattleboro, 22, 23, 72, 74, 164, 260
Brecht on Brecht, 182–183
Brecht, Bertolt, 182
Breckinridge, John C., 92
Britton, Nan, 96
Bristol, 107
Brokaw, Tom, 232
Brown v. The Board of Education of Topeka, 158
Brown, Rufus, 120
Bryan, Frank, v, 5, 9, 146, 221–224, 235, 258
Buchanan, James, 91
Buckley, T. Garry, 163
    Lieutenant Governor, 164
Building Trades Union, 129, 198
Burchard, Jedediah, 47–48
Bureau of Publicity, 106
Burlington, ii, 48, 54, 65, 72, 83, 101, 113–116, 120–123, 127, 162, 169, 192, 201–203, 205–210, 228, 242, 246, 264
    board of aldermen, 206
    Dean presidential announcement, 230
    Whig Party Convention, 83
Burlington City Council. See Board of Aldermen, 114, 206, 222
Burlington Free Press, The, ii, 118, 121, 124, 130, 143, 145, 172, 195, 243
Burlington Gas Light Company, 115
Burlington Light and Power, 115
Burlington light plant, 114, 121
Burlington progressives, 244, 246, 149–250
Burlington Traction Company, 117
Burr, Aaron, 15–16
Bush, George W., 260
Buttigieg, Pete, 263

Caledonia County, 61
Carrara, Italy, 61, 100
Carter, Harvey, 185–187
Casey, Leo, 148
Cavendish, 4
Central Labor Union, 101
Central Vermont Public Service Corporation, 200
Central Vermont Railroad, 106, 115
Chicago, Ill., 92, 93, 95, 227
Chittenden County, 172, 202
Chittenden County Correctional Facility, 198
Chittenden County Democratic Committee, 228
Chittenden County Republicans, 169
Chittenden, Martin, 237
Chittenden, Thomas, 7, 41
citizen legislature, 5, 224, 253, 255
Citizens for Responsible Growth, 202
Citizens Party, 115, 128, 206, 208
Citizens Waterfront Group, 228
civil unions, 229
Civil War, 71–72
    and Chester Arthur, 93
Clavelle, Peter, 242
Clay, Henry, 59, 83, 90
Clement, Percival, 117–120
    alliance with James Burke, 117
    and fusion politics, 119
    campaign for governor, 120
    as governor, 80
    war with Proctors, 118
climate, 3, 65, 77, 246, 249
Clinton, Bill, 214
Club for Growth, 231
Colby, Michael, 153
Colden, Cadwallader, 29
Commission on Country Life, 26

Index

Commission on Environmental Control, 257
Commission to Study State Government. *See* Little Hoover Commission, 225, 254
Commonwoman, 192
Communist Party, 159
Community College of Vermont, 211
Congressional Progressive Caucus, 217
Connecticut River, 19, 21, 22, 41
Consolidated Electric, 115
Constitution Party, 92
Continental Congress, 30, 35, 36, 38–39
    and Vermont statehood, 41
Coolidge, Calvin, 25, 95–97
    and business interests, 97
    and right to strike, 95
    in Harding administration, 96
Coolidge, Carlos, 84
Councils of Safety, 30, 37
counterculture, 258
Craig, William, 171
Craven, Jay, 3
Crispe, A. Luke, 163
    reapportionment lawsuit, 164

Danville, 59–60, 79
David-Friedman, Ellen, 212
Davis, Deane, 152, 185, 198, 225, 253, 257
de Champlain, Samuel, 19, 20
Dean, Howard, 174, 237–234
    50 State Strategy, 233
    and Iraq, 227
    as governor, 228
    critics, 231, 233
    Deaniacs, 232
    education, 227–228
    in state legislature, 228
    Internet strategy, 230
    Iowa Caucus, 231–232
    national coverage, 232-233
    on gay marriage, 229–230
    scream incident, 233
Debs, Eugene, 96, 133
decentralism, 9, 255
Declaration of Independence, 36–37, 39
Defense of Marriage Act, 229

Democratic National Committee, 234
Democratic Party, 85, 91, 127, 162, 200, 206, 216, 242, 244
Dennett, Charlotte, 260
Department of Labor, 103
DeWolfe, Florence, 96
Donovan, T.J., 265
Dorset, 35–36, 99
Dorset Convention, 35
Douglas, James, 242, 245
Douglas, Stephen, 91–93
    1860 presidential race, 92
Driscoll, Carina, 250

Earth Day, 184–187
East India Company, 34
Eclipse, The, 193
education, 6, 27, 51, 54, 55, 73, 107–108, 135, 158, 165, 211, 228, 243, 255
    and Bennington, 178–184
    and Republicans, 172, 225
    and women, 76–79
    funding, 138
    industrial, 167, 225
    Vermont Design for, 181
elections, 7, 37, 59, 62, 77, 159, 162, 223, 247
Electoral College, 91
    Roosevelt vote, 147
Eli Copper Mine, 101
Emerson, Lee, 156
eugenics movement, 25–26, 131-132
exceptionalism, 9, 17, 86, 235

F-35 Fighter Jet, 249
Fairbanks, Erastus, 73
Fairfield, 93
Fellows Gear, 102
Fillmore, Millard, 239
Fisher, Dorothy Canfield, 9
Flanders, Ralph, 155–160
    break with Republicans, 159
    itemized complaints, 159
    mocks McCarthy, 157
    religious beliefs, 155
Food & Water, 153

forests, 4, 65, 257
Fort Dummer, 21, 23
France, 4, 12, 13, 24, 44
Frankenthaler, Helen, 177
Franklin, Benjamin, 13
Free Soil Party, 84
Freedom & Unity: The Vermont Movie,
    v, 3, 145
Freemasons, 57–64
    and Henry Clay, 59
    in Pennsylvania, 60–61, 63–64
Frémont, John Charles, 86
French Canadians, 26, 114, 113, 132,
    135, 139, 205
Freyne, Peter, 194, 212, 243
Friends of Equal Rights, 51
Froines, John, 189
Fugitive Slave Act, 85, 239
Fusion, 113, 117–120, 241-144, 247

Garfield, James, 93–94
Garibaldi, Guiseppe, 133
Garrison, William LLoyd, 51, 53
gay marriage, 9, 229–230, 234
General Electric, 197
Gibson III, Ernest, 163
Gibson, Jr, Ernest, 150
    accusations of communist leanings,
        157
    governor, 151
    reforms, 151
    social services expanded, 150-151
Gibson, Sr, Ernest, 150
Gillies, Paul, 136
Gitlin, Todd, 108–151
Goldman, Emma, 123–126
Gold Rush, 70
Goodkind, Steve, 250
Gordon, Robert, 136
Gore, Al, 230
Gorges, Ferdinando, 20
Graham, Martha, 177
Granai, Cornelius, 133,134,
    work with strikers, 138
Grange movement, 108
Granite Cutters International, 133
Great Depression, 97, 102, 143
Great Seal, 260

Greater Burlington Industrial
    Corporation (GBIC), 169–170
Green Mountain Boys, 12, 30–32,
    35–36, 177
Green Mountain Parkway, 140–146
    media coverage, 143
    referendum, 145
Green Mountain Parkway Act, 144
Green Mountain Power, 116, 201
Green Mountain Television, 169
Green Up Day, 185
Greenberg, Clement, 177
Grey Lock, 23
Griswold, Roger, 11
Guatemala coup, 159
Gulf War, 118
Gun Owners of Vermont, 243

Habeas Corpus Law, 239
Hackel, Stella, 171
Hackett, Luther, 152
Haiti, 12
Haldimand negotiations, 39
Harding, Warren G., 95
    death, 96
Harrison, William Henry, 64, 83
Hartness, James, 155
Hawley, Donley C., 213
Hayes, Thomas, 185
Haynes, Lemuel, 53
health practitioners, 78
Highgate, 43
highway construction, 126, 137, 202,
    205, 225
Hines, Wanda, 246
Hiss, Alger, 157
Hoff, Phil, 161–167
    court appointments, 164
    fighting racism, 161–162
    on local control, 165
    young Turks, 163
Hoffer, Doug, 244
Holbrook, Frederick, 73
Home for Colored Orphans, 77
Hoover, Herbert, 97, 254
Howe, Julia Ward, 80, 101
Howes, Harvey, 80
Humphreys, David, 67

Illinois, 85, 89, 91
    Joseph Smith shot in, 90–91
immigrants, iii, 12, 25, 74, 85, 95, 100, 133, 139, 259
independence, 5, 29, 33, 35–39, 70, 135, 145, 192, 238
Industrial Workers of the World, 135–136
Irasburg, 162
Isle La Motte, 21, 118
Italy, 4, 11, 135

Jackson, Andrew, 58, 89
Jackson, J. Holmes, 127–128
Jackson, Jesse, 212
Jarvis, William, 67
Jefferson, Thomas, 15
    electoral votes, 15–16
Jeffords, James, iii, 5, 152–153, 185, 189, 228, 241, 243
Jenison, Silas, 62
Johnson, Rev. David, 162
Jones and Lamson, 101-102
Joseph, Joseph E., 185, 187

Kake Walk, 55
Kansas, 77
Kentucky Resolve, 239
Kerry, John, 232,
    New Hampshire primary, 233
Keyser, F. Ray, 163, 197
Kiss, Bob, 210, 246, 247
Klu Klux Klan, 54
Know-Nothings, 86
Kunin, Madeleine, 80–81, 210–212
    record as governor, 211
    Sanders criticism, 211

Lake Champlain, 19, 20, 35, 65, 121, 228
Larrow, Robert, 162
    reapportionment, 164
Law, William, 90
Lawrence, MA, 135
Lawson, John, 136–138
Leahy, Patrick, 213, 249

versus Snelling 172–173
Lee, Mother Ann, 78
Leddy, Bernard, 163
Liberal Extracts, 57
Liberty Party, 55, 83
Liberty Union Party, 199–200
Lincoln, Abraham, 92
    and secession, 93
    votes in 1860, 92
Little Hoover Commission, 225, 254
local control, 5, 165, 180, 255
local option, 45, 118, 119, 225, 254
Luntz, Frank, 232
Lyman, Elias, 116, 120
Lyndon State College, 256
Lyon, Matthew, 11–17
    presidential vote, 16

Madison, James, 15, 239
Maine, State of, 3, 20, 180, 198, 240
Mallory, Richard, 152
Man and Nature, 257
Mansfield, Mike, 151
manufacturing, 65, 72, 97, 102, 105, 137, 151, 197, 249
maple syrup, 2, 5, 107
Maple Tree Place, 202, 203
marble, 99–100, 117, 119
    and federal buildings, 100
marble workers, 98–99
marble workers strike, 143, 197
Marlboro, 78, 260
Marsh, George Perkins, 257
Marshall, John, 158
Mason, Steven Thompson, 15
Massachusetts Bay Colony, 8
McCarthy, Joseph, 154–160
    censure, 159
    Flanders resolution, 159
McClaughry, John, 5, 9, 193, 235
McKibben, Bill, 238
McKinley, William, 113, 118
meetups, 230
Merinos, 67–68
Mexican War, 83
Meyer, William, 163, 200
Middlebury Institute, 237
Milk War, 107

281

Miller, William, 46, 50
modern art colony, 177
Monroe, James, 15, 17
Montpelier, 54, 59, 72, 85, 124, 185, 201, 247, 264
Moonlight in Vermont, 1–2
Morgan, William, 57, 58
Mormons, 89
    and Chester Arthur, 95
    and polygamy, 91, 95
Morrill, Justin, 108
Morris, Kiah, 265
Moser, Howard Frank, 3
Mount Anthony, 20
Mountain Rule, 150, 256
Mt. Anthony Union High School, 178
Mt. Mansfield, 20, 257
Muller III, H. Nicholas, 6
myths, 5, 24, 145, 165, 224

Nader, Ralph, 232
National Abortion Rights Action League (NARAL), 153
National Committee for an Effective Congress, 159
National Guard, 101, 138, 249
National Hydraulic Company, 101
National Park Service, 144, 145
National Reform Party, 89
National Republican Club, 148
National Republicans, 58–59
Nauvoo community, 89
    riot, 91
Naylor, Thomas, 235, 238
Nebraska Act, 85
Nelson, Gaylord, 184
neutrality, 42
New Connecticut, 37
New Deal, 102, 103, 142, 147–148, 258
    Gibson supported, 150
New England Farmer, The, 73
New Hampshire Grants, 29, 32
New Hampshire, State of, 3, 4, 19, 20–22, 24, 29, 32, 34, 38, 55, 91, 188, 232
New York, 1, 4, 15, 16, 20, 24, 29, 47, 65, 70, 78, 99, 161, 256
    and Bennington arts, 177
    and Chester Arthur, 93
    and Henry Clay, 59
    and Clarina Nichols, 77
    and Joseph Smith, 89
    and Vermont statehood, 43
    Anti-Masons, 57–59
    Constitution, 36
    Grants, 30
    in American Revolution, 32, 34, 35–36, 38, 57, 58
    land seizures, 30
    Oneida community, 49
    Rutland Marble, 99
    youth project, 161
Newhart, 2
Nichols, Clarina, 74–77
    legislative testimony, 77
    move to Kansas, 77
Nichols, George, 77
Nixon, Richard, 82, 178, 198
North Country Star, The, 192
Novikoff, Alex, 157
Noyes, John Humphrey, 48–50, 52–53
Nuclear Review Committee, 190
nullification, 238–240

oaths, 58, 61, 63
Obama, Barack, 214, 232, 233, 234, 238
Occupy movement, 247, 250–251
open shop, 102, 137, 138, 198
Order of Industrial Reform, 101
Orleans Historical Society, 54
Orwell, George, ii
out-migration, 67, 70

Palmer, William, 61–63
    and secret societies, 63
    election victories, 62
Page, John B., 73
Pape, C. Herbert, 115
Paquette, Gordon, 194, 205–207
    debate with Sanders, 207
Parenti, Michael, 200
Peacham, 157
Peacham Academy, 60
Peck, Hamilton, 123–124
Pegler, Westbrook, 156

Perelman's Hall, 125
Perfectionism, 49
Perkins, Harry, 26
Pfenning, Joshua, 247
Philadelphia, 11, 12, 13, 35, 44, 59, 63–64, 170
Pierce, Franklin, 53, 85, 91
Pittsfield, 50
Pizzagalli Construction, 198
Plumley, Charles, 157
Plymouth Notch, 95
polarization, 264
Polk, James K., 63, 83, 90
Pollina, Anthony, 241–244
Polston, Pamela, 194, 195
Pomerleau, Antonio, 171, 207
population, 4, 9, 22, 41, 66–67, 70, 72, 135, 164
Post, Bruce S., 145
presidential elections
    1800, 15
    1832, 62
    1836, 63
    1840, 83
    1844, 83, 89
    1848, 84
    1852, 91
    1856, 86, 91
    1860, 92
    1880, 93
    1884, 95
    1920, 95
    1924, 97
    2004, 226–233
    2016, 216
Prince, Lucy Terry, 53
prisons, 165
Proctor, Town of, 99, 102, 103, 144
Proctor Republicans, 117, 120, 150
Proctor, Fletcher, 99, 118, 120, 126, 224
Proctor, Mortimer, 143, 150
Proctor, Redfield, 99
    Spanish-American War, 100
Proctor strike, 197
Progressive Party, 156
property tax, 204, 206, 213, 225, 226
Prouty, George, 126
Prouty, Winston, 161
Public Occurrence, 192–193

public health, 151, 264
public wharf, 115, 120–121
Pure Water Act, 185
Pyramid Mall, 202

Quarry Workers Association, 137
Quebec, Canada, 20, 39, 41, 42, 44, 55, 65, 139

Raid, The, 72
railroads, 69–70, 105–106, 120–123
Randolph, 79, 156
Reagan, Ronald, 153, 173, 207
reapportionment, 164
Red Scare, 135–136, 160
Republicrats, 132, 205
Resch, Tyler, iv, 178
Resources and Attractions of Vermont, The, 105
revivals, 47-48
Ridgely, C. Herbert, 171
Right to Work Committee, 170
Ritner, Joseph, 64
Roberts, Robert, 120, 123
Robertson, John, 23–24
Robinson, Rowland T., 75
Rock of Age Company, 137
Roosevelt, Franklin D., 142, 147, 149, 226, 253, 266
Roosevelt, Theodore, 113, 114, 117, 118, 120, 126, 190, 257
Routly, Paula, 195
Royce, Stephen, 85, 86
Rural Electrification Program, 108
Russia, 4–5, 91
Rutland Herald, The, 77, 103, 117, 143
Rutland Railroad, 118, 120, 122, 123

Sabotage Prevention Act, 157
Sacco and Vanzetti, 135
sales tax, 170, 198–199, 234
Salmon, Thomas, 24, 164, 198–199, 200
Same-sex marriage, 229, 255, 259
Sanders, Bernie, ii, 192, 194, 200, 205–226, 228, 235, 241, 242–243, 246, 249, 250, 263–264, 266

1981 mayoral campaign, 206, 208
and exceptionalism, 9
and Federal Reserve, 218
and Peter Smith, 211
approach in Congress, 218–219
as mayor, 210
Bookchin critique, 212
campaign for governor, 210–214
campaign slogan, 208
mini-filibuster, 214
presidential races, 218–217, 263–264
on Yugoslavia, 218
Sanford, Gregory, 236
Scalia, Antonin, 240
Scribner, Harvey, 181
Scott, Phil, 244
Seabrook nuclear plant, 188
secession, 234–238
and U.S. Supreme Court, 240
defined, 238
support for, 237
Second Great Awakening, 47
Second Vermont Republic, 235
self-rule, 255
self-sufficiency, 33, 65, 238
Seven Days, 195
Shelburne, 171, 203
Shelburne Industries, 171
Sherman Antitrust Act, 107
Shumlin, Peter, 217, 241, 246, 249
silicosis, 135, 151
Signs of the Times, 50
sit-down strike ban, 103
ski industry, 141, 199
Slade, William, 51, 53, 61, 64, 83–84
slavery, 47, 49, 51–54, 55, 60, 71, 75, 83–85, 91–93, 256
Sleeman, George, 179–180, 184
Sleeman, Richard, 180–181, 184
Smalley, B.B., 115
Smith, Charles, 147
Smith, John Gregory, 73
Civil War, 73–74
Smith, Joseph, 89–91
killed by mob, 91
presidential campaign, 89–90
Smith, Peter, 210–212
on Kunin and Sanders, 211

Snelling, Richard, 24, 168–174, 190, 200, 210
as governor, 172
death, 174
election, 171
family, 170
four year terms, 254
GBIC, 169–171
property tax, 225, 226
Senate race, 173
Shelburne Industries, 171
Socialism, 133, 200, 247, 263
Sons of Temperance, 51
Socialist Party, 133
Sorrell, William, 260
sovereignty, 50, 41, 143, 266
Soviet Union, 4
Spanish-American War, 100
Springfield, 72, 101
Stafford, Robert, 153, 163, 197, 200
St. Albans, 72
Stamp Act, 33
State Legislature, 9, 54, 61, 72, 80, 81, 127, 128, 150, 164, 223, 234, 239
unicameral, 7, 62
State Police, 151, 162, 182
State Senate, 6, 62, 244
statewide development plan, 165
Stevens, Sarah Morill, 60, 61
Stevens, Thaddeus, 59–61
in Pennsylvania, 63–64
Stone, Lucy, 79, 101
strikes
Barre Granite, 102, 138
Rutland General Electric, 197
Pizzagalli Construction, 197
Vermont Copper Mining, 101
Vermont Marble, 161, 197
Woodstock Textile Mill, 79
suffrage, 75, 79–80, 101
and Council of Censors, 80
bill passed, 80
Suffolk Resolves, 35
Suffrage Amendment, 80
Suitor, Fred, 133
Sutherland Falls Marble Company, 99
Swanton, 19, 23, 100
Switzerland, 4, 235

Index

Tafts Corner, 202
Taylor, James Paddock, 141–142, 145
Taylor, Zachery, 84
television, 157, 169, 233
    Howard Dean coverage, 230–232
temperance, 48, 50–51, 85
    Society for the Promotion of, 51
    sons of, 51
terms of office, 61, 253, 254
Thompson, Hunter, 3
Ticonderoga, 24, 40
timber, 24, 41, 44, 65, 257
tourism, 26, 137, 201
tourists, 9, 106, 143
Town Meeting, 3–4, 8, 9, 34, 35, 81, 145, 221–224, 226, 249, 254, 255, 258, 260
    Bryan-Clark Research, 223
Townshend Acts, 34
Tracy, Max, 250
trade embargo, 239
Treaty of Paris, 42
trolley system, 137
Truman, Harry, 150, 151
Twilight, Alexander, 54

U.S. Congress, 44, 83, 260
    and Joseph McCarthy, 159
    calls for abolition, 53
    first abolition address, 83
    Sanders in, 214, 217–218
U.S. Supreme Court, 5, 100, 164, 240
Underground Railroad, 55
Union Passenger Station, 123
United Stone and Allied Products Workers, 197
unicameral legislature, 7
University of Vermont, v, 26, 60, 108, 157, 171, 193, 217
urban redevelopment, 205

Van Buren, Martin, 62
Varney-Brownell, Emily, 79
Vergennes, 14, 15
Vermont Advisory Commission on Civil Rights, 162
Vermont Agricultural Society, 107

Vermont Central Railroad, 73
Vermont Chamber of Commerce, 141
Vermont Commons, vi, 237
Vermont Constitution, 6, 7, 32, 37–38, 236, 255
    adopted, 37
    amended, 7
    and extending terms of office, 254
    citizen resistance, 32
    Conventions, 62–63, 79
    escape clause, 236
    public education, 6, 158
    ratification, 44
    Senate created, 62
    slavery banned, 6, 9, 38
Vermont Cynic, 203
Vermont Copper Mining Company, 101
Vermont Council for Effective Government, 171
Vermont Dairyman's Association, 108
Vermont Farm Bureau, 108
Vermont Freeman, 191, 192
Vermont Fish and Wildlife Dept., 27
Vermont Historical Gazetteer, 105
Vermont Independent Party, 163
Vermont Journal, 13
Vermont Marble Company, 99, 102, 143, 197
Vermont Planning Council, 202
Vermont Progressive Party, 228, 241–244, 260
Vermont Rebels Again, 103
Vermont Supreme Court, 7, 85, 115, 121–122, 123, 124, 164, 229
Vermont, State of
    budget, 138, 171, 172, 228
    citizen legislature, 5, 224, 253, 255
    civil unions, 229–230
    climate, 3–42
    constitutional time lock, 254
    Council of Censors, 7
    Council with the Governor, 6
    Declaration of the Rights of Inhabitants, 37
    education reform, 108, 180, 255
    gay marriage, 229–231,
    Gross Domestic Product, 3
    General Assembly, 8, 26, 61, 69, 227

independent republic, 9, 42, 44, 235, 237
population, 3
size, 3
statehood, 38
Vermont Times, The, v, 202
Vermont Way, iii, 5, 160, 260–261
Vermont Woman, 192
Vermont Women's Suffrage Association, 79, 101
Vermont Vanguard Press, The, iv, 191, 193–194
Vermont Yankee nuclear plant, 187–188, 211, 213, 246, 260
Vernon, 187
Vershire, 101
Vietnam War, 151, 176, 192, 200, 226, 251
Vonnegut, Kurt, 187
Voting rights, 7, 44, 77, 259
    extended to women, 80
    in school elections, 80

Wallace, Henry, 156
Wallingford, 11
Walloomsac River, 20
Walton, Ezekiel P., 85
War of 1812, 17, 40, 42, 68, 237, 258
Wasco, David, 185
Washington, George, 13, 33, 38, 42
Water Resources Board, 185
Weathersfield, 69
Webster, Daniel, 64
Webster, Noah, 13
Weinberger, Miro, 244–245, 246, 247, 249–250
welfare, 151, 164, 165, 172, 192, 199
Wentworth, Bennington, 29
West Townsend, 76
Westminster, 32, 37
Westminster Massacre, 32
Whig Party, 55, 65, 83
Whitmore, Elizabeth, 78–79
Willard, Ema Hart, 78
Williams, Rob, 237, 138
Williston, 41, 113, 165, 171, 201–202
Wilson, Stanley C., 138
Wilson, Woodrow, 95

Windham County Democrat, The, 77
Windsor Riot, 31
Winooski, 19, 21, 35, 72, 202
Winthrop, Nat, 193, 194
women's rights, 77, 80, 101, 266
Women's Rights Convention, 77
Woodbridge, 43
Woodbury, Urban, 113, 257
Woodstock, 57, 79, 141, 163
Woodstock Textile Mill, 79, 101
woolen mills, 68
Working-man's Gazette, The, 55
Workingmen's Societies, 55
Workman's Compensation, 151
Works Progress Administration, 141
World War I, ii, 1, 95, 108, 137
World War II, ii, 1, 150, 197
Wright, Kurt, 236, 249

Young, Brigham, 91
Young, Thomas, 37

Zuckerman, David, 244
Zwicker, Ralph, 159

www.ingramcontent.com/pod-product-compliance
Lightning Source LLC
Chambersburg PA
CBHW030851170426
43193CB00009BA/570